The Bidens

The Bidens

★★★

Inside the First Family's Fifty-Year Rise to Power

BEN SCHRECKINGER

TWELVE

New York   Boston

Twelve
Hachette Book Group
1290 Avenue of the Americas, New York, NY 10104
twelvebooks.com
twitter.com/twelvebooks

First Edition: September 2021

Twelve is an imprint of Grand Central Publishing. The Twelve name and logo are
trademarks of Hachette Book Group, Inc.

The publisher is not responsible for websites (or their content)
that are not owned by the publisher.

The Hachette Speakers Bureau provides a wide range of authors for speaking events.
To find out more, go to www.hachettespeakersbureau.com or call (866) 376-6591.

Library of Congress Control Number: 2021939695

ISBN: 978-1-5387-3800-9 (hardcover), 978-1-5387-3799-6 (ebook)

Printed in the United States of America

33614082400739   LSC-C

Printing 1, 2021

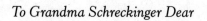

To Grandma Schreckinger Dear

Contents

Contents

Author's Note

In the summer of 2019 I set out with a vague notion of profiling Hunter Biden, who was then beginning to attract media attention. My initial research quickly led me instead to a more investigative story for *Politico Magazine* about Hunter's business ventures, those of his uncle Jim Biden, and the ways in which they intersected with Joe Biden's political career and public office.

There are more fun ways to spend a summer than digging through documents and piecing together old newspaper clippings in order to assemble a story about a sensitive, contentious topic, and I assumed this first piece on the Biden family would also be my last.

But between the time I started working on that piece and the time it was published, new allegations from Jim's former business partners had emerged in a lawsuit in Tennessee that fit the pattern I had documented. From there, I received a steady trickle of new tips and leads related, primarily, to the business ventures and finances of Biden relatives.

Soon, Donald Trump's ham-handed efforts to pressure Ukrainian authorities into investigating the Bidens came to light and the topic of the family's business dealings suddenly became central to a presidential impeachment. Then, Joe staged a dramatic comeback in the Democratic primary and won the presidency, even as Trump sought to make Hunter an issue in the race.

The Bidens, and the efforts of Trump's allies to sully them, became my de facto beat.

We live in an age of distrust and of coordinated campaigns to manipulate public opinion. Readers have every right to wonder whether an extended inquiry into the Biden family, emphasizing its finances, is just some instrument of a broader effort to create a political narrative. After all, as this book covers, there really was a conspiracy against the Bidens, or several loosely aligned conspiracies.

When I started to publish articles about the Bidens, I received a fair number of offers of professional opposition research. Mostly, the research I was offered amounted to compilations of old, unflattering news articles. These could provide useful context but were hardly the stuff of a masterful information campaign.

Instead, almost all my reporting resulted from my own research or tips from regular people. One article did result primarily from a piece of professional opposition research, though even that required weeks' worth of additional reporting.

At times, I struggled to reconcile the folksy image of the Bidens that had become familiar to me as a news consumer and young journalist during the Obama era with the messier portrait that emerged from my recent reporting for *Politico*.

This book, which grows out of that reporting, represents my attempt to grapple with the Bidens' story—an epic saga of an American political family—in its entirety. To understand any world leader it is helpful to understand their family, but I believe that in Joe Biden's case it is more crucial than in most.

Because both the campaign controversies and my own reporting dealt with the Bidens' finances, this telling of their story includes a special emphasis on that subject and the ethical questions raised by it. Journalists have produced reams of excellent reporting about the ethical problems posed by the Trumps' finances, which in many cases were more direct, more clear-cut, and on a grander scale than the issues raised here. This book does not deal with that subject in any depth other than to note it undermined Trump's ability to make a convincing case against his opponent.

At the highest levels, even the appearance of a conflict of interest or of special treatment threatens to undermine public faith in government. Did any of the Bidens' activities go further and create undue influence, allow hostile actors to compromise a member of the first family, or otherwise cross ethical lines? Joe has maintained that he has never discussed his relatives' business dealings with them, and several of those relatives have repeatedly denied allegations that they used their family connections for profit.

I believe that reasonable people may reach different conclusions about the motives of the people depicted in this book and about the significance of the episodes described.

I also believe that the best way to understand people in power, and subjects of international controversy, is to attempt a thorough, timely examination, provide context, and lay out the available evidence, though it may often be inconclusive and in places seem contradictory.

Too often people interpret the news of the day through the lens of their own political sympathies, and a more nuanced understanding of our leaders emerges only much later, when political pressures have eased.

This phenomenon seems to have gotten worse during the Trump era. In response to destabilizing social forces, a president who frequently spouted falsehoods, and a deluge of online information, Americans retreated into competing, inconsistent versions of reality (some more unhinged than others). As subjects like Donald Trump's relationship to Russia and the origins of COVID-19 illustrate, our understanding of complex stories often evolves with time, and many questions may not be definitively settled for years, if ever.

The Bidens' story isn't over, but I hope that this early attempt at a holistic telling of that story will help people understand events from a common set of facts, even if it inevitably remains incomplete and open to multiple interpretations.

Chekhov's Laptop

"If in the first act you have hung a pistol on the wall, then in the following one it should be fired. Otherwise don't put it there."

—Russian playwright Anton Chekhov, laying out the dramatic principle known as "Chekhov's gun"

In the spring of 2019, as Joe Biden set out on the first leg of his third presidential campaign, his son, Hunter, was sowing the seeds for the campaign's dramatic conclusion.

Even by the standards of Hunter's tumultuous life, the past few months had been eventful ones for America's future first son.

The previous October, his girlfriend, Hallie, had taken his .38 revolver from the center console of his pickup truck and thrown it into a trash can outside Janssen's, a high-end grocery store near Wilmington that the Biden family had long frequented.

When Hunter discovered his gun was missing, he told Hallie—who was also the widow of his late brother, Beau—to go back and retrieve it. But when she returned to the store later the same day, the gun was no longer in the trash can.

The Delaware State Police were called, and Hunter was summoned to the grocery store for questioning.

Curiously for a call about a missing handgun, the Federal Bureau of Investigation showed up, too.

Even more curious, two Secret Service agents showed up at Starquest, the store where Hunter had recently purchased the gun, according to two people familiar with the incident. At the time, the Bidens were not under Secret Service protection, but the agents wanted the paperwork Hunter had filled out to purchase the gun. The owner of the store refused to give it to them, because the paperwork fell under the jurisdiction of the Bureau of Alcohol, Tobacco, Firearms and Explosives. (The Secret Service has denied any involvement in the incident).[1]

Not long after the agents left, the ATF paid its own visit to the store to get the paperwork.

The frantic search for the gun ended within a few days when an old man known to rummage through Janssen's trash for recyclables turned it in.

The incident did not lead to any charges. Hunter had skipped town, anyway. A few days after the gun fiasco, Hallie dropped him off in Newburyport, a scenic old port city on the north shore of Massachusetts. Hunter was there to get clean with the help of ketamine therapy and Keith Ablow, a well-known psychiatrist. Ablow was an odd choice for a confidant. He was a regular guest on Fox News, where he was recognizable by his clean-shaven head. And he had made headlines back in 2012 for suggesting on air that Hunter's father, a teetotaler, had either been drunk during his vice presidential debate with Paul Ryan or was showing signs of dementia.[2]

But Hunter seemed to enjoy his time with Ablow in New England. He talked of writing a memoir, and of rearranging his troubled life so that he could spend more time with his family. He practiced yoga, took art lessons, and received intravenous infusions of vitamins and minerals.

He skied at Wachusett Mountain and went to a local theatre to see

Crippled Inside, a play written by a psychologist from nearby Rockport,[3] that deals with mental health and addiction. In it, a middle-aged man, Jimmy, reflects on his teenage years, when his father, John, a top Justice Department official, bailed him out of scrapes while playing politics in Washington.[4]

Hunter was an ideal viewer for this particular drama. At forty-eight, his own personal problems were still complicating his father's ambitions in Washington. His business ventures entangled him again and again with shady characters and people with an interest in influencing Joe. He drank too much and was hopelessly addicted to crack cocaine. A few years earlier, he had been kicked out of the Navy reserves for failing a drug test.

Then his marriage to his first wife, Kathleen, had unraveled as he embarked on a tabloid-worthy affair with his late brother's wife. He had just fathered a son out of wedlock with another woman, a graduate student moonlighting as a stripper, setting up what would soon become a messy paternity fight. But through it all, as Hunter's political liabilities piled up, Joe had stood steadfastly by him.

In mid-January, Hunter visited tiny Plum Island Airport and took an introductory flying lesson. For five or ten minutes, he got to take over the steering himself. He seemed happy up in the air over Ipswich Bay. Here, at least, he was in control, gliding along far above the troubles of the world below. He told the instructor he would like to have more lessons, but he never came back.

Hunter moved on to other plans. He began talking to a local man he wanted to hire as an assistant. In late January, they met at a Starbucks near the waterfront to discuss Hunter's goals, big and small.

He wanted to spend more time with his father and go to more of his daughters' lacrosse games; to get Lasik eye surgery; to get back in touch with a business associate, Jimmy Bulger, the Boston-based scion of another Irish-Catholic political family.

He also wanted help getting his arms around his finances. He had something on the order of twenty bank accounts, but his life was in such disarray that he did not have the log-in credentials to access many of them. He had business interests around the world, and he wanted to sign up for a TSA program that would let him speed through airport lines.

Then, just as Hunter seemed ready to pull his life back together, he was gone. He got in his truck and left Newburyport in early February, a hard time of year for him ever since his older brother died of brain cancer in 2015. The sudden departure coincided with what would have been Beau's fiftieth birthday on February 3 and with his own forty-ninth birthday the following day.

In his haste, Hunter left behind some of his belongings at Ablow's office, including a laptop.

=====

The months leading up to Joe's launch were also eventful ones for the president's personal lawyer.

In his latest act, former New York City mayor Rudy Giuliani was representing Donald Trump in Special Counsel Robert Mueller's Russia investigation. The work was pro bono, but Giuliani made his money representing wealthy foreigners with thorny legal and political problems, so the proximity to the president was well worth the trouble.

Not long after Hunter showed up in Newburyport, a private investigator approached Giuliani saying he had information implicating Ukraine in efforts to interfere in the 2016 presidential election.

Claims that Democrats had colluded with Ukraine in 2016 could be very useful to his client. At the time, Mueller was investigating Russia's covert efforts to boost Trump's first presidential campaign, seeking to determine whether Trump was complicit in those efforts.

As Giuliani stuck his nose into Ukrainian politics, other claims wafted up, claims about Hunter's work for a Ukrainian energy company, Burisma, and Joe's role overseeing U.S. policy toward the embattled Eastern European nation. Giuliani smelled pay dirt.

For one thing, Joe was the 2020 presidential contender who most troubled Trump, so anything that muddied Joe up was good for his client.

For another thing, Giuliani had his own history with the Bidens. Once upon a time, Joe had called Giuliani for a favor: His niece, Missy, wanted a job in Giuliani's mayoral administration. Giuliani obliged, and Missy took a job on his legislative affairs staff.[5]

The courtesies extended by America's bipartisan favor mill went only so far: Giuliani had been on the butt end of the most memorable line of Joe's short-lived second presidential campaign—or at least the most memorable line that was not a gaffe. Back in 2007, Joe had skewered Giuliani's penchant for bringing up his role in responding to the September 11 terror attacks, saying that the only three things Giuliani needed to string together a sentence were "a noun and a verb and 9/11." The line stung, and the rap stuck.

Hunter, meanwhile, had grown into something of a competitor with Giuliani in the lucrative market of well-connected Americans selling their legal services and political help to deep-pocketed foreigners.

In one instance, the men were more like indirect collaborators. In 2015, a fabulously wealthy Romanian businessman had hired Hunter to help fend off corruption charges in his home country. Hunter then pulled Louis Freeh, a former FBI director, into the effort to defend the businessman, who was eventually convicted. Freeh later brought on Giuliani to work for the same oligarch as they pressured Romanian authorities to ease up on the man.[6]

To hunt for Biden dirt, Giuliani teamed up with two Florida-based Soviet émigrés straight out of political skullduggery central casting.

Lev Parnas, born in Ukraine and raised in Brooklyn, reportedly led a colorful life before his turn in the global spotlight. In one memo-rable 2008 incident, which he denied, his landlord claimed Parnas had put a gun to his head when he was trying to evict Parnas from a South Florida condominium. "This is my last warning to you," Parnas alleg-edly told him, then got into a Porsche and drove away. The condo in question was on the forty-second floor of Trump Palace in Sunny Isles Beach.[7]

Lev's partner, Igor Fruman, was born in Belarus and became a suc-cessful businessman with interests in Ukraine. They included a beach club he owned in Odessa, on the Black Sea, called Mafia Rave. He also reportedly enjoyed personal ties to the most powerful businessman in that region—a man known locally by the nicknames "the Lightbulb" and "the Gray Cardinal."

During the Trump years, Lev and Igor spread money around Republican circles and pushed for the ouster of the U.S. ambassador to Ukraine, a career diplomat intent on cracking down on corruption there.

When Rudy went digging into claims about Hunter, Lev and Igor were there to help. They connected him with Ukraine's prosecutor gen-eral, Yuriy Lutsenko.

While Hunter was piecing his life back together in Newbury-port, Giuliani was meeting with Lutsenko in New York, urging him to investigate the Bidens. They met again in Warsaw. In March 2019, Lutsenko rekindled a dormant investigation of Mykola Zlochevsky, the Russia-aligned magnate who had hired Hunter to the board of his energy company.[8]

This was not enough to appease Giuliani's client. Soon, Trump would threaten to withhold military aid from Ukraine in a bid to pres-sure the country's president to announce an investigation of Hunter. Trump's threats led to the third presidential impeachment in American history.

But in a grand irony of history, while Trump was getting himself impeached for trying to force the Ukrainians to investigate Hunter, his own Justice Department was doing just that, right under his nose.

The FBI had responded to the case of Hunter's missing revolver because it already had him under surveillance.

In conjunction with the Internal Revenue Service, the FBI and the U.S. Attorney's office in Delaware had been investigating his finances, looking at potential violations of money laundering and tax laws, as well as the Foreign Agents Registration Act. Investigators took an interest, too, in Hunter's business partner and uncle, Jim, Joe's younger brother.[9]

Hunter's and Jim's dealings with a Chinese oil tycoon and the tycoon's corrupt deputy had drawn the interest of the FBI's counterintelligence division.[10] So, too, had Hunter's payments to a number of Eastern European women, over concerns that they could be used to compromise him with evidence of embarrassing activities.[11] (A report by Senate Republicans later stated that some of the payments show apparent links to "an Eastern European prostitution or human trafficking ring." Lawyers for Hunter did not respond to questions about the payments or about his dealings with the Chinese tycoon.)

This was not even the full extent of the Justice Department's interest in Hunter's activities. Prosecutors in the securities fraud division in the Southern District of New York also began scrutinizing overseas payments to Hunter that had surfaced in an unrelated prosecution of one of his business partners, looking for signs of possible money laundering.

By all indications, neither Trump nor Hunter had any idea this was happening.

After Newburyport, Hunter went on an extended crack binge in Connecticut, holed up in seedy motels along I-95, in the company of prostitutes and drug dealers. Then, in the weeks before Joe's campaign launch, he briefly materialized in Delaware.[12]

That's when John Paul Mac Isaac says Hunter brought three other laptops, MacBook Pros—one affixed with a sticker for the Beau Biden

Foundation—to Mac Isaac's computer repair shop inside a drab, brick shopping plaza near Hunter's home in Wilmington, leaving one behind for data recovery. (Hunter has acknowledged the laptop "certainly" could be his, and that he was not keeping track of his possessions during this time, but he has not directly addressed whether he ever dropped off equipment at Mac Isaac's store, and he has suggested he may instead have been hacked.)

A few weeks later, Joe held his campaign kickoff rally in Philadelphia. His children and grandchildren were on hand to support him, save for one notable exception. Among the gathered Bidens, where Hunter should have been sat a single, empty chair.[13]

His presence would be felt in the campaign soon enough, and hang over its closing weeks, when the laptop said to be sitting in that drab shopping plaza became the subject of international controversy.

Joe's close relationship with his family had always been the central fact of his public life. When Joe was nobody, his relatives ran his campaigns. Weeks after he pulled off a shocking Senate upset at the age of twenty-nine, his first wife and infant daughter died in a car accident. Joe's story of heartbreaking personal loss became an important part of his public profile, and the basis for his unusual capacity to connect with voters on a deeply personal level. The death of his eldest son from brain cancer in 2015, just as Beau was poised to enter the prime of his own political career, precluded Joe's anticipated 2016 presidential run, one that many, in hindsight, believed would have prevented the Trump presidency from happening.

Likewise, for the Bidens, a normal family that came out of nowhere to win a seemingly unwinnable Senate seat, Joe's political career became a central fact in their lives. It led some of them to their own careers in politics and public service. It also opened the door to job opportunities, loans, and favors from people who wanted to be in Joe's good graces. Over the course of five decades, at a time when the country's wealth and power were reaching new heights, they learned how to leverage their proximity to Joe in order to make it in America, and to get themselves to the right side of the divide that was making life harder and more disordered for many normal families.

Now, thanks in large part to the machinations of Trump and Giuliani, much of American politics—not to mention global geopolitics—would soon come to revolve around Hunter and his relationship with his father. To understand that, and almost everything else about Joe, you have to understand the Biden clan, America's middle-class Kennedys. And to understand them, it is best to start at the beginning.

The Clan

"If you ever speak to my son like that again, I'll come back and rip that bonnet off your head. Do you understand me?"

—Eugenia "Jean" Finnegan Biden, dressing down a nun

The wrought-iron gates of Archmere Academy are intricately worked with accents of gold paint. Large and imposing, they open onto a grand, sandy-colored brick walkway. The walkway leads to an old manor house, the former home of a twentieth-century industrialist.

Though Archmere sounds, and looks, like it should be an English boarding school, it is Catholic and situated in Claymont, Delaware, just south of the Pennsylvania state line.

By November 2020, its gates had seen better days. They were sealed shut with rusty padlocks, the bricks underneath them faded and strewn with litter.[14]

But in 1953, in the eyes of a ten-year-old Joseph Robinette Biden Jr., they might as well have been the pearly gates to heaven.

Joe had just moved to Claymont, to an apartment complex that represented a step down from the home he had departed in Scranton, Pennsylvania. From his bedroom, he enjoyed a clear view of Archmere's gates, and he dreamed of one day being welcomed inside.[15] The gates were just across the street. In other ways, the world beyond them was further out of reach than young Joe appreciated.

Thanks to a family connection, Joe's father had spent the war years flush. Joe Sr.'s uncle, Bill Sheen Sr., was in industrial materials, and he was rich.

When Joe Sr. moved to Scranton, Pennsylvania, at the end of high school and the middle of the Great Depression, he brought with him a worldliness that the local boys lacked. Scranton beauty Jean Finnegan found it attractive, and the pair coupled up.

After Joe Sr. came of age, he went to work for his uncle and alongside his cousin. The company did good business. Then the war came, and the real money flowed. The sort of money created by governments and wars. As tensions with Nazi Germany mounted, Congress mandated that all ships engaged in the North Atlantic trade armor their sides using one of Sheen's products.

Joe Sr.—"Big Joe," people called him—managed the Boston operation. He spent time on yachts. He flew around the Eastern seaboard in company planes, hunted pheasant, and drove Buick convertibles gifted by his uncle.[16]

Joe was born on November 20, 1942. When he was young, and the end of the war money came within sight, Joe Sr. went looking for his next big thing. He tried crop-dusting with his cousin, but Bill Jr. was a layabout and a drunk. He went into a furniture store with a friend, but the friend absconded with the money.[17]

At one point, Joe Sr. was going to go into business with Russell Preno, a Scranton pal whose Italian restaurant, Preno's, was a local institution and Biden family favorite. The pair wanted to open a plant to can tomatoes and sauce in East Mountain, a part of town by Lake Scranton. The plan never took off.[18]

As Joe was reaching school age, the family was back in a modest home in Scranton, surrounded by his mother's family. The Finnegans, born and bred to modest means, sometimes got the feeling that Joe Sr. was putting on airs.

Except for Jean, who didn't mind a little bit of airs. "Joey, remember, you're a Biden," she would tell her firstborn son. "You're every man's equal. No man is better than you."

"It was like we were talking about some dynasty," Joe later reflected on these childhood pep talks. "But it was real. It was real. It was palpable. You could taste it. You could feel it."[19]

The four Biden children could also see it, or vestiges of it, in the back of their father's closet, where he still kept a pair of riding boots and a polo mallet.[20]

When Joe was a toddler he was joined by a baby sister, Valerie. A few years after Val came Jimmy. Finally, eleven years after Joe came Frank.[21]

Joe's biographer, the veteran journalist Jules Witcover, described the Bidens as a "particularly tight Irish Catholic family that put loyalty, along with religion, above all other considerations."

Shacking up with down-on-their-luck relatives was a part of this ethos, and the kids shared a house with their mother's brother, Edward Blewitt, and their great-aunt, Gertie.

One winter in Scranton, Joe and his friends were making mischief in the neighborhood when a snowball aimed at the outside of a truck sailed into the cabin and then into the driver's face. The driver chased the gang up Joe's driveway, but he was turned back when Aunt Gertie came roaring out of the house, brandishing a broomstick and hollering, "Get outta here, you son of a bitch!"[22]

As the oldest son, Joe inherited the role of protector in his generation. During their playground years, this meant letting Val tag along on his adventures. She'd hitch a ride on the handlebars of his bike, hopping off at the foot of big hills to run alongside him.[23] Once, when Joe's pals imposed a "No girls allowed" rule on a fort they had built in the woods, Joe ditched them to go off with Val and build a new fort of their own.[24]

"I was his sidekick," Val recalled. "Wherever he went, he took me. I was part of the deal."[25] Joe would tell other kids, "If you like me, you like my sister." Val, in return, watched her brother's back.[26]

If Jimmy or Frank was having problems with a kid at school, Jean would tell them, "Why don't you take your brother Joe along? He'll show you how to throw a punch." Once, according to Richard Ben Cramer's *What It Takes*, she even gave Jimmy two dollars to punch another kid in the face.[27] Cracking wise about Jean would, likewise, earn a kid a punch on the nose from Joe.[28]

The Biden children learned that their bonds to one another trumped all else. "There is no one on Earth closer than brother and sister," their mother advised. "They're the same blood. Even closer than parent and child."[29]

From a young age, their parents instilled in them, too, the overriding importance of displaying a united front to the world. "Mom and Dad always told us that we were responsible for each other," Val recalled of this upbringing. "There were four kids, and once we walked outside that door and that door shut, we were in the outside world and we were the Bidens. If we had something to say, if you wanted to punch somebody in the nose, you walked inside the house and did it, but you didn't get in a fight outside."

To hash out their disagreements, the Biden kids regularly called meetings among themselves, behind closed doors, without parental intrusion.[30]

This way of doing things could present problems. For a brief period during his parochial school days, Joe's teachers deputized him for the school's "safety patrol." His job was to monitor his schoolmates' behavior on the bus. His stint proved short-lived. When Val acted out, Joe faced a dilemma between his duties to the nuns and the blood ties the Bidens prized above all. Joe Sr. made him quit the safety patrol rather than turn in Val.[31]

(The us-against-the-world attitude endured through the generations. Decades later, when Joe would drive Beau and Hunter to school, the trio made a pastime of turning up the radio and singing along to the songs. They especially enjoyed Helen Reddy's 1974 hit, "You and Me Against the World.")[32]

The Bidens learned to stick together for a reason. Conditions in the outside world could be harsh. When work dried up with the oil company, Joe Sr. had to take a job cleaning boilers in Delaware, and he relocated his family there.[33] Later, he found work as a car salesman. It was a good fit, because he loved to drive cars, and drive them fast. He would joke that he should have become an ambulance driver.[34]

Despite the family's money woes, Joe's childhood was the stuff of an all-American yesteryear—remarkable for just how ordinary it was. He liked to play baseball and football with kids from the neighborhood. Later, he came to like girls and cars. "We were, like, normal kids at the time," as Val neatly sums it up.[35]

A visit to Scranton and a drive through northern Delaware offers a tour of the Bidens' changing fortunes during these years. His childhood home in Scranton sits in a solidly middle-class neighborhood, though today, some of the houses there could use a fresh coat of paint.[36]

Their next neighborhood, in Claymont, was a step down. It didn't have trees. On the car ride to their new home, Joe's mother, sitting in the passenger seat, cried.[37] Today, outside the manicured campus of Archmere Academy lies a busy street lined by a small strip mall, a gas station, and a billboard advertising the Delaware Hope Line, a government hotline for accessing substance abuse and mental health resources.

After a few years across from Archmere, the Bidens moved to Wilson Road in Mayfield, a few miles away. Today, the squat house is painted gray and has a poured concrete driveway. The neighborhood is quieter, but still modest.[38]

Joe learned to be on the lookout for the next move up. In fact, he had his eyes on the presidency more or less from the start.

As a precocious adolescent, he seemed to be cut out well enough for the role that a waitress at a lunch counter around the corner from the Mayfield house took to calling him "President Biden."[39]

As a schoolboy, he had written about his presidential ambitions for a classroom assignment, but when he returned decades later to address students as a first-term senator, he disavowed any plans for a White House run. This prompted a nun to fish his old paper out of her habit and confront Joe with hard evidence to the contrary.[40]

He was motivated to succeed in part by the regular presence in the family home of Uncle Edward. Boo-Boo, as they called him, had a stutter, and the speech impediment shot his confidence. He gave up on his career ambitions, descending into bitterness and drink.[41]

Joe struggled with a bad stutter of his own, and he did not want to go the way of Uncle Boo-Boo. In Mayfield, he transferred to a new school, Saint Helena's. He was used to getting teased by his classmates, but at Saint Helena's a nun mocked his stammered answer to a question by addressing him as "Mr. Bu-bu-bu-bu-Biden." Joe walked straight out of her classroom and marched home. When he explained to his mother what had happened, she drove him back to school, walked him in, and told the nun, "If you ever speak to my son like that again, I'll come back and rip that bonnet off your head. Do you understand me?"[42]

Dignity was important to the family. When Joe was a teenager, his parents went off to a Christmas party at his father's dealership only to come back home while the night was still young. At the party, the owner of the dealership had thrown a bucket of silver dollars out onto the dance floor and watched the ensuing frenzy as his employees rushed to pick them up. The stunt disgusted Joe Sr., who quit his job and stormed out.[43]

A family friend explained that episodes like this one affected both Jimmy and Joe, but in different ways. "With Joe it translated into, 'I want respect.' With Jimmy it translated into, 'I want money.' "[44]

In eighth grade, after hearing a presentation from a priest during his school's vocation month, February, Joe came home and announced he might want to enter the seminary himself. That could start as soon as ninth grade. Jean told him he had to complete high school and college before he could become a priest.[45]

If it was to be high school, rather than the seminary, his heart remained set on Archmere. Despite the strain it put on the family's budget, they scrounged up the money for tuition.

Joe made the most of his time at Archmere. To overcome his stutter, he recited the poetry of William Butler Yeats into the mirror in his bedroom.[46] Inspired by a story about the Greek orator Demosthenes, he also tried filling his mouth with pebbles and shouting at a wall outside his house.[47] That method proved less fruitful, but he nonetheless conquered the tic and flourished. He played for the school's standout football team and, with Val running the campaign,[48] got himself elected class president.

He did not lose sight of the other presidency. The big one. When Joe first met his future mother-in-law, she asked him about his career goals. What was he aiming for? "President," he responded. After a moment of silence, he clarified, "Of the United States."[49]

It was an audacious answer for the son of a car salesman, but Joe was continuing to hone his knack for crashing the gates. That's how he had met the stunned woman's daughter, Neilia Hunter, in the first place.

Joe was a junior at the University of Delaware when he took a spring break trip down to Fort Lauderdale. From there, he and some buddies decided to jump a cut-rate flight to the Bahamas. In Nassau, they noticed that the public beach they were making use of was not nearly as nice as the British Colonial Hotel's next door. The British Colonial was blocked off by a chain-link fence, so Joe and his friends nicked some towels emblazoned with the hotel's insignia that were hanging on the fence and waltzed in past security, right through the front door.

It was Archmere all over again: Joe peered inside, liked what he saw, and went for it.

Encountering a pair of attractive coeds poolside, Joe declared, "I've got the blonde," and introduced himself to Neilia.

They hit it off and started dating. The draws of college life gave way to a single-minded focus on Neilia.

Joe was not particularly scholarly in college, much to his father' chagrin. "I was looking for Bs, a C-plus," Joe Sr. groused about the low bar his son often failed to hit.[50] Despite Joe's lackluster grades, he resolved to attend Syracuse Law School to be close to Neilia, and he got in.[51]

Jimmy was not focused on academics, either. But when he was graduating high school, Joe took his younger brother to meet the dean of the University of Delaware's college of agriculture. "It was the easiest one to get into," Jimmy explained. It worked. Jimmy got in, and later transferred into the college of arts and sciences.[52]

Things tended to work out for the siblings. The Bidens were attractive, athletic, and popular.

Jimmy had a rascally sense of humor and was something of a rogue, always on the make. Frank, like Joe, struggled with a stutter, and idolized his confident oldest brother, who overcame it with greater ease. "I was considered a dummy," recalled Frank, who came to consider Joe his hero.[53] As a teenager, he bounced around from high school to high school,[54] but he earned a reputation as an athlete along the way. He was a high-scoring guard on the basketball court[55] and a standout football kicker.[56]

Val, the responsible one, was studious. She followed Joe to the University of Delaware, where she made the dean's list.[57] She was also named Homecoming Queen.

For his part, Joe quit the college football team to spend more time with Neilia (or Joe Sr. made him quit because his grades were suffering, depending on which source you consult).[58] She was from upstate New York, where her family had a big spread up on one of the Finger Lakes,

Skaneateles. After the Bahamas, Joe began driving up there on week-ends to be with her. To pay for the sojourns, he drove cars that his father's Chevrolet dealership needed moved from one location to another.[59]

Law school did not make Joe any more scholarly. A botched citation on a paper got him investigated for plagiarism. He talked his way out of it and survived the rest of law school by the skin of his teeth. To make ends meet, he took on part-time work driving a school bus.[60]

Between his first and second years, he and Neilia married. As a wedding gift, Joe Sr. gave him a green Corvette convertible.[61]

After his graduation in 1968, the couple moved back to Wilmington. He took a job at a white-shoe, Republican law firm but soon left to work as a public defender.

They had their first child, Joseph Robinette Biden III, on February 3, 1969. They called him Beau. A year and a day after Beau, Robert Hunter Biden came along. The next year brought Naomi Christina Biden. They called her Amy, and sometimes Caspy, on account of a resemblance to Casper the Friendly Ghost.[62] Rounding out the happy family were two dogs, a Great Dane and a German shepherd.[63]

Joe was determined to give them a home fit for a Biden. As a student at Archmere, he would fantasize about the fine houses he glimpsed from the school bus window. "I'd been seduced by real estate," he later confessed.[64]

So, after law school, he embarked on a frantic climb up the property ladder. With money from his father-in-law, he bought one house to rent out and flip. Then, he set his eyes on another house nestled into some woods at the end of a cul-de-sac.[65] The house was out of Joe's price range, so he convinced his parents to buy it and move in, sitting on it until Joe could afford it himself. His parents, in turn, sold to Joe the house he had grown up in on Wilson Road, and Joe planned to move back into it. But then he was offered a deal on a cottage set on seventeen acres. He and his young family could live there rent free if he managed a swimming club on the grounds. Joe took the deal and rented out his boyhood home to tenants.

While living on the grounds of the swim club, he soon set his eyes on another property, a farm over the Delaware state line. At eighty-five acres, there was room for Joe's siblings and parents to build houses of their own: a proper Biden compound at last. Joe bought it. Jimmy fixed it up and found some more tenants.[66] Still shy of thirty, Joe was presiding over a small property empire.

But he was still striving when it came to real estate. On the weekends, he took his family on drives around the region, looking for their dream home.[67] They found a handsome Colonial with a swimming pool, situated on three acres on North Star Road, in a leafy neighborhood west of Wilmington proper.

He bought it, but the purchase was complicated by Joe's other new pastime: politics.

In the late '60s, Joe did not fully identify with either party. The Finnegans were Truman Democrats, but the party's Southern wing represented white racial reaction. Joe briefly fancied himself a Republican and considered running for office as one, but he had no love for Richard Nixon.[68]

Instead, he cast his lot with the local Democrats and won a seat on the New Castle County Council in 1970. Neilia and Val ran the campaign. The whole clan helped to canvass the county. "There was a Biden at every door," Val recalled.[69]

When Joe won, his taste for real estate collided with his political career. The North Star house was outside of his county council district. He enlisted his parents in another game of property musical chairs. Joe Sr. and Jean moved into the newly purchased North Star house, while Joe and his family moved into the house his parents vacated, which was inside the bounds of his district.[70] (Years later, it emerged that the house, which remained Joe's residence through the beginning of his Senate tenure, came with a restrictive covenant barring it from being "owned or occupied by any Negro or person of Negro extraction." Joe said that the clause, which had long been rendered unenforceable by the Supreme Court, had appeared on a separate document from the deed his father had signed, and that his parents had filed a declaration disavowing the covenant.)[71]

Joe's new duties gave him another early glimpse of the uncomfortable tensions between family life and public duty. After he took his seat on the council, a local bigwig, John Rollins, came seeking permission to install a helipad at his corporate headquarters. Joe's constituents did not want a helicopter coming and going over their neighborhoods. So Joe killed the helipad. But the decision was uncomfortable. In addition to being a former lieutenant governor, Rollins had employed Joe's father at a car dealership.

A subsequent encounter with Rollins was awkward, but the onetime officeholder reassured Joe, "I'd have done the same damn thing."[72]

It soon became clear that zoning fights and tiptoeing around the bigshots of the Brandywine Valley held little interest for Joe. He had barely settled into the county council when he decided to run for the U.S. Senate.

This was to be the most audacious gate-crash yet. The incumbent, Republican Caleb Boggs, was widely revered. Joe, on the other hand, had barely been out of diapers when Delawareans had first sent Boggs to Congress. Joe's résumé did not exactly scream out for membership in the nation's most august body, either. He was juggling barely launched careers in law and local politics. He would be twenty-nine years old on Election Day, and become age-eligible for the chamber only in the interval between the vote and the January swearing-in.

In other ways, though, Joe was prepared to leapfrog to the top of the American pecking order more than anybody outside of the Biden clan could hope to realize.

Some of the hints were less subtle than others. While Joe was living on the grounds of the swim club, his future Senate colleague Bill Roth was already a neighbor. They got to know each other on account of their dogs. Roth's dog was a Saint Bernard, Ludwig. One of Joe's dogs was named Governor.

Joe explained the name away as some sort of Biden family inside joke. The same went for the name of Joe's other dog: Senator.[73]

The Children's Crusade

"I just hope I see him before my brother does."

—Joe, condemning a volunteer who betrayed his campaign

On March 20, 1972, Joe announced his run for the Senate with a speech at the Hotel DuPont in Wilmington, then boarded a prop plane, stuck Beau on his lap, and took off to barnstorm the state with his family.[74]

He didn't have money, or name recognition, or experience, or a political machine. What he had was his youth, his charm, and the Bidens.

Val served as his campaign manager. Her husband, Bruce Saunders, was budget director.[75]

Neilia was involved in nearly all aspects of the campaign.[76] Jimmy was in charge of fund-raising. Frank, all of eighteen years old, oversaw the campaign headquarters.[77]

Joe Sr. served as a surrogate at events that Joe could not make.[78] It was a role that confused many voters, who assumed the more senior Biden was the one running. This could occur even at events where his son was standing onstage with him.[79]

The family's early strategy boiled down to providing voters, particularly women voters, an intimate glimpse of Joe. Before he announced, the family put on a never-ending series of coffee klatches around the state to give the housewives of Delaware a chance to see Joe up close. Jean, known to campaign volunteers as "Mama Biden," scheduled the coffees.[80] After each get-together, Neilia and Val sent a handwritten note to each attendee.[81]

They had gotten the idea from the Kennedys, who hosted family teas as part of Jack's 1952 Massachusetts Senate campaign, another long shot challenge to an entrenched Republican incumbent. The Bidens even hired a Kennedy aide, Matt Reese, to help them pull it off.[82]

Such parallels did not go unnoticed. Pointing to the family-run campaign, *Time* magazine described him as a candidate "in the Kennedy mold."[83]

"He has a Kennedy style about him," a Republican aide conceded to the AP.[84]

This was all before describing a young pol as Kennedy-esque became a cliché, and well before "You, sir, are no Jack Kennedy," entered the lexicon.

Of course, a little charisma and mystique were no substitutes for a campaign, so the Bidens campaigned. Doggedly. They put in seventeen-hour days.[85] Joe would sometimes get home from a day of campaigning close to midnight, his wife and three children in the car with him, fast asleep.[86] Sometimes, Neilia would take the wheel so that Joe could get out of the car at every red light and shake a few hands before it changed.[87]

Enduring this sort of slog to slowly flip a few votes came naturally to a family steeped in the great midcentury American tradition of sales. Both Joe Sr. and his brother, Uncle Frank, worked car lots in Wilmington. Uncle Boo Boo was a traveling mattress salesman.[88] This was like second nature to them. "In the Biden family," the younger Frank Biden, Joe's brother, explained, "we call it door-to-door, store to store, 'til there ain't no more."[89]

To keep the operation funded, Jimmy learned to be an aggressive deal closer. He would take the train to Washington, or zip around the country, hanging around labor leaders and various other poobahs, trying to get them to take him and his big brother seriously.

When enough money was rolling in to hire outside help, Joe interviewed some professional consultants. They advised him to get his family out of the campaign and their pictures out of the mailers that were blanketing the state. It sent the wrong message. "They said that people don't equate strength with a family man," Val recalled later, "and they said Joey needed to look strong in order to have a chance to win."

Joe showed those consultants the door.[90] They didn't understand that the Bidens *were* the message.

Joe did sign up Pat Caddell, a twenty-two-year-old pollster out of Harvard, and John Marttila, another young consultant from Boston. A DuPont engineer, Ted Kaufman, came on as a volunteer, and quickly became a trusted consigliere.

Naturally, Joe set himself up as the candidate of change.

Vietnam was still raging, and in response to discontent over the draft, the Twenty-Sixth Amendment had just passed, lowering the voting age by three years. This was to be the first national election in which eighteen-, nineteen-, and twenty-year-olds could vote, and youth was one of the few clear advantages Joe held over his sexagenarian opponent.

With a shoestring budget and no notion of what a U.S. Senate campaign looked like from the inside, the Bidens improvised. "We created a brand-new campaign because we had no option," Val explained.[91]

Jimmy and Frank recruited their friends into a massive youth volunteer operation, which swelled to hundreds of members. Val enlisted her students at the Wilmington Friends School. (According to Richard Ben Cramer's *What It Takes*, she told them they had to volunteer if they wanted to pass her class.)[92]

The campaign printed up faux newspapers touting Joe's promise and the volunteers distributed them by hand. They'd blanket the state with two hundred thousand copies in a weekend. Joe might have been a long shot, but the newsprint made him seem real. "People believed newspapers then," recalled Tom Stiltz, one of the campaign's youthful volunteers.[93]

In their rare off hours, the youthful staff socialized together, swimming and playing touch football. "I guess we thought we were the Kennedys," recalled Richard Heffron, who worked on the campaign.[94]

Val dubbed the effort a latter-day "Children's Crusade."[95] The Bidens were counting on those children to help them win converts. Joe figured that teenagers had more influence over their elders than vice versa, so he campaigned at high schools in Republican areas, knowing the students would go home and talk him up to their parents.[96]

Boggs, meanwhile, barely lifted a finger. Despite these upstart Bidens, his seat was still considered safe. By Labor Day, Joe was down twenty-eight points in the polls.[97] But every day the clan kept grinding, and every day it added up.

Slowly, Joe started to get national attention. At the time, his law school buddy, Jack Owens, was working for Milton Shapp, a Democrat and the first Jewish governor of Pennsylvania. He enlisted Shapp to come south and campaign for Joe at an event at the Hotel DuPont. The crowd could have been bigger, but Joe and Shapp were competing with a Jewish wedding being held at the Brandywine Country Club. So, after the hotel event, they decided to crash the wedding.[98]

At the end of September, the campaign got an even bigger boost when Ted Kennedy came to town, with a Secret Service escort in tow.

At St. Mark's High School, nuns flocked to Teddy like teenyboppers to the Beatles. At the state party's annual Jefferson-Jackson dinner, the $50-dollar-a-plate filet mignon was more like a lump of brown beef roast, but what the event lacked in gastronomy, it made up for in enthusiasm. State party chairman Michael Poppiti suggested Teddy should run for president, and the crowd roared.

In his remarks, Teddy singled Joe out for praise. It was a Saturday night, and after dinner, Joe and Teddy hit the town in their tuxes. With Neilia in tow, they cruised over to a dance hall in the Polish section of town for "Patriotic Night," where the band, complete with an accordion player, performed next to an American flag.

"We don't want to interrupt your dance," Teddy announced. "But Joe Biden and I thought we'd drop by and see if we could find somebody to dance with." Women squealed.

Afterward, Teddy zipped back to Washington on a private plane owned by local magnate John Rollins, Joe Sr.'s old boss, who evidently was not suffering for his lack of a helipad.[99]

Clearly, the Biden campaign was starting to catch on. In the final weeks before the election, Boggs started to wake up. At a rally hosted by the Wilmington Republican Committee at the Hotel DuPont in mid-October, the incumbent complained of "distortions and innuendos" in a Biden ad on his tax record. As Boggs spoke, Neilia sat in the crowd with a tape recorder. That night, she was playing the role of campaign tracker—the person, usually a young staffer, tasked with attending all the opposing candidate's events and recording them in hopes of catching a misstep. Wilmington's Republican mayor spotted her and called out her presence, prompting Neilia to smile and clap, according to reporter Curtis Wilkie.[100]

To counter Joe's newsprint strategy, the Republicans ordered advertising inserts to go out in the state's largest newspapers, the *Morning News* and *Evening Journal*, which were under common ownership. Just like Joe's campaign literature, the inserts looked like real newspapers. One featured a picture of a kitchen sink on the cover and the caption, "The only thing that Joe Biden hasn't promised you."[101]

The weekend before the election, the Republicans were going to run an insert with a picture of the moon on the cover and the same caption. The empire was striking back.

Joe had already taken out a mortgage on his house to keep the campaign afloat. The Bidens were out of money to counter Boggs's last-minute push with ads of their own.

To make matters worse, on the Thursday before the election, the

Morning News ran a front page story about a volunteer, Victor Livingston, who had quit the Biden campaign in outrage over Joe's opinions on Israel. Livingston said Joe instructed him to author a campaign position paper that offered strong support for Israel, even though Joe did not believe in it, because Joe was courting Jewish donors.[102]

Joe, who contested Livingston's version of events, was furious. The former volunteer expressed fear that the Bidens were going to come after him, evidently with good reason.

"I just hope I see him before my brother does," the candidate told Robert Schwabach, a Wilmington-based reporter for the *Philadelphia Inquirer*. When Schwabach asked Joe if that was because his brother would attack Livingston, the candidate responded, "Naw, he would just kiss him on the cheek."[103]

Then, on Thursday night, the Bidens' luck turned. The unionized truck drivers who distributed the newspapers went on strike, bringing production and distribution of the News Journal Company papers to a halt. A brawl broke out at the printing plant between picketing truck drivers and printers trying to enter the facility. Several people were injured, forcing police to intervene. The papers did not get out in any number again until Monday, the day before the election. Neither did the Republicans' anti-Biden insert.[104]

A group of Republican volunteers scrambled to pass out as many copies of the insert as they could by hand, but they got nowhere close to saturating the state.[105]

Then, on the eve of the election, Joe got another gift from the Kennedys. George McGovern's running mate, Sargent Shriver, and his wife, Eunice Kennedy—Jack and Teddy's sister—came to New Castle to campaign for the Democratic slate. The rally kicked off with a torchlit parade to the courthouse square. Joe and Shriver drew the biggest cheers that night.[106]

Luckily for Joe, his fortunes were not as hitched to McGovern's and Shriver's as they normally would be. Delaware had just done away with voting machines that allowed for straight-ballot voting with a single pull of the lever. The Nixon landslide that was materializing would not so easily sweep Joe's campaign away with it.

On Election Day, there was more good news. The skies over Delaware were clear, pointing to higher turnout, a boon to a Democratic candidate.

Joe and his supporters gathered in a ballroom at the Hotel DuPont. As the results trickled in, he and Boggs traded the lead throughout the night.

In the end, the weather, the strike, the youth vote, the end of the straight-ticket machines, all came together for the upstart Biden campaign. Just before the clocks tolled midnight, Val made it official. "We won!" she announced over the sound system. They had eked it out by three thousand votes.

The band struck up "Happy Days Are Here Again." Joe waited another half hour or so for official confirmation of his win, then he and his young supporters partied into the wee hours.[107]

Among the revelers that night was a college student, Jill Jacobs. Her husband, a rock club owner, was a big supporter of Joe's. Jill took notice of Neilia, an island of calm among the frenzy in the ballroom, and introduced herself. "Congratulations on your win," Jill told her. Neilia smiled back at her, and responded, "Thank you so much."[108]

As it happened, at the end of the night, Jill and her husband retired to a hotel room two doors down from Joe and Neilia's.[109]

The Bidens had done it. From there on out, the family saw Joe's political career as their collective endeavor. They took on the habit of speaking of it in terms of "we"—"We haven't decided what our position is on that," or "We aren't running for President."[110]

Joe was among the youngest people ever elected to the Senate, having won an unwinnable race. The achievement was all the more remarkable because Nixon had carried forty-nine states. Joe's win was the rare bright spot for Democrats that November, and the biggest upset of the cycle.

Just as remarkable was that the campaign had been managed by his twenty-seven-year-old kid sister.

Today, if a twentysomething woman with no political experience were to manage the biggest upset campaign of a whole election cycle, her face would be on magazine covers. She would likely become a household name, especially, if like Val, she had done it while recovering from a miscarriage.[111] The feat was even more extraordinary back in 1972. When Joe took office, there were no female senators in the chamber.[112] The first woman had just been permitted to serve as an elevator operator in the Senate the year before.[113]

In fact, plenty of people felt Val should have been the Biden on the ticket. After all, she had gotten better marks than her older brother in college and been voted homecoming queen. Instead of a Senate seat or a magazine cover, she got a profile in the local paper that dubbed her "the best-looking campaign manager in the country." The reporter told her, "It must have been fun playing touch football with you, especially for the other team." Val laughed it off.[114] Another profile of the campaign described her as "all steel sinews under beauty."[115]

When Joe earned ink in *Time* magazine on the eve of the election, Val's name didn't make the profile, though Neilia was mentioned as a "pretty blonde."[116]

Of course, this says a lot about American attitudes toward gender in the early 1970s. But there was also a class element to the short shrift given Val. Three years earlier, Hillary Clinton had delivered a commencement address at Wellesley, the elite, northeastern women's college, in which she spoke up in favor of protest and criticized the other commencement speaker, Massachusetts Republican senator Ed Brooks. The act of delivering some controversial remarks on a prestigious campus got her featured in *Life* magazine.[117] She was invited to address the fiftieth-anniversary convention of the League of Women Voters.[118]

Clinton went on to spend the summer of 1972 campaigning in Texas for McGovern's flameout of a campaign.

Val, with her good grades from the University of Delaware, and her methodical approach to winning, didn't take on the same cachet.

It was a pattern that endured over the decades. The Bidens never seemed to get the same respect, or inspire the same awe—or hatred, for that matter—as the Clintons, with their Ivy league degrees, or the Obamas, who had those *and* global celebrity, or the Kennedys, who also had both, and a family fortune to boot.

Despite all the Camelot comparisons, the Bidens lacked those ingredients of the Kennedy mystique.

And there was another missing element that made the Kennedy comparison incomplete, but that would abruptly change.

On December 18, Joe and Val were in Washington assembling a staff. Among others, they were bringing on Wes Barthelmes, a former Bobby Kennedy aide.[119]

While the Senate was in recess, the Bidens had temporarily set up their DC headquarters in the offices of West Virginia senator Robert Byrd, where a phone call came in for Val. It was Jimmy.[120] He told her there had been a car accident. A truck coming down a hill had plowed into the side of Neilia's car at an intersection while she was out shopping for a Christmas tree. Neilia and Naomi were dead. Beau and Hunter were seriously injured.[121]

"There's been a slight accident," Val told Joe. "Nothing to be worried about. But we ought to go home."[122]

Jimmy arranged for a plane to rush Joe and Val back to Delaware.

As their footsteps echoed through the empty hallways of the Russell Senate Office Building, Joe turned to Val and said, "She's dead, isn't she?"

Val could not bear to break it to him. "I don't know, Joey," she said. They flew home in silence.[123]

The campaign had made the Bidens a lively subplot of the 1972 election cycle. The crash seared their story into the national consciousness.

Reporters and cameras were a constant presence at Wilmington Medical Center, where Hunter, two, and Beau, three, lay recovering. Ted Kennedy sent a doctor to look after Beau and Hunter.[124]

Hunter's first memory was lying next to his big brother in a hospital bed, while Beau held his hand, looked into his eyes, and repeated, "I love you. I love you."[125] He does not remember a time before his family drama became national news.

Joe slept in their hospital room. In the weeks afterward, he was inconsolable and filled with rage at the blow he had been dealt by fate.

He considered quitting the Senate before he started. He went to the bishop of Wilmington to ask about getting a special dispensation to become a priest.[126] Jimmy began talks with Sherman Tribbitt, the newly elected governor, about the process of appointing a successor. But the Senate majority leader, Mike Mansfield of Montana, was not having it, and he convinced Joe to give the Senate a shot.[127]

On Friday, January 5, 1973, Joe took his oath of office at the hospital chapel on a massive Bible with a Celtic cross on the cover that had been in the family since 1893.[128] Hunter had been released from the hospital's care, but Beau remained bedridden. Before the swearing-in, Beau and Hunter presented their father with a pair of gold pens in Beau's hospital room, with news crews looking on. The media swarm grew too large for Beau's room, so he was wheeled into the chapel, where Joe's old headmaster from Archmere gave an invocation.

Beau tried to make a speech. Hunter tried to play with the microphones the networks had set up on a podium. Joe took the oath with his back facing the cameras from the national networks, so an NBC correspondent induced him to turn around and take it again.

The *Morning News* described the scene as "both tragedy and carnival."[129]

Joe went through severe depression. The title of his memoir, *Promises to Keep*, is an allusion to Robert Frost's 1923 poem, "Stopping by

Woods on a Snowy Evening." In it, the narrator pauses his journey on a cold winter's night to entertain a temptation to wander off into a frozen forest.

It ends:

The woods are lovely, dark and deep,
But I have promises to keep,
And miles to go before I sleep,
And miles to go before I sleep.

The poem is widely interpreted to be about the contemplation of suicide. In the aftermath of the accident, Joe did consider killing himself. "Suicide wasn't just an option, but a *rational* option," he wrote in the memoir. Instead, he decided he owed it to his sons to keep going.[130]

Val and her husband moved in with Joe so that she could take care of Beau and Hunter. Jimmy, too, took on the role of surrogate parent, setting up an apartment in Joe's garage.[131] In Washington, Joe barely attended to his Senate duties, spending all day on the phone with Val, Jimmy, his sons, his parents.

Jimmy, Joe's steady companion during this time, would sometimes take leave of Joe as his older brother sat at his home study at the end of the night, only to find Joe still planted in the same spot in the morning, staring at the wall. "I'm not sure how much he valued in his life in those days," Jimmy recalled. "Except the boys."[132]

Joe's memoir does not mention Frank's role during this time, but he did not stray far from his grieving big brother. Reports issued by the Architect of the Capitol show he got work as an elevator operator in the Senate in Joe's first year there.[133]

In the immediate aftermath of the crash, Joe and Jimmy would walk silently through the streets of Wilmington's roughest neighborhoods at night, looking for a fight.[134]

Two months into his Senate term, Joe traveled to New Orleans with

Jimmy to give a speech at Tulane University. Late at night, the brothers came across four men walking toward them. Neither group was going to give ground so they walked right into each other. Joe thought to himself, *Take 'em on.* As they all stood facing each other, wondering who would throw the first punch, a cop came around the corner. It finally dawned on Joe, *What the hell am I doing? I'm a United States senator.*[135]

How the Bidens Became Irish

"I am not an EYE-talian, but an Italo-American and proud of my ethnic background!"

—Providence mayor Buddy Cianci, 1976

On March 17, 1973, the Friendly Sons of Saint Patrick of Lacka-wanna County hosted its sixty-eighth annual feast in the ballroom of Scranton's Casey Inn. The room that night was packed with revelers. They were there to see the local kid whose life had become national news.

In the run-up to the event, organizers feared their recently widowed keynote speaker would be a no-show. But when the doors of the luxe ballroom swung open, there was Joe Biden, striding in shoulder to shoulder with his father and three uncles. One attendee compared the entrance to the Gunfight at the OK Corral.

When Joe took the stage, he praised the Irish love of liberty and criticized London's heavy hand in Northern Ireland.

As he reflected on the loss of his wife and daughter, the holiday feast morphed into an Irish wake of sorts. He remarked that life had shaken his hand and given him a kick at the same time. "That's the Irish of it," he said, a line he would still be dropping at St. Patrick's Day Celebrations forty years later.[136]

As Joe explained years later, the Friendly Sons dinners drew a different crowd than the ones he usually faced at Irish gatherings in Delaware, where the ancestors of attendees had mostly come over as laborers recruited by the DuPont company, under relatively favorable conditions. Like many things in Delaware, the Friends of Ireland dinners there were genteel affairs, Joe told *Irish America* magazine in 1987. Protestants and Catholics broke bread together. The Irish who came to Scranton, on the other hand, had mainly fled the famine, and their descendants tended to harbor anti-Protestant sentiment. " 'Friendly Sons,' means you don't have any orange on your body anywhere, do you? Check your underwear," Joe joked, referring to the color associated with Irish protestants. "You know, it's no foolin' around."[137] The Friendly Sons dinners were also all men.[138]

Joe's speech roused the room to its feet three times.[139] This was his crowd, and a homecoming in the truest sense.

On his mother's side, all eight of Joe's great-grandparents could be traced back to Ireland. His Blewitt ancestors fled from Ballina, in County Mayo, one of the areas most ravished by the Famine. Joe's great-great-great-grandfather, Edward Blewitt, set up shop as a land surveyor in Scranton in the middle of the nineteenth century.[140]

Edward's grandson, Joe's great-grandfather, Edward F. Blewitt, had been a state senator from Scranton, sometimes credited as the first Irish Catholic in that body, and had cofounded the Irish-American Society of Lackawanna County, the group that later became the Friendly Sons.[141]

The venue for Joe's speech that night was a fitting one as well. Opened in 1911, the Casey Inn, originally the Hotel Casey, had been built downtown by industrious Irish immigrants, Patrick and Andrew Casey. The hotel went up on the site where the home of city father George W. Scranton once stood.[142]

This was the Scranton that Joe's maternal grandfather, Ambrose Finnegan, the son of apple pickers, was born into—one rife with tensions between the descendants of Irish immigrants and the old WASP elite.

Joe gets all of a dozen paragraphs into the prologue of his memoir before we learn what "Pop" Finnegan thought of that tension. Joe describes one of the weekly gatherings his grandfather hosted in his home after Sunday Mass during Joe's childhood. At this one, talk turned to "Patrick," a local machine politician Joe describes as "a slick Irish operator, friend to the diocese, friend to the working man, friend to his neighbors, friend to his family— maybe too good a friend...Patrick's political favors, even in the days of patronage, had often caught the attention of the local newspapers."

While the others gathered around the kitchen table dragged the slick pol, Pop Finnegan kept defending the man. Then, he surprised his grandson by turning to him and saying, "Joey, you're wondering why Pop likes Patrick." Indeed, Joe was. Pop Finnegan explained that whenever he needed a favor, Patrick gave it to him straight. "Whatever Patrick has to say, he's gonna say it to my face. I might not agree with him, but he thinks enough of me to tell me to my face."

Joe's grandfather contrasted that with the style of William Scranton, a descendant of the city's founding family, and a Republican politician, whom young Joe naturally revered as a leading citizen. Pop Finnegan explained that if he went to ask Scranton for a favor, Scranton's butler would escort him to the library of Scranton's mansion, where he would explain his problem over sherry. Imitating Scranton's response, Pop Finnegan said, "I'd be happy to help," then he hit his grandson on the back hard enough to startle him.

"Joey," he explained, "it wouldn't be until I got my coat, got out the door, and reached the first landing that I felt a warm trickle of blood down my spine."

The moral of the story: "Joey, remember this: Men like Mr. Scranton would never do to their friends at the country club what they would do to us on the street. They think politics is beneath them. They think politics is only for the Poles and the Irish and Italians and Jews."

━━━━━━━

Joe's Irish heritage and his Catholicism informed his worldview and, later, became integral to his political persona. While these aspects of his identity sometimes presented challenges, such as when conservative Catholic teachings ran into conflict with his liberal political positions, he learned to wield them skillfully in public life.

Joe expresses ambivalence about Pop Finnegan's view of the world,[143] but his childhood left him with a deep sense of his Irishness, imbuing him with an appreciation for the bittersweetness of life and a black, self-deprecating sense of humor.

It's an ethos that continues to suffuse Joe's old Scranton neighborhood. A couple blocks from Joe's childhood home is Hank's Hoagies, a small sub shop that Joe still makes a habit of visiting when he returns to his hometown. Inside, the place is decorated with fading sports memorabilia. It seems to have changed little since Joe left town in 1952, save for the addition of a cardboard cutout of an adult Joe Biden, sporting, during the coronavirus pandemic, a new facemask. Behind cardboard Joe, a laminated piece of paper, browned with age and crumpling at the edges, lists "Murphy's Laws—And other truths." It includes morsels of wisdom like, "If you're feeling good, don't worry, you'll get over it."

A sign on another wall declares, "The Irish Way: Now don't be talking about yourself while you're here. We'll surely be doing that after you leave."[144]

Raised in parochial schools and in neighborhoods ruled by nuns and priests, Joe's Irish Catholic community offered an oasis in a sometimes hostile world.

(Joe seems to suffer no illusions about the fact that the Irish in America have had their own problems with the treatment of outsiders, sometimes in ways that were far bloodier than Mr. Scranton's figurative back-stabbing. In his memoir, he describes the time a group of Black boys he had befriended during a summer lifeguarding job visited him in an Irish neighborhood in the 1960s. They were beaten badly for drinking out of the wrong water fountain.)[145]

The importance of weathering this hostility was imprinted on Joe. He ends the preface of his memoir with a familial lesson about which he shows no ambivalence: his father's insistence that when life knocks you on your ass, you get back up. "Bad grade? *Get Up!*" he writes, describing this ethos. "The girl's parents won't let her go out with a Catholic boy? *Get up!*"[146]

Joe's Catholicism actually did present a minor roadblock in his relationship with Neilia, whose aunt was active in the Presbyterian Church. But a little Protestant snobbery proved no match for the young lovers, and Neilia's father even consented to holding the ceremony in a Catholic church.[147]

As a politician, Joe even learned to use anti-Catholic sentiment to his advantage. In the fall of 1984, as he cruised to his second reelection, Joe decided to have a little fun at a candidates' forum held right before Sunday services at First Baptist Church near New Castle. The church had described its criteria for a winning candidate as "pro-life, pro-American, pro-family and pro-moral." This conservative Christian congregation was not Joe's crowd, but he did not shrink from making his case. To put a fine point on his opposition to organized school prayer, Joe made a sign of the cross and recited a Catholic prayer to the Baptist congregants. "How many of you want your children to pray that way?" he asked. The Baptists were properly scandalized.[148]

Joe's Irish Catholicism was also an important part of his political image from the start. "The Washington press corps ushered me to town as a kind of poor Kennedy cousin: I was Irish, Catholic, young, toothsome," he recalls in his memoir. "The reporters were sure I was a liberal."[149]

Asked as a senator who his heroes were, Joe would usually answer Wolfe Tone, an eighteenth-century Protestant Irishman sentenced to death for his role leading a revolt against British rule. "He had nothing to gain on the face of it," Biden told *Irish America* magazine in 1987, "but he sought to relieve the oppression of the Catholics caused by the Penal Laws. He gave his life for the principle of civil rights for all people."[150]

Later, Joe began citing the Irishman Seamus Heaney as his favorite poet. He is especially fond of a passage from "The Cure at Troy," a 1991 adaptation of a Sophocles play about the end of the Trojan War, known for the lines:

The longed-for tidal wave
Of justice can rise up,
And hope and history rhyme.

Bill Clinton quoted the passage during a speech in Northern Ireland in 1995,[151] and Joe has cited it in settings from the campaign trail to a think tank, a memorial service, and his 2020 acceptance speech at the Democratic National Convention.

It makes for a subtle contrast with one of Obama's favorite lines, "The arc of the moral universe is long, but it bends toward justice," which traces back to Martin Luther King Jr. and the nineteenth-century Unitarian theologian Theodore Parker. It expresses a confident view of progress, as something that may be painstakingly slow but is inevitable.

Joe has been citing those lines of Heaney's since at least 2005.[152] But perhaps it took four years of Donald Trump, who forced millions of Americans to reevaluate their metaphysical assumptions about the world, for the electorate to come around to Joe's more wizened, more Irish view of hope, history, and justice.

Joe, who continues to attend Mass regularly, has attributed his sense of justice to his Catholic upbringing. This has influenced his approach to foreign policy. Imbued with this sympathy for the little guy, Joe became the champion of Catholic Croats and Bosnian Muslims in the face of Orthodox Serbian aggression. His efforts were instrumental to international interventions in the ethnic conflicts that tore apart the country. He credits his interest in the Balkans to a Croatian monk who began showing up at his Senate office in the early '90s, decked out in traditional robes, to implore him to intervene there, and invoking his Catholicism.[153]

Throughout the Troubles, Joe expressed support for the Irish cause and sometimes took action in the Senate. In 1985, he voiced opposition to an extradition treaty with Britain that would have affected members of the Irish Republican Army who had fled to the United States, taking issue with the British administration of justice in Northern Ireland,[154] and he helped force Republicans to water down the agreement.[155]

Efforts such as these were apparently enough to anger one group of Brits who tried, and failed, to buy the domain name Biden2004.com to air their grievances when Joe was considering challenging George W. Bush's reelection.[156]

Though Northern Ireland never became a marquee Biden issue, Joe came to be indelibly associated with his Irishness. During her vice presidential debate preparations, Sarah Palin famously struggled with his name. She kept calling him "O'Biden." The Secret Service, meanwhile, assigned him the code name Celtic.

———————

But that's only half the story of Joe's heritage—or, more precisely, five-eighths of it.

On his father's side, Joe's ancestry is mostly English.

"The ambiance is probably stronger than the lineage," he conceded to *Irish America* magazine in that 1987 interview. "I grew up in Scranton, in a predominantly Irish neighborhood in an overwhelmingly Irish parish."

"There is an ongoing debate as to whether Biden is an Irish, English or German name," Joe told the magazine, but his Scranton relatives preferred not to dwell on the likelihood that they were sleeping with the enemy. "My grandfather and my mother were never crazy about it being English and used to say, 'Tell him it's Dutch,'" he recalled.

When Joe was a young boy, his great-aunt Gertie once told him, "Your father's not a bad man. He's just English."[157]

Joe Sr. seemed to take Aunt Gertie's side at times, expressing the belief that the name Biden *was* Irish.

At least that's the way Joe recalled it to *Irish America* as he prepared for his presidential run. Expressions of identity have a way of adapting themselves to the political moment. In America, the German Trumps, during the World Wars, took to passing as Swedish.

There was little reason, or outlet, for Joe to express an English side to his identity as an up-and-coming Democratic politician in Delaware in the early '70s. The French Huegenout du Pont family and their allies dominated Republican politics in the state, an extension of a broader Northern pattern in which native WASPs generally aligned with the Republican Party against white ethnic and Black Democrats.

In that context, English American identity was not politically potent as such. For white ethnic immigrant groups, on the other hand, pride over their heritage formed the identity politics of that era.

Joe's Irishness continued to prove an asset in the Obama years. In the 2008 primary, white Catholic voters broke decisively for Hillary Clinton, leading the staid Pew Research Center to opine on "Obama's Catholic voter problem."[158] Joe's addition to the ticket was greeted as a potential remedy to that problem.[159]

Occasionally, this presented complications, such as when Catholic prelates, including one in Scranton in 2008, barred Joe from receiving communion over his support of abortion rights, a common Church rebuke of Catholic Democrats.[160] The Obama administration's signature legislation, the Affordable Care Act, likewise encountered resistance from Catholic leaders. The United States Conference of Catholic Bishops objected to provisions that allowed federal funding for abortions, compelled employers to help cover the costs of contraception, and barred undocumented immigrants from accessing health insurance exchanges.[161]

During the papacy of Pope Benedict, a conservative, the Vatican stepped up its oversight of American nuns in response to their perceived leftward drift. In June 2011, Joe met with Benedict at the Vatican and reportedly spoke up for the nuns, telling the pontifex to "lighten up."[162]

Joe's Irish Catholicism has also provided material for theatrical ice-breakers. When he hosted British prime minister David Cameron for a state luncheon in 2012 in the ornate Franklin Dining Room in Foggy Bottom, he joked about his Irish family's traditional antipathy for the English. "Ambrose Finnegan," he called out toward the ceiling, perhaps mindful of that warning Pop had given about trying to make deals with WASPs in fancy rooms. "Things have changed."[163]

After being introduced by his daughter Ashley's husband, Howard Krein, at a health care event during Obama's second term, Joe cracked, "As usual I'm going to say something that I shouldn't. Every Irish Catholic father looks forward to the day that his daughter will marry a Jewish surgeon."[164]

With Catholics shaping up as a swing bloc ahead of Obama's reelection, the president himself briefly became "O'Bama," nodding to his maternal Irish ancestry with a 2011 visit to the tiny village northeast of Limerick from which his great-great-great-grandfather had hailed. "I'm Barack Obama, from the Moneygall O'Bamas," he joked in an address there. "And I've come home to find the apostrophe that we lost somewhere along the way." The visit at least played well in Ireland, where Obama's eighth cousin, Henry Healy, parlayed the distant family tie into minor celebrity.[165]

Just after St. Patrick's Day in 2013, Joe accepted his induction into *Irish America*'s Hall of Fame with a speech that tied his Irish ancestors' ocean-crossing experience with his administration's priorities on immigration reform.[166]

Three years later, Joe and a gaggle of Bidens made an official trip to Ireland to reconnect with their Irish roots.

To accompany the trip, Joe commissioned a genealogy covering his mother's side of the family, which was released to the public. He also gave an interview to Ancestry.com, which ran posts about the genealogists' findings.

There was another, fuller Biden genealogy, but it has not seen the light of day. Back in 2004, Joe cold-called James Petty, a genealogist in Salt Lake City (the Mormon Church runs the world's greatest genealogical research library there). He wanted help researching his Scranton ancestors. Eventually, he commissioned a full genealogy.[167] James Petty died in 2020, according to his widow and professional partner, Mary Petty, who said she worked on the Biden genealogy. Mary Petty told me she sat down with Beau and Hunter as part of the process but declined to provide me any information about the genealogy, citing client confidentiality.

While the findings have not been released to the public, genealogists sometimes talk among themselves. Another prominent genealogist in Salt Lake City told me the Petty genealogy showed that on his father's side, some of Joe's ancestors owned slaves.

The existence of slave owners among Joe's paternal ancestors was confirmed to me by Alexander Bannerman, a genealogist in West Virginia. Along with Gary Boyd Roberts, an expert in presidential lineages, Bannerman coauthored an article on Joe's ancestry for the Winter 2021 issue of *American Ancestors*. The magazine is a publication of the New England Historic Genealogical Society, a widely cited authority in the field of ancestry.

"Not a lot of ancestors, and not a lot of slaves," said Bannerman.

He cited Joe's great-great-great-grandfather, George Robinett, who owned two slaves in Allegany County in the 1800 census. Another great-great-great grandfather, Thomas Randle, owned a slave in Baltimore in 1850.

Bannerman explained it is common for Americans with colonial-era roots on the continent to have slave-owning ancestors, and a prepublication version of his article, which he shared with me, did not note that these two ancestors owned slaves.

In the article, Bannerman and his coauthor, Gary Boyd Roberts, did note a distant tie to Varina Anne Banks Howell, the wife of Confederate President Jefferson Davis, via Joe's ancestor Allen Robanet. Bannerman said it was the first presidential kinship tie to Howell that he has come across in his research.

Robanet, who later changed his name to Robinett, probably came to Pennsylvania from England in the 1680s. (Bannerman said he found no evidence that any of Joe's paternal ancestors were French Huguenots, as is sometimes claimed.)

It turns out that one of the more remarkable people that Joe may have ancestral ties to is a freedman named Michael G. Shiner. The possible ties come via some Maryland ancestors, the Pumphreys.

(Joe's ties to Shiner are not confirmed because the link between Joe's great-great-grandmother Jane Eliza Pumphrey of Maryland and her possible father, James Pumphrey, are only putative. Bannerman and Roberts did not find sufficient documentation to say definitively that Jane Eliza's father was James.)

James Pumphrey and his brother, William Pumphrey Jr., both farmers, between them owned Shiner and his wife, Phillis, for much of their respective lives.

Shiner is now known to history for a personal diary he kept for most of the nineteenth century recording life in Washington, DC. Beginning with the British invasion of Washington during the War of 1812, which he witnessed firsthand as a boy, Shiner's accounts have become a trove for scholars, including Navy historian John Sharp, who in recent years has produced studies of Shiner's diary and his life.

Shiner was born into slavery in 1805. Later, Jane Eliza's putative uncle, William Jr., rented his labor to the U.S. Navy for use in Washington's Navy Yard—a common practice in the area at that time—where records indicate he worked on older ships being held in reserve.

William Jr. died in the summer of 1827. He willed that his slaves be sold on the condition that each be freed after a number of years—in Shiner's case, fifteen—a period that his subsequent owner cut in half.

After finally gaining his freedom, Shiner declared, "The only master I have now is the Constitution."

The path to freedom for Phillis was more harrowing. Jane Eliza's putative father, James, died with debts. Her putative brother, Levi, bought Phillis and two of her children from James's estate, then turned around and sold them to Franklin and Armfield, the largest slave dealers in the country. Shiner records in his diary that they "wher snacht away from me and sold."

The trio was held in Alexandria, Virginia, where they could expect to be shipped farther South and encounter harsher conditions. Shiner, though, was able to secure their release both from jail and from slavery.

His family free, Shiner continued working in the Navy Yard, for wages now, as a painter. Later in life, as a Republican activist, he advocated for the cause of former slaves. He became locally prominent, and when he died in 1880, his obituary ran on the front page of one of the local newspapers, the *Evening Star*. It credited him with possessing "the most retentive memory of anyone in the city, being able to give the name and date of every event which came under his observation, even in his boyhood."[168]

———

The existence of slave-owning ancestors can present a conundrum to an American politician, especially a white Democrat who must attract overwhelming support from Black voters to win a national election.

One of Seamus Heaney's most famous poems deals with the perils of interpersonal interaction in a divided society, and the risks posed by divulging seemingly mundane personal details. Its title advises, "Whatever you say, say nothing." Joe seems to have absorbed that wisdom when it comes to this aspect of his background.

While he made a habit of name-checking his father's Irish Hanafee ancestors,[169] Joe's non-Irish ancestry has not played a prominent a role in his public image.

In many contexts, a candidate having distant ancestors who owned slaves would not have much relevance to a campaign. But in the summer of 2020, racial justice protests triggered by a police officer's murder of an unarmed Black man, George Floyd, roiled the country like they had not done in decades.

Beneath the raw outpourings of outrage and frustration, the unrest was fueled in part by the connection between the centuries-old origins of slavery in America and the injustices of the present day. (Some of the statues of slaveholders toppled during the unrest were spray-painted with "1619," a reference to the year slaves were first taken to the future United States. This is also the name of a recent *New York Times Magazine* project exploring the influence of slavery on the course of American history.[170])

If ever there was a time that Joe's slaveholding ancestors could present a political problem for him, it was in that moment.

In June, with the unrest at its height, an internet meme circulated widely claiming that a Biden ancestor, Joseph J. Biden, owned slaves and fought for the Confederacy. At the time, there was not yet an authoritative study of Joe's paternal ancestry available to the public, so it was left to mainstream fact-checkers to investigate the meme. *USA Today*, and the fact-checking sites Politifact and Snopes, all concluded that the meme's claim was unfounded and that the photo supposedly showing a Biden forebear was of some other man.[171] In passing, the Snopes article mentions the possibility that Joe was descended from the Maryland Robinettes, who owned slaves.

In August, the fact-checking website followed up. It evaluated evidence submitted by a reader that Joe's ancestor Thomas Randle owned a slave in Maryland in 1850, according to census records and a slave schedule. Snopes found the evidence was compelling that the Biden forebear and the man listed as owner on the slave schedule were one and the same, but it rated the claim "unproven."[172] Other mainstream sources of information did not pursue the question during the election.

It was not until after Joe won the presidency that an authoritative genealogy was produced for public consumption, and that its coauthor confirmed to me what some people online had been already claiming about Thomas Randle and the Robinettes. So Joe's ancestry never became part of the raging inferno of an election year fight over race and American history.

It could be because Joe has subtly managed the public perception of his background in a way that deflected that sort of uncomfortable scrutiny. Or it could just be the luck of the Irish.

Glory Days

"It ain't no sin to be glad you're alive."

—Bruce Springsteen, "Badlands"

With time, Joe's overwhelming grief subsided, permitting him room to focus on the challenges of raising a young family and learning to legislate. Over the course of his first term, the Bidens also learned about some of the perks of their new lot in life. They were suddenly famous, at least in Delaware. They were driving fast cars. Jimmy opened his own rock club.

Eventually, Joe started dating again, and he was one of the most eligible bachelors in the mid-Atlantic. His most notable love interest was Francie Barnard, a young correspondent for the *Fort Worth Star-Telegram*, who had met the senator at a dinner on Capitol Hill in the summer of 1973. The legendary Washington correspondent Helen Thomas, then with United Press International, had published a rumor in 1974 that the two were secretly engaged to be married.[173] Instead, Barnard married Bob Woodward later that year.[174]

Not that Joe had to worry about finding another date. As the youngest senator in Washington, Joe carried a certain mystique. Even before he was elected, the city had greeted him like he was a movie star. During the campaign, Joe traveled with the photographer Tom Stiltz to the

Capitol to pose with several Democratic senators for some campaign literature.

A young elevator operator in the Senate asked Joe, "Have you seen *The Candidate?*" Joe hadn't. "You're it!" the young woman told him.[175]

The movie, which had just come out, stars Robert Redford as a young Senate candidate running a Hail Mary campaign against an unbeatable opponent. In the end, Redford's character wins.

It was not the last time Biden drew comparisons to Redford, either. Admiring Joe's "natty pin-striped suits, elegant silk ties, and black tasseled loafers," the journalist Kitty Kelley compared him to the actor's portrayal of Jay Gatsby in her 1974 profile, "Death and the All-American Boy."

The profile was his first high-stakes encounter with the national press. Joe's family had always been the central fact of his public persona, but when the profile came out, he realized he had opened up too much about wounds that were too raw. The experience left him distrustful of the press in general, and permanently peeved about that profile in particular.

It was still sticking in his craw eight years later, when a writer for *Esquire* magazine explained, "He has been burned by a reporter before. That was years ago, and the interviewer then was, like Neilia, a blonde, and Biden, with his weakness for blondes, told her everything."[176]

Five years after that, Joe was still steamed. "She sat there and cried at my desk," he claimed in 1987, though Kelley said she had no memory of crying. "I found myself consoling her saying, 'Don't worry . . . It's okay, I'm going to be fine.' "[177]

Another twenty years after that, Kelley *still* remained on his mind. He wrote in 2007 that she made him look "unhinged," and that her profile caused him to "actively hate" the press.[178]

In many ways, though, the picture Kelley painted of freshman senator Joe Biden was a flattering one. She noted that many Joe watchers, including Val, considered him to be the second coming of Jack Kennedy:

"The Irish Catholic similarities were obvious," she wrote. "Both campaigned with glamor. Both were sexy. Both were elected to Congress before the age of 30. And both were struck by tragedy."

The real Kennedys embraced the up-and-comer, too. "Rose Kennedy is always calling me to come to dinner," Joe told Kelley. "She has invited me at least ten times and I've only gone once. Most guys would kill to get invitations like that but I don't accept them because I like to be with my children as much as possible. Whenever Ted and Joan Kennedy call me for dinner—and they call quite a bit—I usually say I have to go home. They are great because they understand why."[179]

Such comparisons did not impress Jean. "I don't know the Kennedys," she said. "But I don't think they could be half as great as the Bidens."[180]

Later that summer, Joe brought his own Rose Kennedy to the Capitol. He had been imploring his mother to pay him a visit in Washington since the start of his term, but she kept demurring. As the drama of Watergate reached its August denouement, Joe finally insisted during a family vacation to Rehoboth Beach.

Jean accompanied Joe back to Washington to hear Gerald Ford address a joint session of Congress on the new president's third day in office. She sat in the third row of the House gallery, right behind Ford's family. Out in the Senate lobby afterward, Ted Kennedy embraced Jean in a bear hug, as if the Bidens really were Kennedy cousins. "Mom, you've stayed away too long!" Kennedy told her. "I'm glad you made it."

Jean got a private tour of the Senate, taking a seat at the rostrum in the chair reserved for the chamber's presiding officer, then Joe took her out for Italian. "The food was good," she told the paper back home in Scranton. "But not as good as at Preno's."[181]

———

The only person having more fun in Delaware than Joe and his suddenly famous relatives was Bill Stevenson.

Stevenson had been a University of Delaware football player who dropped out to start a bar, rock club, and liquor store called the Stone Balloon.

The same year Joe caught the tail end of the '60s awakening— casting himself as the spirit of change, but in a suit—Stevenson was beginning to capitalize on the political fatigue that followed. He set up shop by campus on Main Street in Newark, just southwest of Wilmington, in early 1972.

The Stone Balloon became a place where patrons, the same young people who propelled Joe's campaign, could leave politics behind. Rather than protest the war in Vietnam, plenty of them were looking for a place to just forget about it. A bigger concern for Stevenson's crowd became, as he described it, "the war between rock 'n' roll and disco."[182]

Stevenson battled constantly with local authorities, who were not thrilled with the arrival of rock in their sleepy part of the world, and he heard regularly from the FBI, which had an ongoing interest in both local corruption and the club's finances. It was these clashes with local government that motivated his support for Joe's first Senate run.

Whether or not the powers that be approved, Delaware was ready to rock. In the club's early years, it booked the likes of Hall and Oates, Pat Benatar, Wolfman Jack, Herman's Hermits, Blue Öyster Cult, and Steppenwolf. The place was wildly popular. *Playboy* named it one of America's top college bars.[183]

Bill was also married to one of the most beautiful women in Delaware: Jill Jacobs. The couple met in 1969, when Jill had enrolled at Brandywine Junior College and Stevenson had returned from partying at Woodstock. Stevenson was charming and drove a yellow Camaro. After a few months of courtship, they married in 1970, when she was still just eighteen.

Jill soon transferred to the University of Delaware. Stevenson bought her a Cutlass convertible, just one of the perks of marrying a successful nightclub owner. In early 1974, Stevenson brought Jill along on a road trip to visit the Stone Pony, a dive bar in Asbury Park, New Jersey. They were there to scout the house act, an up-and-coming group called Bruce Springsteen and the E Street Band.[184]

In August, Springsteen came to play the Stone Balloon. It was mayhem. Fans started to line up 10 a.m. for the 10 p.m. show. As showtime approached, an overflow crowd of a thousand people flooded Main Street. The police showed up. So did a TV crew from Philadelphia. As Stevenson attempted crowd control outside, Jill pranked him by telling him his own staff would not even admit her into the overflowing club. Jill did make it inside, and Bruce ended up playing past two in the morning.

Nights like that were not enough to sustain their marriage. In her memoir, Jill writes vaguely of falling out of love with Stevenson. "We were young, and it didn't take long before we grew in different directions," she writes.

While Barack and Michelle Obama's courtship is the subject of a movie, *Southside with You*, how Joe and Jill first met is a subject of dispute. Some of the details in their account are fuzzy, and Stevenson maintains that the two knew each other and began dating earlier than they claim.

In her memoir, Jill writes of befriending Joe's youngest brother when they were both students at the University of Delaware: "I met a gregarious young guy from Wilmington, a student named Frank. He and I would say hi to each other, occasionally stopping to chat. It wasn't until much later that I took note of his last name: Biden . . . Of course, at that point I'd never heard of Joe Biden. Joe was a councilman in New Castle County then, a local attorney who no one expected would run for Senate."[185]

That timeline, though, looks to be off. Frank graduated from high school at the Wilmington Friends School in June 1972,[186] when Joe's first Senate run was well underway and her husband was backing it.

According to her memoir, Jill had little interest in the campaign, but she began to notice her husband's support for Joe that summer.[187] In his own memoir, published in 2005, Stevenson writes that he hosted two meet-and-greets for Joe at the Stone Balloon and that Jill enthusiastically supported the campaign, making phone calls to get out the student vote.

Joe and Jill, though, place their first meeting in early 1975. In his memoir, Joe dates the first time he took notice of Jill to Friday, March 7, of that year, about two months before Jill and Stevenson were granted their divorce.[188] That was when he recalled seeing Jill's photograph in a tourism ad at the Wilmington airport. "I remember thinking to myself, *That's the kind of woman I'd like to meet,*" he writes. That night, his account continues, Frank gave Joe the phone number of a woman to ask out. Joe called it the next day, and when he later met the woman in person, he discovered she was the same one he had seen on the airport wall.[189]

Joe's version of events gives the impression that Frank giving him Jill's number was some sort of serendipitous coincidence. Jill's recounting of their setup makes more sense. In it, Frank picks Joe up at the airport and Joe points out Jill, telling his younger brother, "That's the kind of girl I'd like to date."

Frank responds, "Well, why don't you then? I know her," and then procures her number.

Jill writes that she had let her photographer friend Tom Stiltz photograph her as a favor because he wanted his pictures for the tourism ad campaign to have some people in them.[190]

Stiltz, who also took photographs for Joe's first Senate campaign, remembers some of the details differently. Stiltz said he did take a photograph of Jill that was displayed at the Wilmington airport around that time. He also said Jill, at the age of twenty-three, was "stunning."

"I almost couldn't talk to her," he told me. "Her presence made me wobble at the knees."

But he denied that Jill posed in the photos as a favor to him. Stiltz said that he and Jill were not friends, and that the photo shoot was the only time he remembers interacting with her. He said Stevenson had hired him to help Jill jump-start a modeling career. "The irony," Stilz said, "is he paid me to take the photos that she credits with her meeting Joe."

Stiltz did not seem to have any ax to grind. He emailed me out of the blue in August 2019 to share his reminiscences of the 1972 campaign. We spoke by phone in September 2020. He told me he was a Democrat and described his recollections of his photo shoot on the condition they not be used before the 2020 election. Stiltz said he is friendly with Stevenson, but he attributed the couple's breakup to the excesses of Stevenson's life as a rock club owner, rather than anything Jill did.

Stevenson, who does have an ax to grind, also disputes Joe's and Jill's versions of events. He maintains that during the 1972 campaign, Jill met Joe when the couple went to Joe's house as part of their volunteering for the campaign. "Jill, Joe, Neilia and I were in his kitchen," he said. "How do you forget that?"[191]

When I met him, on a Sunday afternoon a few weeks after the 2020 election, we returned to the site of the Stone Balloon. New owners had recycled the name and the brand for a restaurant that pays homage to the original rock club. The stonework that inspired the original establishment's name is still there,

Stevenson's years of hard partying have not worn him down. He is filled with boisterous energy as he revels in the club's old days, widening his eyes as he looks into yours to emphasize this or that point. He looks like the legendary football announcer John Madden, except that his salt-and-pepper hair stands on end, as if an electric current is moving through him. Stevenson's second wife, Linda—who, if she is not long-suffering, is at least very patient—joined us for lunch.

Stevenson was eager to dish on the Bidens. The family figures into his first memoir, an out-of-print tome he published in 2005. But with Joe charging toward the presidency, he began work on a second memoir, and in the summer of 2020, news of the project leaked, along with the fact that it would challenge the family's narrative of how and when Joe and Jill began dating.

After the leak, Stevenson told me that he was approached by supporters of both Joe and Trump who made competing offers. He would not name the people involved, but he said Trump's supporters offered to pay him to lie. They wanted him to claim that Joe and Jill began having an affair when Neilia was still alive, and that the affair drove Neilia to her death. Joe's supporters, he said, wanted him to delay publication until after the election.

He opted to delay publication. Though he voted for Trump, he said he hadn't wanted to lie or to hurt Jill's chances of becoming first lady. In the days since the election, he had been rather embracing the role of "the first lady's first husband," boning up on the life of William G. Warren, Betty Ford's first husband, and, he says, the only other person in American history to hold this particular distinction.

Stevenson said he was motivated to write the second memoir because he had reason to believe that Joe was behind a federal bank fraud prosecution that hit him a few years after his contentious divorce from Jill.[192]

He said that Joe and Jill were dating by 1974: Stevenson had purchased a Corvette for her birthday and registered it to the address of the Stone Balloon. He said a man driving a big Buick Electra stopped by in September of that year to complain that Jill's Corvette had backed into his car and he hadn't received any payment for the damage. The man also told him that Joe had been behind the wheel of the Corvette, which Stevenson knew had a dent in it.

A spokesman for Jill has dismissed Stevenson's version of events, saying, "These claims are fictitious, seemingly to sell and promote a book. The relationship of Joe and Jill Biden is well documented."[193]

According to Joe and Jill, it was the following spring when they first met. Jill had been separated from Stevenson for months at that point, living alone in a one-bedroom town house on the Pennsylvania side of the state line, casually dating other men. Joe sweet-talked Jill into breaking a date, sight unseen. He took her out for dinner and a movie in Pennsylvania, where he was less likely to be recognized.

When he showed up in his suit and fancy shoes—Joe was earning a reputation at the Capitol as a natty dresser—it was all a bit much for the twenty-three-year-old wife of a rock club owner. Jill recalls that they went to see *Un homme et une femme*, a 1966 French movie about a widow and a widower who hook up but remain haunted by the memories of their dead lovers.

Over dinner, Joe won Jill over. She went home and called her mother to tell her, "Mom, I've finally met a real gentleman." Joe talked Jill into another date the next night. Then he asked her out again for the following night. Pretty soon, they were going steady.[194]

Things moved quickly, and Jill learned just how tight-knit Joe's family was: "The Bidens prized loyalty to each other over almost anything else," she observed. "Joe, Valerie, Jimmy, Frank, and their parents weren't just close; being a Biden was their identity."[195]

The daughter of a banker and a homemaker from the Philadelphia suburbs, and the eldest of five sisters, Jill knew a thing or two about fierce family loyalty: "We might squabble with each other," she explained of her own brood. "But if anyone outside the family hurt one of us, they'd find all five of the Jacobs girls ready to fight back."[196] Once, when she was thirteen, she sought out an eleven-year-old boy who had thrown worms at one of her sisters and punched the kid in the face.[197]

Still, she found the Biden clan intimidating. She already knew Frank and Jimmy, and within a couple of weeks, Joe insisted that she meet Val, too. So Jill came over to the house that the siblings were then sharing, where Val was making tuna sandwiches. Sensing Jill's nervousness, Val broke the ice by imitating a cat as she served Jill her sandwich, saying "meow, meow, meow," and pawing at her future sister-in-law's shoulder.[198]

Jill having passed the sister test, the couple began making a life together. That November, not wanting to choose between either of their parents—or Neilia's parents, who had also issued an invitation—Joe and Jill decided to do Thanksgiving alone with Beau and Hunter. In a Kennedy-esque stroke, they decided to spend the holiday on Nantucket, the island in Massachusetts off of Cape Cod.[199] (The most popular ferries for the island depart from Hyannis Port, where the Kennedy compound is located.)

———

As the younger brothers of Delaware's new political star, Jimmy and Frank spent the mid-'70s living it up. They joined the Delaware Rugby Club, and Jimmy rose to the rank of vice president. Once in a while, Joe snuck in for a scrimmage, too.

"There's always quite a bit of hitting, always some broken arms and legs," Jimmy explained of the exotic sport's appeal. "No one wears any equipment. I think that's one reason rugby is such a crowd pleaser."[200]

Perhaps it was the recognition that people in Delaware wanted something raw and dangerous that led Jimmy to start a rock club.

It seemed to be working for Stevenson, after all. Jimmy and one of Stevenson's friends, Joey Reardon, opened their own bar, Seasons Change, in a shopping plaza north of Wilmington.

At first, Jimmy, whose bar catered to the 27–35 set, was not a competitor of the Stone Balloon's, which drew a younger crowd, and he remained on good terms with Stevenson.

In late 1974, Stevenson took Reardon and Jimmy with him to Chicago to see Stanley Steamer, a band he was scouting for his club, perform. On the flight out, as Stevenson tells it, Jimmy handed a stewardess one of Joe's business cards and informed her that he was Delaware's junior senator. She promptly escorted him to a seat in first class.[201]

Perhaps it was an early indication that for the Bidens, Joe's name served as an all-purpose ticket to the first-class section of American life. Favors, jobs, loans to finance an affluent lifestyle. All of it could be theirs—so long as Joe maintained his political power.

In Chicago, Stevenson introduced Jimmy and Reardon to the band's manager, a move he came to regret several months later when the duo expanded their nightlife venture, opening a rock club next door to Seasons Change and naming it the Other Side.

Now, Jimmy and his partner were in direct competition with the Stone Balloon. Not only were Stevenson and Jimmy vying to book the same bands, they were driving the same model car: the Mercedes 450SL.[202]

(Joe, in addition to his Corvette, started driving a green 1972 Chevrolet Caprice Classic convertible, a big boat of a car, that he picked up at auction for $1,500.)[203]

Stevenson caught word that Jimmy and Reardon were bragging they would put the Stone Balloon out of business—and that they had offered Stanley Steamer and several other bands more money to defect to the Other Side.[204]

He resolved to drive them out of business instead. He scheduled the band Blood, Sweat & Tears, a big get at the time, for the night of the Other Side's grand opening. He advertised the event heavily. Because the Other Side was closer than the Stone Balloon to the Pennsylvania state line, Stevenson offered to waive the minimum for Keystone State residents to induce them to drive past Jimmy's club and come to his.

Stevenson also inserted a clause into his contracts that forbade the bands he booked from playing anywhere else within a twenty-mile radius, effectively blocking Jimmy from booking a lot of established talent.[205]

When Stevenson booked the Grammy-winning R&B group the Pointer Sisters for a Tuesday, Jimmy booked them for Wednesday. Stevenson struck back by calling the group's agent and talking him into canceling on the Other Side in order to do two nights in a row at the Stone Balloon instead.

It may sound extreme, but Stevenson believed he was not engaged in a fair fight. "They had unlimited cash from somewhere and political immunity in Delaware," he complained in his 2005 memoir.[206]

Indeed, Jimmy did land generous financing. Before going into the nightlife business, he was making $15,000 a year at his day job and had a net worth of $10,800.[207]

Despite this, and their lack of experience in the industry, Jimmy and Reardon had obtained tens of thousands of dollars in loans, at least partly unsecured, from Farmers Bank in Wilmington.

Given those circumstances, the financing was unusually generous. As it so happened, Joe had a seat on the Senate Banking Committee.

Another unsecured loan came from Maryland businessman Norman Rales, who did business with Farmers.

Rales, who had risen to fortune after spending his childhood in a New York City orphanage, was active in Democratic circles and made loans to several members of Congress.[208] In an unusual arrangement, Rales loaned to Jimmy indirectly, channeling the money through Joe's former law firm, Walsh, Monzack & Owens. One of the firm's partners, Joe's old friend Jack Owens, became a partner in the nightclub.[209]

Owens also became part of the Biden clan, marrying Val, who by now had divorced her first husband, in 1975.[210] (A year later, Val gave birth to a daughter, Valerie James Owens, who went by Missy. Later came a son, Cuffe, and then another daughter, Catherine Eugenia, who went by Casey.)[211]

Stevenson's efforts to derail the Other Side, coupled with its owners' inexperience, began to take their toll. By 1975, Jimmy was starting to fall behind on his loan payments to Farmers.

This was when Joe got involved. He called the chairman of Farmers and complained that the bank had been harassing Jimmy. Joe later said that he complained only that the bank was invoking his name with Jimmy's by telling its debtor that it would embarrass the senator if his brother defaulted. "They were trying to use me as a bludgeon," Joe complained.

Joe laid the blame for the missed payments not at his brother's feet, but at the bank's. "What I'd like to know," he griped, "is how the guy in charge of loans let it get this far."

None of this stopped Jimmy from obtaining still more financing. He went to another bank, First Pennsylvania, and obtained another loan, this one for $500,000. It helped that Owens had worked as an aide to Milton Shapp, Pennsylvania's Democratic governor, and that Shapp had recommended Jimmy to the bank.

At the time, Shapp was embarking on a long shot bid for the Democratic nomination. Joe, in July 1975, became the first senator to publicly throw his support behind a Democratic candidate, declaring that Shapp was "one of the most qualified men to be president," and adding, "I have no trouble supporting him."[212] Joe's biographer, Jules Witcover, described the endorsement of Shapp, who possessed little in the way of political star power, as "surprising." He described Joe's praise of the governor as "generous."[213] (Joe went on to become an early supporter of Jimmy Carter, after Shapp's campaign flamed out prematurely.)

Jim, though, was not in the clear. Because of concerns about First Pennsylvania's lending practices, the Federal Reserve Board placed the bank on a watch list.

Meanwhile, the bankers at First Pennsylvania found themselves at wit's end trying to get Jimmy to cooperate in righting the club's finances. A loan officer finally implored Joe to help. "He asked me," Joe recalled later, "to intercede with my brother and ask him to change the management. He wanted me to use my influence with my brother. I did talk to him for them, and they finally changed the management."[214]

In 1976, it all started to blow up. Farmers came to the brink of insolvency. The Federal Deposit Insurance Corporation had to swoop in and prop the bank up. The state of Delaware had to take it over. The state had so much exposure to Farmers that the rating agency Moody's downgraded Delaware's creditworthiness.

Amid the meltdown, the loans to Jimmy made the papers.

It emerged that Rales had been dumping bad loans onto Farmers' balance sheet. The Justice Department began investigating the politically connected financier's dealings with the wobbling bank. The DOJ also began investigating the Farmers loan to Jimmy.[215]

To make matters worse, another bank repossessed Jimmy's Mercedes.[216]

———

Jill came to appreciate that she was not just entering into a relationship with Joe. The Bidens came as a package deal. About a year into their relationship, Beau, seven, and Hunter, six, confronted Joe in the bathroom during his morning shave. "Beau thinks we should get married," Hunter informed him.

"We think we should marry Jill," Beau clarified. Joe agreed, but Jill had reservations about taking on the life of a senator's wife.[217]

The Bidens had reservations of their own. As the relationship started to head toward marriage, Jimmy and Frank took Jill out to dinner to have a chat. "They told me it was a dream of this family that Joe would be president and did I have any problem with that," Jill recalled.[218]

She did not, so Joe and Jill were married at the United Nations Chapel in Manhattan on June 17, 1977. At the beginning of the ceremony, Beau and Hunter rose from the pews to stand next to Joe. "They just instinctively understood that this was a marriage of four of us," Jill wrote.

The foursome got along grandly: Beau was like his father; he was conscientious and wore his heart on his sleeve. Hunter was more reserved, and more mischievous.[219]

They all honeymooned together with a hotel stay in New York, a brief respite from the outside world.[220]

To the boys, Neilia remained "Mommy," but Jill was now "Mom," fully inducted into the family's circle of intimacy. The concept of step-mother did not compute. As Joe put it, "There's no step-anything in our family."[221]

This new life took some adjusting to. Neilia had not just been a natural in the role of political wife, she had been a driving force in Joe's campaigns. Jill was shy, and her first marriage remained a sensitive subject.

When the *News Journal* requested an interview with the bride of the state's junior senator, he declined to make her available, saying, "I don't want to get her into the political thing."[222] He offered to tell the reporter about Jill instead, but he left her marriage to Stevenson out of her back-story. The omission caused some embarrassment for the reporter, who printed an item a week later saying that the oversight gave Delaware's introduction to Jill a "doctored tinge," and relaying Joe's excuse for leaving it out. "I thought the fact that Jill was married before had no relevance," the senator told the paper.[223]

Divorce was still taboo in large parts of American society, especially the Catholic parts, though Jill was hardly alone. In addition to Val, Jimmy and Frank both eventually went through divorces, too.

———

Jimmy stepped away from the management of the Other Side in April 1977, as the Bidens were gearing up for Joe's first reelection campaign. That year, Joe also left the Senate Banking Committee to join the Judiciary Committee.

But the nightclub continued to rear its head. Before the Other Side went bankrupt, First Pennsylvania arranged for its ownership to be transferred to another businessman, Salvatore Cardile. Cardile went on to sue the bank, saying it tricked him into taking on ownership of the floundering business in a botched attempt to head off a scandal. "The bank didn't want the senator's brother to be on the paper when the disco folded," he claimed in June 1978. "They needed a patsy. Me."[224]

While Joe secured his next term, Jimmy and Frank packed off to San Francisco. Jimmy found work with Walt Shorenstein, the billionaire developer and Democratic donor. He did some fund-raising for Joe out West, and Shorenstein contributed to Joe's reelection.[225]

Frank enrolled in San Francisco State University and briefly became a campaign issue himself. Just before the election, Joe's Republican challenger, James Baxter, a county recorder of deeds, brought him up at a debate. Frank had tagged along with Joe on a taxpayer-funded congressional trip to Africa. Though Frank got free airfare, Joe countered that his little brother paid his other expenses out of pocket.[226]

For the first time, Joe faced the prospect that his greatest political assets—his relatives—could become a liability, as the newspaper and Joe's opponent zeroed in on them. In this race, though, the threat remained well contained, and he notched a commanding reelection victory.

He cruised into his second term and the next decade, poised to build his national profile, to continue to rebuild his family, and even to have a little fun.

Over Labor Day weekend in 1980, Joe went to a birthday party at Val's house near the Pennsylvania state line. Catching sight of a car speeding recklessly on a nearby abandoned road, Joe jumped into his car and chased the twenty-six-year-old driver into Pennsylvania, where he hailed the man down and placed him under citizen's arrest. Then Joe dragged the joyrider into magistrate court, where state law allowed anyone to prosecute a traffic violation themselves. Joe later agreed to drop the charges after the motorist convinced him the reckless driving was a one-off, though the senator had been looking forward to slipping back into the role of courtroom lawyer to make the prosecution. "It would have been fun," Joe said, relishing his turn as a crime stopper.

This was not the first time the young lawmaker had taken to

enforcing the law directly: Three years earlier, Joe reportedly leapt out of his car and snatched a stolen purse back from a couple of thieves.[227]

A year later, in June 1981, Joe and Jill had a daughter, Ashley. Beau and Hunter had chosen the name. The new child was greeted in a manner befitting the times. After Jill started going into labor, but before leaving for the hospital, she took the time to curl her hair. "What can I say?" Jill wrote decades later. "It was the '80s."[228]

Working Men

"They were Truman Democrats, working men, or sons of working men."

—Joe, on the participants in his grandfather's kitchen-table
political debates

More than thirty years after the Bidens' big Senate upset, a different story about how they pulled it off began to circulate in the Brandywine Valley. The Republicans who had worked in vain to hand-deliver Caleb Boggs's last-ditch advertising insert had long harbored suspicions about the timing of the pre-election truck drivers' strike that derailed delivery of the *News Journal*.

They remained just that, vague suspicions, until 2004, when a Delaware attorney, former homicide prosecutor Charles Brandt, published *I Heard You Paint Houses*, a book based on extensive interviews with Frank "the Irishman" Sheeran, a dying mob hitman.[229]

(As it happens, Brandt was Delaware's deputy attorney general at the time of Joe's first Senate win, and one of the people who went to the scene of Neilia's car accident to investigate.)[230]

Martin Scorsese adapted the book into the 2019 epic film *The Irishman*, starring Robert De Niro, Al Pacino, and Joe Pesci.

The book's big reveal is Sheeran's claim that he killed Teamsters boss Jimmy Hoffa. That claim and others he makes in the book have been subjected to journalistic debunkings,[231] though the publisher has responded to at least one with a detailed defense.[232]

The claim that lit up Delaware, though, related to Sheeran's activities in the fall of 1972.

At the time, Sheeran had been working as a local Teamsters official in Wilmington. Earlier in the campaign season, he related to Brandt, he had denied Boggs's request to address the union rank-and-file, deeming the Republican incumbent too anti-labor. But he allowed Joe to speak to them, and the challenger acquitted himself well.

In the closing stretch of the campaign, the book recounts, an unnamed Democratic lawyer visited Sheeran in his office on Front Street, near the Wilmington train station, about a block from the Christina River.

The lawyer had brought along an employee of the News Journal Company, which put out the state's two top papers, the *Morning News* and the *Evening Journal*, which ran as a single edition, the *News Journal*, on weekends and holidays.

The lawyer explained about the advertising inserts Boggs was planning to run in the closing days of the campaign. As Sheeran recounted:

> The lawyer didn't want those newspapers to be delivered...
> The guy who was there who worked on the paper said that he
> wanted to put up an informational picket line, but he didn't have
> any good people that worked with him in the newspaper he could
> trust to walk the line.... I told him I would hire some people and
> put them on the picket line for him. They were people nobody
> would mess with.... I told him that once we put up the picket
> line I would see to it that no truck driver crossed that picket line.
> The teamsters would honor the informational picket line of the
> other union, whatever name they used.
>
> The line went up and the newspapers were printed, but they
> stayed in the warehouse and they never were delivered.... I have

no way of knowing if Joe Biden knew if that picket line thing was done on purpose on his behalf. If he did know he never let on to me.[233]

After the book was published, a spokeswoman for Joe said he knew nothing about the alleged events described by Sheeran.[234]

But Bill Stevenson claims to know a thing or two about the newspaper strike as well. He told me that toward the end of the campaign, Frank paid him a visit and asked for some cash. "There's a plan that will probably win us the election," he said Frank told him. So Stevenson said he scrounged up just under $3,000 and handed it over.

After the election, Stevenson said that one of the Bidens, he could not remember which one, told him his money had paid for the strike. Stevenson said that after the new senator was sworn in, his friend Joe "Boom" Beck, an official with the Carpenters Union, took Sheeran around to the Stone Balloon, where he introduced Stevenson to the Teamsters boss as "the guy who took care of the tab for the News Journal strike."

Stevenson, who is not a small man, said that when Sheeran reached out to greet him, the hitman's hand was so large it enveloped his own, like a baseball glove.

Sheeran's presence at the bar made Stevenson nervous. The rock club owner knew the Teamsters official by reputation, and at the time, organized labor was trying to unionize bar staff, something that Stevenson did not want to happen at his establishment. But he said that Sheeran and Beck just ordered a couple beers, left a $200 tip, and walked out. Stevenson also said that one of the Biden brothers later mentioned the name of the lawyer who had fixed up the strike, and he gave me the name of a labor-connected lawyer who was a longtime ally of Joe's.

While Brandt, now in his late seventies, left the name of the lawyer Sheeran described out of the book, he was more forthcoming with me and provided a different name, that of a well-known labor-connected lawyer in that region. I reached out to both lawyers. A representative for one lawyer emphatically denied any involvement, and the other lawyer did not respond. Because neither Stevenson nor Brandt has any first-hand knowledge of their alleged involvement, I'm leaving out the names of both.

Brandt said he never heard of any involvement from the lawyer Stevenson named but that he considered Stevenson's account credible, down to the baseball glove–like hand.

"Sheeran had an incredible hand!" Brandt exclaimed. "And an incredible head! He had the largest head of anyone you've ever seen."

Brandt said Sheeran never mentioned getting paid for the strike, but he said that "Money did talk with Frank Sheeran" and "$3,000 sounds about right."

Brandt also said he believes Sheeran was responsible for an explosion of a train boxcar carrying newspaper supplies shortly after Joe's election, as the strike raged on. "That may sound strange, but Sheeran dealt with a lot of dynamite, and his last conviction dealt with dynamite," Brandt said.

Indeed, the explosion occurred as the train rolled along Front Street, right by Sheeran's office.[235] When I emailed Frank questions about several topics, including Stevenson's claims, he wrote back, "You have so many things factually wrong it's hard to [know] where to start," but he did not directly address the strike. He said he would consider speaking to me at more length about my queries, but he did not end up doing so.

Whether or not the Bidens played any role in ginning up the strike as Stevenson claims, their 1972 campaign sealed an alliance with organized labor that would last for decades. At the time, organized labor had its fair share of tough guys and corruption. Joe never got wrapped up in the big scandals that shook the unions, but as he hit his stride as a lawmaker in Washington, he and his relatives kept a foot in the more rough-and-tumble world of working men.

Back then, labor was a force to be reckoned with. But Joe's ascent to the Senate coincided with a high point in its power, and in the fortunes of the middle class that had been built on its back. The rise of free trade, the growing power of global corporations, and concerted anti-union activism by the likes of the billionaire brothers Charles and David Koch all contributed to a long, slow decline.

In many cases, as labor's pie shrank, union bosses saw to it that they, and their friends, got their pieces first, while rank-and-file members were the first to feel the diminishment of the American labor movement's hard-won spoils.

Joe has described the decline of unions as a key culprit in the broader collapse of the American middle class that has occurred over the course of his political career. "History shows that when the union movement is strong, the middle class is strong," he declared from the Senate floor, as he made that case during his second presidential run. "The union movement and our middle class are under attack," he warned.[236]

As his ties to organized labor deepened, his family had a unique vantage point on this great divergence, as the fortunes of normal families stagnated and life kept getting better at the top.

———

Jimmy was the first Biden to learn how to play ball with the unions. During Joe's first Senate campaign, he had been point man with labor. He haunted the Washington offices of big unions, trying to make the case that Joe was viable. In the process, at the age of twenty-three, he got an up-close look at political sausage making.

Jimmy proved a quick study. Despite running a long shot campaign with an unknown candidate in a tiny state, Joe took in $36,000 from labor groups in 1972, which was more than all but seven candidates in the country that year—three of them presidential candidates.[237]

A few weeks before the election, after he had courted the machinists' union for the better part of a year, a top union official made an offer: He would write the campaign a $5,000 check if Joe would come out to his office to accept it in person.

So the brothers went out to pay him a visit. At the meeting, the union boss, chomping on a cigar, with the check sitting in plain sight on his desk, asked Joe, "Let's say the Lockheed bailout comes up again in the next session, and you're a sitting United States senator. My guys are losing jobs, ya know, Joe. How do you vote?"

As Joe recalled it in his memoir, he sensed he was being asked to stake out a position in exchange for a contribution, and he told the boss, "You can take that check and stick it," angrily storming out. Jimmy talked Joe back into the room, but he still refused to take the check from the union boss's hand.

So, Jimmy took it.[238]

Most of Joe's interactions with union officials were more amicable. In 1976, when he became the first prominent Democrat to endorse Jimmy Carter's long shot presidential primary bid, he told a local Democratic club in Delaware that Carter needed him for his contacts with national labor leaders.[239] When Joe ran for reelection 1978, roughly 20 percent of his campaign funding came from labor groups.[240]

The alliance brought Joe into contact with some dubious characters. In June 1979, the Pennsylvania AFL-CIO scored him as a keynote speaker for a dinner honoring a handful of its top leaders during the union's annual convention at the Philadelphia Sheraton.[241]

One of the leaders was the state union's executive vice president, James J. Mahoney. Mahoney had been treasurer of the Council for Revitalization of Employment and Industry in Philadelphia, or CREIP. CREIP was a government-funded job creation initiative overseen by organized labor.

Four months after the dinner, a federal grand jury indicted Mahoney on forty-seven counts, including mail fraud and filing false tax returns. Mahoney eventually pleaded guilty to promising contractors millions of dollars in CREIP contracts to builders in exchange for working for free on his home.[242]

By then, CREIP had changed its name to the Council for Labor and Industry, or CLI.[243] The group, a quasi-governmental organization incorporated as a nonprofit, was described as having "strong political and labor ties."[244]

In fact, those political and labor ties were stronger than almost anyone realized. After Joe won his Senate seat, Joseph Robinette Biden Sr. decided it was unbecoming for a senator's father to work as a car salesman, so he quit his job to work in real estate.

Not much is known about Joe Sr.'s late career venture into real estate. Newspaper ads show he bounced around several Wilmington area real estate agencies over the years. He had a good run in the late '70s, when ads for Patterson Schwartz Realtors list him among the few dozen of their agents in Delaware to have racked up more than $1 million worth of sales in a year.[245]

But in the early '80s, the housing market hit the skids, with interest rates hovering around 20 percent and the number of new houses starting construction falling in 1981 to half the level of 1978.[246]

Luckily for Joe Sr., he landed a client with less exposure to market forces. Starting in December 1981 and continuing into the next month, a handful of classified ads appeared in the *Philadelphia Inquirer* advertising space in a warehousing and manufacturing complex owned by CLI. The ads were placed by J. R. Biden, the style in which Joe Sr. often rendered his name.[247]

In conjunction with its efforts to attract business to the city, the Council maintained the Wissahickon Industrial Center in the Germantown neighborhood. Earlier that year, Philadelphia's city commissioners, in charge of administering elections, ended a contract they had with CLI to store the city's voting machines in the industrial center, despite receiving a steep discount. The commission cited leaks in the roof and faulty heating.[248] This may explain why the Council needed help finding a tenant for a warehousing space.

The exact length and extent of Joe Sr.'s business relationship with the council is not clear. Several years after the ads ran, in June 1986, serial entrepreneur Rich Thoma recalled seeing him at CLI's headquarters at One East Penn Square, just across from city hall.

At the time, Thoma was in a dispute with CLI. The council had extended financing to one of his ventures—an early hard disk storage company called People & Technology—through a loan fund it administered with the stated goal of fostering economic development in the city.

Thoma recalled stepping off the elevator on the eighth floor and being greeted by a female council staffer, then looking up and catching sight of an older man entering an office down the hall. He recalled the staffer telling him, "Oh, that's Mr. Biden" or "That's Joe Biden," and adding, "He comes up by train from Wilmington." Thoma said he could see the man was too old to be Joe Biden the fortysomething senator.

During his meeting, Thoma said the council's executive director, the late James Toomey, offered to make the dispute go away if Thoma let CLI buy a stake in his company. After Thoma refused, the council sued his company, and Thoma described Toomey's offer under oath in a September 1986 deposition.

Thoma, who first reached out to me in July 2020, said he considers Toomey's entreaty that day to be attempted extortion.[249]

CLI's dispute with Thoma was the least of its problems, which steadily mounted over the years. In 1982, the group was delinquent on $500,000 in municipal taxes.[250] Three years later, investigators at the U.S. Commerce Department's Inspector General's Office discovered financial irregularities and recommended that the department cut off its funding to the council, but they were overruled by superiors.[251]

Then, at the beginning of 1989, a nonprofit that subcontracted to CLI issued a report finding a "pervasive pattern of impropriety" in the council's administration of a job training program. The state labor secretary, future Democratic senator Harris Wofford, called for state and federal investigations.[252] The mayor stopped all payments to the council,[253] and the U.S. Department of Housing and Urban Development weighed in with a report that faulted the city Commerce Department for failing to keep the council in check.[254] CLI soon disbanded, unable to weather its second big scandal in less than a decade.

But by that time, Joe Sr. was working at a new job. He joined the Delaware Realtor Lit Dryden & Associates as a project marketing manager and director of sales in January 1987, just as his son was gearing up for his first presidential bid.[255]

Joe has not spoken much about his father's turn as a Realtor, but he did relay one anecdote to the *Los Angeles Times* for a profile that ran a month later in anticipation of his primary run. The senator recounted that when his father had been selling condominiums on the Delaware coast, he became friendly with a middle-aged gay couple, and upon finding out they were supporters of his son, he asked his son to pay them a visit during a beach trip. When Joe Jr. tried to push it off, Joe Sr. grew angry, telling him, "Look, damn it, you're my son, aren't you? I'm telling you they're good people. It's important to me that you meet them. Where the hell have you been raised?" So Joe hauled himself up to the couple's apartment in his bathing suit, and three men shared a glass of iced tea.[256]

———

In Washington, Joe remained a friend to labor. In the spring of 1984, the Judiciary Committee held hearings on whether to amend labor laws to allow federal prosecution of violence committed by union members. Sigmund Kaye, a Philadelphia man, testified he temporarily lost the use of an arm after he was attacked by a "goon squad" from the local carpenters union, some of them wearing shirts that read, "Union carpenters hit harder." Kaye was among those arguing for more federal power to prosecute. He said that the local district attorney's office refused to follow up on his case, telling his lawyer, "It's an election year."

Joe was not swayed. He sided with the AFL-CIO in opposing an expansion of federal jurisdiction.[257]

In June 1986, Joe traveled to Chicago to speak to the annual convention of the Hotel Employees and Restaurant Employees International Union. The visit came three months after a presidential commission named it one of the four labor unions with the closest ties to organized crime. The appearance earned Joe a mention in a *Chicago Tribune* story headlined, "Big Political Names Drop In on Union Linked with Mob."[258]

Joe could also take a hard line with his union allies. In the '80s, Reagan Democrats—working-class whites in the Rust Belt, many of them from union backgrounds—were bolting the party. At the annual convention of the Florida AFL-CIO in Miami Beach in September 1985, he took the unions to task, accusing them of complacency. "When members of organized labor end up with two cars and a camper, they become Republicans," he said. The senator suggested that unions too often thought in terms of Ronald Reagan's "Are you better off now than you were four years ago?" when they should be thinking in terms of Jack Kennedy's "Ask not what your country can do for you."

The tough talk worked. Joe got a standing ovation. One attendee insisted on shaking Joe's hand and told him, "One of the best speeches I ever heard. You got any Kennedy blood in you?"[259]

Trial Run

"The Kennedys quoted the Greeks; Biden quoted the Kennedys."

—old Capitol Hill wisecrack

Kennedy-esque was exactly what Joe was going for as he prepared to mount his first run at the presidency.

He had passed up the chance to challenge Reagan's reelection in 1984, despite the urging of advisors like the pollster Pat Caddell. Or, more precisely, the Bidens passed up the chance. "We aren't running for president in '84," various family members told a writer profiling the family for *Esquire* magazine in the run-up to the election cycle.[260]

But a couple years later, with Joe's speeches around the country finding an enthusiastic reception, the Bidens decided it was time to get in the ring in '88.

"We thought about it and said, 'Well, you know, let's just see what's out there,'" Val recalled later of the family's decision-making process. "We would form an exploratory committee and just see. He wasn't sure whether we wanted to run or how well we—what he thought would mesh with the rest of the party. So we decided to do some preliminary work. And we were incredibly more successful than we thought that we would be."[261]

As Joe carved out a national profile, he had positioned himself as a tough-on-crime Democrat, pushing the war on drugs.

As ranking member on Judiciary, he coauthored the Comprehensive Crime Control Act of 1984 with the committee's Republican chairman, Strom Thurmond of South Carolina. The new law increased the penalty for possession of marijuana and established mandatory minimum sentences for drug-related crimes. Two years later, as crack cocaine tore through American cities, the pair teamed up for the 1986 Anti–Drug Abuse Act. The law stiffened drug crime penalties and mandated notoriously disparate sentencing for the possession of crack, associated with Black users, and powder cocaine, more popular with affluent whites: Possession of either five grams of crack or five hundred grams of powder cocaine carried a minimum of five years in prison.[262]

Joe leavened stances like these with soaring rhetoric as he barnstormed the country ahead of a potential run. He even went so far as to hire a twentysomething from San Diego who had studied the Kennedys, and was working on a compilation of RFK's speeches, as a speechwriter.[263]

In February 1987, he addressed the California State Democratic Convention, where he decried excessive focus on the dreary metrics of economic output.

"It doesn't measure the beauty of our poetry, the strength of our marriages, the intelligence of our public debate, the integrity of our public officials," Joe declared. "It counts neither our wit nor our wisdom, neither our compassion nor our devotion to our country."[264]

Such Kennedy-esque flourishes gained notice. *Newsweek* called him a "masterful orator."[265] Others saw a "soul-stirring rhetorician."[266]

At forty-four, Joe was still young and strapping by the standards of presidential politics. His thinning hair had even regained some of its fullness, leading to speculation about a hair transplant. Joe played coy about the transplant, telling a reporter who asked him if he had had one, "I've got to keep some mystery in my life."[267]

Youth had its drawbacks, too. Joe was seen as ambitious and untested.

Democrats' experience in 1984, when front-runner Gary Hart's campaign fell apart on revelations of an extramarital affair, loomed large over the primary process. Questions of character took on "greater importance than ever," as the *Los Angeles Times* explained in the run-up to Joe's entry, and the press was on high alert for flaws.[268]

Joe's image at the time was a far cry from the one that would crystallize in the Obama years, of a gaffe-prone but time-tested "Uncle Joe." He was seen as a silver-tongued politician, perhaps an overly ambitious one.

One constant was that family was central to his image. It was also top of mind for Joe, and the scrutiny his relatives could face weighed on him. He worried that Jim's finances and Val's divorce from her first husband would become fodder, and that, as Richard Ben Cramer wrote, "Every paper in the country would be turning over rocks on Frankie."[269]

Joe entered the race on June 9. He delivered a speech from Wilmington's train station. Then he boarded a train to Washington, accompanied by a full complement of children, siblings, and assorted other Bidens.[270]

Val once again ran the campaign, which got off to a strong start.

This was thanks in part to a growing force in politics. Fund-raisers were beginning to reshape national campaigns. These well-connected figures could connect candidates with pools of donors. They were also prompting concerns that "the tail has started to wag the dog," as one columnist, Robert Wagman, put it in 1987. To explain the growing importance of these fund-raisers, Wagman cited Walt Shorenstein, who had employed Jimmy in San Francisco after his nightclub venture blew up. He pointed, too, to New York businessman Joel Boyarsky, who was credited with a disproportionate share of Joe's impressive $1.7 million haul in the first weeks of his campaign.[271]

In addition to being Joe's campaign finance chairman, Boyarsky was Jimmy's new employer at Improved Funding Techniques, a company that provided actuarial and consulting services to pension plans.[272]

At an August debate at the Iowa State Fair, Joe concluded with a rousing closing statement about his family's history. "I started thinking as I was coming over here, why is it that Joe Biden is the first in his family ever to go to a university?" he asked. "Why is it that my wife who is sitting out there in the audience is the first in her family to ever go to college? Is it because our fathers and mothers were not bright? Is it because I'm the first Biden in a thousand generations to get a college and a graduate degree that I was smarter than the rest?"

He continued, "Is it because they didn't work hard? My ancestors, who worked in the coal mines of Northeast Pennsylvania and would come up after twelve hours and play football for four hours?"[273]

Minus the references to the Bidens and Pennsylvania, much of the closing statement had been lifted word-for-word from British Labour leader Neil Kinnock, who had movingly invoked his family's Welsh coal mining roots in a losing campaign against Margaret Thatcher's Tories earlier that year.

In other campaign stops, Biden had credited Kinnock for the language, but a few weeks after the state fair, the press had caught the slipup, thanks to a tip-off from an aide to the eventual nominee, Massachusetts governor Mike Dukakis.[274] The *New York Times* ran an exposé on the second Saturday in September, when Biden was in Washington for the christening of his niece Caroline, Jimmy's daughter.[275]

Soon the press discovered that Biden had been disciplined for plagiarism as a first-year law student at Syracuse—the school determined his botched paper citation had been accidental—and that months earlier he had exaggerated his academic record in a heated campaign trail exchange with a voter in New Hampshire.[276]

Reporters uncovered, too, that some of Joe's moving words at the California state convention were not just Kennedy-esque, they were among several passages filled with language he had borrowed directly from Bobby Kennedy without attribution.[277]

Joe's campaign said he was paying homage to Robert Kennedy's words, not plagiarizing them.

As the media firestorm enveloped Joe's campaign, he hunkered down in Delaware and Washington. He was preparing to oversee Robert Bork's Supreme Court nomination for his day job as chairman of the Senate Judiciary Committee. Jill was dispatched to Iowa as his surrogate.[278]

The press showed no signs of letting up. The *New York Times* began poking around on Jimmy's financial problems.

With the Bork hearings heating up and his campaign scandal in full bloom, Joe gathered his family, including his siblings and parents, in his living room on a Tuesday night later that month.

As he describes in his memoir, Beau and Hunter took the assault on the family honor especially hard. They wanted their dad to stand and fight for the family's good name.

Joe's mother advised him to drop out.

Alone with Jill later that night, he weighed the dual challenges of salvaging his campaign and guiding the Bork hearings.

They chose the Bork hearings. The next day, with Jill at his side and Jimmy and Val standing by, he announced his withdrawal from the race from the Judiciary Committee's hearing room. After giving his statement, and before he took the gavel back up to resume Bork's hearing, Jill told him, "You have to win this thing!"

Joe convinced a majority of the Senate that the nominee's judicial philosophy was too extreme, and with his wife's encouragement, helped inaugurate an era of contentious Supreme Court nomination fights, forcing presidents to go to great lengths to ensure their picks do not get "Borked."

Joe had gotten some praise after his withdrawal, but Jill had decided she hated the press for chewing Joe's life up and spitting it out. The rest of the Bidens were similarly incensed. The *Times* dropped its inquiries into Jimmy after Joe dropped out of the race. To the Bidens, that was not just normal journalistic practice. They saw something like that as more like, Cramer wrote, "blackmail."[279]

Even thirty years later, Val struggled to reconcile the objective truth (that Joe had flubbed his closing statement in Iowa) with her natural position as a Biden (that Joe had done nothing wrong). "By all accounts—not by his sister—but by all accounts, he made a mistake," she told PBS in 2020. "He had quoted Kinnock in every speech. The press corps knew it, knew his speech by heart, which means it's—that's a good thing; you keep saying the same thing. And—but he—but he didn't, at the end of the Iowa State Fair, for a good reason. But it doesn't matter. He made a mistake. He didn't say it." She was still mad at the Dukakis campaign, too: "I am really, you know, not very forgiving in what I think was a kick to the gut. It was dirty pool."[280]

Jill, in her own 2020 interview with PBS, went even further in absolving her husband: "It was so unfair what happened to him, and that he had to pull out of the race," she said, "because it just seemed that it was through no fault of his own that the plagiarism occurred. You know, he was reading a speech that someone had written for him. He didn't realize that the lines were used, and I just felt it was so unfair."[281]

In his memoir, Joe does not maintain, as Jill does, that the missed attribution was the fault of someone else's botched speechwriting. Instead, Joe writes that an aide suggested to him before the debate that he use the Kinnock quote that had been playing well on the trail in his closing remarks. In the downtime before the debate began, Joe meant to write down a closing statement using the quote but he got distracted. When it came time to deliver a closing statement, Joe ad-libbed it, and botched the delivery. He writes, "I hadn't found a place to stop and slip in the standard attribution."[282]

⸻

The day after Joe dropped out (and three years after Arnold Schwarzenegger starred in *The Terminator*) he promised his supporters, "I'll be back." He suggested he could mount another run in 1992.[283] He even met with Kinnock a few months later in London. Joe gave the Labour leader a compilation of his own speeches, joking that Kinnock was free to borrow from it "with or without attribution."[284]

Despite the brave face, Joe's career was dead in the water. "Biden's Belly Flop," was how *Newsweek* played his exit from the race.[285] As the Associated Press framed it, Joe had lost his "respectability." The AP cast doubt on Joe's hopes to one day regain the status of a presidential contender. "Critics," it noted, "said the episode had laid bare Biden's main weakness—glibness, shallowness—and he would have trouble overcoming what happened."[286]

Wags in Washington made him a punchline. "The Kennedys quoted the Greeks," went the crack. "Biden quoted the Kennedys."[287]

The frenetic pace and stress of the campaign had also taken their toll on Joe's body. On the trail, he suffered from chronic neck pains and headaches. In the middle of one speech at a Rotary Club in New Hampshire, he abruptly left the stage and began vomiting. To deal with the pain, he took to popping Tylenols.[288]

In February 1988, he traveled to Rochester, New York, for a speaking engagement. He collapsed in his hotel room there, felled by an aneurysm that nearly killed him. Then, he had another one. At one point, a priest began to administer last rites as he lay in a hospital bed, only to have Jill come upon the morbid scene and shoo the man away.

Joe's presidential ambitions became even more distant. As he recovered at home from surgery, his family put an embargo on all contact from Washington. Even Reagan's calls could not get through. So Ted Kennedy did an end run around the blockade, taking a train to Wilmington, and barging into Joe's home to present him with a framed etching of a horned Irish deer, writing on it, "To my Irish chairman."

Joe took several months to recover. He whiled away the days puttering around Wilmington or playing with an archery set, a gift from Jimmy. It was the rare quiet period in Joe's otherwise nonstop life.[289]

When he returned to the Senate that September, Joe, with his parents looking on in the gallery, delivered an emotional address to the chamber. "I remember something Pat Moynihan once told me," Joe recalled, citing his Democratic colleague from New York. "He said that to fail to understand that life is going to knock you down is to fail to understand the Irishness of life."[290]

Domestic Policy

"Are you trying to say we both should have been doctors?"

—Beau Biden, 1996, responding to a question
about Hunter and nepotism

The twin setbacks of the Kinnock debacle and the aneurysms had a silver lining: Joe was once again able to focus on family and home life.

Home for Joe was a ten-thousand-square-foot mansion outside of Wilmington in an area thick with du Pont heirs, known to the locals as "chateau country." The Biden house had an outdoor pool, a library, and a ballroom. It looked like an English country estate. He called it "the Station." He had bought the place after Neilia died, paying $185,000 in a soft real estate market, and sold off some of the surrounding land to help finance the purchase.

Improving it, with Jimmy's help, became Joe's favorite pastime, bordering on obsession. "If politics hadn't worked," Val once explained, "Joe and Jimmy could have gone into business as the Biden Brothers—Joe as a frustrated architect and landscaper, Jimmy as an interior decorator."[291]

The basement of the Station was full of asbestos, so rather than pay for professional removal, Joe would don a full-body protective suit and take it out himself.

He and his sons spent weekends improving the property, planting hemlock trees or putting up fencing.[292] The extensive fencing earned the house a second nickname: Fort Apache.[293]

All the time spent working with Beau and Hunter on the Station fit with Joe's philosophy of parenting. "There's no such thing as quality time," he once opined. "It's all quantity. It's all quantity. Every important thing that's ever happened to me with my children has been on unscheduled time. It's not like, 'Well now, son, we're gonna go fishing and we're gonna have quality time.'"[294]

In that spirit, Joe instituted a Biden family rule he called "Wild Card" in the aftermath of Neilia's death. Whenever they felt like it, Joe's kids could call "Wild Card" and take the day off to tag along on whatever their father was doing.[295]

As a result, the boys became regular fixtures on Capitol Hill. They goofed off in the Senate gym, where they would eavesdrop on weighty deliberations being made in the steam room,[296] or sit in on their father's meetings.[297] Later, Ashley followed in her brothers' footsteps. By the time she was in second grade, she was stalking the halls of Congress, buttonholing senators on the plight of dolphins.[298]

The Biden children took these early brushes with authority to heart. Beau developed into a precocious do-gooder and rule follower. When he was still in grade school and one of Jill's friends got a flat tire, he offered to fix it for her.[299] His younger brother and their friends took to calling him "the Sheriff."[300]

At first, people who knew the family pegged Hunter as the real comer of the two Biden sons. He might have been smarter than his older brother, and he showed early flashes of ambition. Once, when he was a boy, Joe asked him what he wanted to be when he grew up. "I want to be important," Hunter responded.[301]

But in adolescence, it became clear that Beau was the more serious-minded brother. Like many teens, Hunter did not take much to rule-following and did take up drinking. Beau, like his father, was a teetotaler. He abstained in high school and college and again after the age of thirty.[302] He took an early shine to politics and was elected class president at Archmere.[303]

Beau even bore an uncanny resemblance to Joe. Charles Brandt, whose children were friends with the Bidens in high school, recalled coming home one day and being momentarily alarmed to find Delaware's junior senator sitting on his couch. He quickly realized it was only Beau.[304]

In high school, the brothers worked together at a cold storage business, preparing large slabs of meat for USDA inspection. But then Beau started to take desk jobs, while Hunter kept working on his feet. He unloaded meat from boxcars, waited tables, and parked cars as a valet.[305]

Despite their differences, the brothers remained inseparable. When Hunter would drink, Beau would drive.[306] Eventually Ashley, too, took to tagging along with her much-older brothers, as Val had with Joe. She earned herself the nickname "Flea."

When it came time to apply to college, Joe wanted his children to aim higher than he had.

Back when the kids were young, he had offered a group of Delaware pals a glimpse of what he had learned in Washington about the workings of the world. At a gathering in a friend's backyard, Joe asked one friend where he would send his son to college. Joe's buddy didn't have any idea: His son was only eight years old.

Joe began to lecture them, according to an account of the episode in *What It Takes*.

"Lemme tell you guys something," he said. "There's a river of power that flows through this country.

"Some people, most people, don't even know the river is there. But it's there. Some people know about the river, but they can't get in. They only stand at the edge. And some people, a few, get to swim in the river. All the time. They get to swim their whole lives, anywhere they want to go, always in the river of power."

During his time in Washington, Joe had managed to locate the headwaters. "That river," he told them, "flows from the Ivy League."[307]

Both sons followed in their father's footsteps to Archmere. But when Beau graduated, he packed off for the nearest Ivy League school, the University of Pennsylvania.

A year later, Hunter was arrested for cocaine possession in Stone Harbor on the Jersey Shore, a regular site of Biden family getaways. This scrape with the law resulted in a pretrial intervention, which allowed Hunter to have his record expunged.[308]

The arrest came the summer after his high school graduation, but the episode did not keep Hunter from attending a prestigious college. He went off that year to Georgetown, which is not in the Ivy League, but is close enough to be considered part of the river of power. As a student there, he continued his hard-partying ways. In addition to picking up a pack-a-day cigarette habit,[309] he tried crack cocaine for the first time after buying it late at night from a homeless woman riding a bike near the White House. Hunter stayed in touch with the woman and came to nickname her "Bicycles."[310]

After graduating college in 1992, he headed out west to Portland, Oregon, to put in a year of service with the Jesuit Volunteer Corps. There, he met Kathleen Buhle, a graduate of St. Mary's College—a Catholic school in Minnesota—with roots in Chicago who was also working with the volunteer corps. Within a few months, Kathleen was pregnant, and their engagement was announced.[311]

Hunter and Kathleen headed back east, and Hunter started at Georgetown Law in the fall. He had wanted to go to Yale, the nation's most elite law school, but was rejected. In December, Kathleen gave birth to a daughter. Hunter, in the middle of his final exam for civil procedure, rushed to the hospital.[312] The baby arrived twenty-one years after the fatal car crash that defined Hunter's first memories of life. They named her Naomi, after Hunter's late sister.

———

In 1990, the voters of Delaware proved far more forgiving than the national press corps had been. Joe easily won election to a fourth Senate term. The one hiccup came in October, when the campaign was caught misattributing a gushing quote about Joe to the *Delaware State News*. In fact, the passage—"Voters view Mr. Biden as 'trustworthy,' 'strong' and possessing the 'character and integrity' we need in a U.S. Senator"— came from a poll Biden himself had commissioned. A *State News* columnist had merely quoted that wording in a column critical of the poll. This time, Val took the fall, and the issue went away.

In the Senate, Joe's highest-profile turns came through his role as chairman of the Judiciary Committee.

In 1991, he presided over another charged Supreme Court nomination hearing, this time for Clarence Thomas. The initial hearings proceeded without incident, but in the middle of the nomination process, allegations emerged that Thomas had sexually harassed a former employee.

The former employee, Anita Hill, a young Black woman, came forward to testify. With Joe presiding, she faced harsh questioning from many of the committee's older, white male senators at a public hearing. When potential corroborating witnesses came forward, Joe did not arrange for them to provide their own public testimony, and Thomas's nomination survived. Hill, and many observers, faulted Joe's handling of the proceedings, something for which he later expressed regret.[313]

The episode, which does not appear in his memoir, undermined Joe's standing with women. It also motivated a bumper crop of female candidates to run for office in 1992, which was dubbed "the Year of the

Woman." That year, Carol Moseley Braun of Illinois became the first Black woman elected to the Senate. In an effort to repair the damage, Joe recruited her and another Democrat elected that year, Dianne Feinstein of California, to the Judiciary Committee.[314]

Joe's tough-on-crime stance softened slightly in these years. He proposed that some mandatory minimums be rolled back and stepped up his support for alternatives to prison for first-time drug offenders.

But he continued to relish a law-and-order image. In March 1991, video emerged of Los Angeles police beating a Black motorist, Rodney King, following a high-speed chase. The video sparked outrage, leading to investigations, and later indictments of the police officers involved, though they were ultimately acquitted.

As the controversy over police brutality played out, Joe introduced the Police Officers' Bill of Rights Act of 1991 in May. The bill, which did not move, would have mandated protections for officers facing internal disciplinary proceedings.[315]

Three years later, as chairman of Judiciary, he successfully shepherded the 1994 crime bill, which he sometimes referred to as the Biden Crime Bill, through the Senate.

In a floor speech on behalf of the bill, Joe declared, "Every time Richard Nixon, when he was running in 1972, would say, 'Law and order,' the Democratic match or response was, 'Law and order with justice'— whatever that meant. And I would say, 'Lock the S.O.B.s up.' "

The Violent Crime Control and Law Enforcement Act increased funding for police and included the Violence Against Women Act, which expanded the federal government's role in policing domestic violence. The law contributed to both declining crime rates and the rise of mass incarceration.[316]

Joe was making his mark in the Senate at a time when the culture of Washington and the legislative process were changing. In the era preceding Joe's arrival in the capital, lobbying played a limited role in the legislative process. In 1967, a few years before his election, Washington had just over sixty active, registered lobbyists, according to the *Atlantic*.

But the industry was growing rapidly. It began to take off during the Reagan years, and kept getting bigger into the '90s, when the ranks of registered lobbyists reached ten thousand.[317] It became commonplace for former congressional staffers, even former legislators, to leave government employment and go to work lobbying their former bosses and colleagues.[318]

Typical of this trend was Scott Green. In the '70s, Green had played linebacker at the University of Delaware, where he overlapped with Jimmy for a few semesters. In the '80s, Green went to work for Joe as a staffer on the Senate Judiciary Committee.

Then in the '90s, Green became a lobbyist and government contractor, focused on law enforcement and national security. He founded his own lobbying shop, the Lafayette Group.

Green's old boss sometimes went to bat for the Lafayette Group's clients, including the Drug Abuse Resistance Education program, which sent police officers into schools to tell kids to say no to drugs. The program became wildly popular in the '80s and '90s and was implemented in most public schools, with support from both parties.

Joe ensured that the program was eligible for a nine-figure pool of public funding in his 1994 crime bill, but the program fell out of favor as studies by university researchers and government agencies piled up showing DARE was not actually effective at lowering drug abuse. As support for DARE waned, Joe remained a steadfast supporter. Throughout his time in the Senate, he continued to secure funding for the program, which was paying Green $40,000 a year in lobbying fees.[319]

While good government advocates often frown upon such arrangements, positions like these made Joe, and by extension his family, popular with law enforcement. Once, when Beau and a friend were pulled over for speeding near Scranton, the cop said he recognized Beau's name and offered to let him off with a warning on account of his father's relationship with the police. The Sheriff insisted that the cop give him a ticket anyways.[320]

For Beau, this affinity with law enforcement led to a career path. After graduating from Penn, he followed in his father's footsteps to Syracuse Law School, graduating in 1994. He clerked for a year with a federal judge in New Hampshire. The judge went on to praise Beau's judgment and work ethic.

But being a Biden meant scrutiny, and both Biden brothers faced questions of nepotism and favoritism from the starts of their careers.

After the clerkship, Beau got a job in a highly selective Justice Department program, while Joe, as ranking member on the Judiciary Committee, oversaw the department. The hiring caught the notice of the *News Journal*. "I don't see any conflict," Joe told the paper. "Why would there be? The Justice Department is a gigantic department and he's qualified. At least they assumed he was."

Beau's boss also vouched that nepotism played no role in the hiring: "Beau came in and got the job on his own merits," said Eleanor Acheson, the undersecretary who hired him and the granddaughter of former Secretary of State Dean Acheson.

Beau balked at any suggestion of impropriety: "The fact that I am his son doesn't mean I can't be involved with helping to enforce or defend the law," he said. "I would be closed out of doing just about anything if you follow that logic." He pointed out that he had been rejected from a job with DOJ's criminal division.

Beau also served up some advice for Hunter, who would soon be navigating the legal job market himself. "I would tell my brother to do what he wants to do and to be honorable doing it," he said. Then he asked the reporter, "Are you trying to say we both should have been doctors?"[321]

―――――――

While the growth of lobbying was reshaping Washington, a new neoliberal consensus in Washington was reshaping the country, and the world. Free trade, financial deregulation, and the rise of high-tech industries made America richer, but it also made life for the middle class more precarious. Joe voted for the North American Free Trade Agreement in 1993 and six years later he voted for the financial deregulation that repealed the Glass-Steagall Act, a move that created the conditions for the next global financial crisis. Years later, Joe came to rue that one, confiding to a writer for the *New Yorker*, "The only vote I can think of that I've ever cast in my years in the Senate that I regret—and I did it out of loyalty, and I wasn't aware that it was gonna be as bad as it was—was Glass-Steagall."[322]

While Joe was helping create this brave new post–Cold War world, Jimmy, who now went by Jim (though Val still called him Jimmy),[323] learned to navigate it. With his older brother on a government salary, the Bidens' financial fortunes rested disproportionately on his shoulders. "Jim's job," one of his former business partners explained to me, "is to ensure the lifestyle is good for the family."

To do so, Jim had to succeed in an economy far more globalized and financialized than the one the Bidens and their neighbors had known in Scranton or Delaware. In this more freewheeling world, political clout and connections could pave the way for lucrative dealmaking. And that could put the family on the right side of the divide that was making many Americans rich while leaving many more of them behind.

Jim divorced his first wife, Michelle, and in August 1995 he remarried, this time to Sara Jones. Sara, a Duke-educated lawyer from Kentucky, had served as general counsel to the congressional committee overseeing the Government Printing Office.[324] Caroline served as a bridesmaid to her new stepmother, and Jamie served as his father's best man.[325]

Joel Boyarsky, still Jim's employer at the time of his wedding, lent the couple $200,000 when they bought a house in a suburb of Philadelphia. But the loan was not enough to shore up Jim's finances. He owed back taxes, and in 1998 the IRS filed a lien on the house.[326]

Jim and Sara were more than life partners; they were also business partners. The couple set up a consulting business, the Lion Hall Group. Joe's old law partner David Walsh served as Lion Hall's registered agent on its Delaware corporate registration.[327]

Lion Hall got business from Dickie Scruggs, a Mississippi trial lawyer who became a billionaire, and perhaps the world's richest lawyer,[328] leading asbestos and tobacco class actions. He was nicknamed "the King of Torts."

In the mid-'90s, Scruggs was working to put together the largest class action settlement in history—a case against the tobacco companies worth hundreds of billions of dollars. For the settlement to be viable, the parties needed Congress to grant the companies immunity from future legal claims. Many Democrats were wary of granting immunity.

Scruggs and his partners put together a Washington influence campaign. Mississippi's former state auditor, Steve Patterson, had worked for Joe's 1988 presidential campaign, and Patterson recommended Jim. Scruggs hired Jim to help him move Joe and his colleagues on the measure.

There is no evidence Jim got Joe to take any action on behalf of Scruggs, who was unable to scare up enough Democratic support to pass the measure. Despite the lack of congressional help, Scruggs found another way to get his megasettlement, and Jim stayed in touch with his Mississippi contacts.[329]

———

Joe has long pointed to his status as one of the least wealthy members of the Senate to prove his regular-guy bona fides, but he was not indigent, either. In 1996, he and Jill sold the Station to John R. Cochran III, vice chairman at MBNA, Delaware's biggest bank. Cochran paid the asking price: $1.2 million.

Joe and Jill then bought a piece of land on a nearby lake and took out a mortgage to build their dream home: a stucco house with an outdoor pool and a dock out on the water. In the meantime, they lived in a series of rentals along with Ashley.[330] She had followed her brothers to Archmere, which had gone co-ed.

Val, meanwhile, continued to run Joe's political operations as he sought his fifth term that year. The biggest hiccup came when his Republican opponent, businessman Ray Clatworthy, implied in a push poll that Cochran had wildly overpaid Joe for the Station. Joe and the bank condemned the claim and released a 1992 appraisal that pegged the value at $1.2 million.[331]

At the time, MBNA was growing into a credit card giant. It was courting politicians from both parties and hiring high-ranking civil servants as it navigated complex federal regulations. Between its employees and its political action committee, it would become, for a time, the second largest source of funding for George W. Bush's campaigns, trailing only Enron.[332] The claim that Cochran overpaid did not stick with voters.

With hands-on participation from the whole family, and with MBNA employees serving as the largest source of campaign contributions, Val guided Joe to an easy victory that year.

Margaret Aitken, a high school classmate of Beau's who volunteered to pass out campaign literature for the '96 reelection effort, went on to serve as Joe's press secretary for a decade. She credits Val for the loyalty many aides showed Joe's political operation. "It wasn't like you were working for Joe Biden," Aitken explained. "You were working with the Biden family."

In the course of working for the family, Aitken learned about the rhetorical lengths the family went to in affirming their loyalty to one another. Once, Val and Aitken were standing in line outside a viewing at a Delaware church, waiting to pay their respects to the deceased. An acquaintance, seeing Aitken in line, asked her, "Do you still work for Joe Biden?"

Aitken explained that she did and that her companion was, in fact, Joe's younger sister.

"Oh, good thing I didn't say anything bad about him," the man said.

"Yeah, good thing," Val retorted jokingly, "because I would hate to have to punch you in front of church."[333]

(At other times, her piety and her family bonds were more harmonious: During her brother's second Senate term, Val had joined the Ministry of Caring, an ecumenical charity for the poor, and helped change state law to encourage local businesses to donate food. She used her pull with Joe in a way the nuns would approve of: getting her brother to speak at a fund-raiser for the charity in 1983.)[334]

After Joe's fifth election, Val, too, got in on the growing business of politics. She came on as an executive at Joe Slade White & Company, a media consulting firm that did work for Joe's campaigns.[335]

===

After a year at Georgetown Law, Hunter tried again for Yale. This time, he got in, and transferred. According to family lore, the ultraselective law school was swayed by a poem he had written for his personal statement.[336]

He graduated from law school in 1996 and served as deputy campaign manager for his father's reelection.[337] Then he took a job at MBNA, where he landed the title of executive vice president. Hunter rejected concerns about the political ties between the firm and his father. "Unfortunately, no matter where I went to work, some people would make an issue of it," he said.[338]

One former Biden aide recalled talking to Hunter about this very question: What sort of work could he pursue without making it look like he was cashing in? The former aide was sympathetic. He came to agree with the conclusion that Hunter was more or less bound to give that appearance no matter what work he pursued. That conclusion may say more about the Washington mindset than about the actual universe of job options open to a graduate of Yale Law School.[339]

Hunter worked at MBNA until 1998, then took a job in the Clinton Commerce Department. In 2001, he left to work as a lobbyist for William Oldaker, who had served as a campaign counsel and treasurer to Joe. In the four years following his return to the private sector, Hunter also received $100,000 a year in consulting fees from MBNA.

Throughout this period, Joe was a steadfast supporter of MBNA's top legislative priority, the Bankruptcy Reform Act, which made it harder for Americans to declare bankruptcy, and thereby shed credit card debt. Consumer advocates fiercely opposed the legislation. Joe went to great lengths to advance it, inserting it into a foreign relations bill in 2000, when he was ranking member on that committee. The gambit fell short, but Joe kept at it.

His efforts put him at odds with an obscure consumer advocate, Harvard Law School professor Elizabeth Warren. "Those who want to say [that] the way to solve rising consumer bankruptcy is by changing the law," she said at the outset of the legislative fight, "are the same people who would have said during a malaria epidemic that the way to cut down on hospital admissions is to lock the door." The two later sparred at a hearing on the bill. Warren told Joe, "You can't take away the last shred of protection from these families."[340]

In total, Joe voted for the bill four times between 1998 and 2005, when it finally passed. Joe has said that neither the bank's payments to his son, nor its gifts to his campaigns, nor even the fact that he represented the bank's home state played any role in his support for the legislation.[341]

═══════

After heading out West during Joe's first reelection bid, Frank took a liking to California. By 1985, he had followed in Jimmy's footsteps and taken work with Walt Shorenstein's real estate empire. That year he married Janine Jaquet, a journalist from Wilmington. The couple set-tled in the Bay Area[342] and had a daughter, Alana.

Then, early in the Clinton years, Frank got a job back east as the director of the Office of Congressional, Legislative and Public Affairs at the Government Printing Office.

He told the *News Journal* that he got the job through a friend, Anthony Zagami, the office's general counsel, not through any help of Joe's. He also said that he avoided taking any jobs from large Delaware businesses because of the complications of being a Biden. "Don't nail me on this," he implored the reporter.[343]

Though he had work and a family, Frank struggled with drinking. His marriage broke up, and he moved to Florida. At one point, he did some work for a printing company in Boca Raton.[344]

By the summer of 1999 he was back in California.

That July, he rented a green-and-tan Jaguar XK8 convertible in Los Angeles using a Florida license that had been suspended. In August, in San Diego, Frank was in the passenger seat of the car when a young acquaintance, Jason Turton, struck and killed a pedestrian, Michael Albano.

Albano's family filed a wrongful death suit against Frank and others in 2000. In their suit, the plaintiffs raised questions about Frank's flush finances, alleging that he "is a forty-seven-year-old individual with no known employment who, nevertheless, was able to come to California, rent a Ford truck and then a new Jaguar for over a month, rent an apart-ment, and live here without working."

Frank did not stick around to contest the claims against him. He went back to Florida, and he never responded to the lawsuit. After more than a year, the court entered a default judgment against him for hun-dreds of thousands of dollars. Albano's daughters were unable to collect on it.[345]

Back in Florida, in the coming years, Frank's drinking problems continued. He got six months of probation for a DUI in 2000. The next year, the court sent him to three months of rehab at the Watershed, a rehab facility in Delray Beach, for driving on a suspended license.[346]

———

As Joe's profile rose, he kept close touch with his roots. In 1999, Preno's—whose original proprietor had talked of launching a sauce-canning operation with Joe's father—closed so that the city could put up a convention center.[347] In the decades since he had left Scranton, Joe had remained a Preno's regular, stopping by on his frequent visits and ordering tubs of the restaurant's signature sauce for family occasions. Not long after it closed, Joe was driving through downtown Scranton when he saw the rubble of the demolished restaurant. He told Beau to pull over, and plucked a brick from the rubble. After that, he kept the brick on his mantel in Delaware.[348]

Then, on September 11, 2001, the world changed during Joe's daily Amtrak commute to Washington. As reports ripped through the train about a plane crashing into the World Trade Center, Joe received a panicked call on his cell phone from Jill. When he arrived in Washington, he proceeded to walk the couple blocks from Union Station to the Capitol. There, he was turned back by security, and so he waited in a nearby park, even as he received another panicked phone call from Ashley about a fourth plane headed for Washington.

Eventually, Joe linked up with Jim, and the brothers hitched a ride home with Bob Brady, a Democratic congressman from Philadelphia who commandeered a van. On the drive, Joe, who had recently taken up the chairmanship of the Foreign Relations Committee, took a call from George W. Bush, then aboard Air Force One. He urged the president to return immediately to Washington, relating a rousing story about how Charles de Gaulle once braved gunfire in the streets of Paris. Bush did not take the advice. When Joe rang off, Jim cracked, "Whatever staffer suggested he call *you* just got fired."

On September 12, Joe was back in the Senate, where he helped organize the logistics of floor speeches and expressed his own view that Americans must not let the attacks warp their values.

Even amid this fear and uncertainty, Wild Card remained inviolable. With the Pentagon in ruins, the remains of the World Trade Center still smoking, and the whiff of impending war in the air, Joe stepped off the Senate floor to take questions about military priorities from a gaggle of reporters.

The back-and-forth was interrupted by a different kind of question: "Uncle Joe?" asked Jim's son, Jamie, who was then studying at Georgetown along with Val's son, Cuffe. Both cousins had come across town with a friend to visit their uncle. Joe broke away from the maelstrom of history to show the three undergrads to the Senate cafeteria.[349]

In the months that followed, he became a fixture on the Sunday shows. Aitken learned to keep a running list of nearby Catholic services, so that at whatever time Joe's television hit ended, she could rush him to the next available Mass.

One Sunday, an exhausted Aitken suggested he skip church this once and take the day off.

"Margaret, something's going to happen to you someday," he told her. "It's going to just—it's going to drop you to your knees. It's going to knock you down. And you have a choice at that time.

"You could either blame God or you could turn towards God for help." He told her, "And I chose to turn towards God for help." So the weekly pilgrimages continued.[350] So did the personal loss that shaped Joe's faith. A year after the attacks, Joe Sr. died at the age of eighty-six.[351]

As the war on terror warped into the Bush administration's drive to invade Iraq, Joe attempted to forge a middle ground between the administration's neoconservative hawks and liberal doves. When Bush sought authorization for war from Congress, Joe proposed compromise language that imposed more restrictions on the use of force than Bush wanted. When his proposal fizzled, Joe voted with the Senate's majority in authorizing Bush to invade. As the increasingly deadly and costly U.S. occupation of the country dragged on, Joe confessed to regretting the vote.

———

After Archmere, Ashley went off to Tulane in New Orleans. Three years later, she was out partying late on a Friday night in Chicago, when a friend allegedly threw a soda can at a police officer trying to keep revelers from walking in the street. Then a second friend allegedly jumped on the cop's back and punched him in the face. Ashley was arrested for "verbally intimidating" a second cop who came to assist the first, and charged with obstructing a police officer.[352] Ashley apologized and the charges were dropped.[353]

At Oldaker's lobbying firm, Hunter did much of his work for Catholic universities seeking earmarks. There, he worked with Eric Schwerin, another veteran of the Commerce Department.

The Bidens have maintained that Joe and Hunter never discussed Hunter's clients. "It wasn't like we all sat down and agreed on it," Hunter has said. "It came naturally."[354]

The lobbying work funded a comfortable lifestyle. With Hunter established in business, he and Kathleen had two more daughters, Finnegan and Maisy. In 2001, they bought a five-thousand-square-foot Colonial on close to two acres of land, less than a mile from Joe and Jill's house, for $617,000.[355] The house was not shabby for a thirty-one-year-old, and Hunter's success did not escape the attention of the neighbors. They noted among themselves that the young lobbyist now lived in the same neighborhood not just as his famous father, but also as Michael Spinks, a retired boxing world champion.[356]

Hunter also joined Fieldstone,[357] a new golf club built on land that belonged to a du Pont family heiress.[358] His increasingly staid lifestyle masked worsening problems with alcohol. With some regularity, he would go out drinking after work in Washington and fail to catch the last train home, leaving Kathleen to take care of their daughters in the mornings.[359]

Beau began to settle down as well. In 2001, he proposed to his girl-friend, Hallie Olivere, during the family's annual Thanksgiving trip to Nantucket. They wed the following autumn, back on the island.[360]

Hunter was a decade ahead of his older brother in starting a family, but in other ways he was still less grown up.

One member of the family's inner circle recalled to me a memorable run-in with Hunter in the aftermath of Beau's rehearsal dinner on Nantucket. Hunter wanted to go out partying.

The foggy little island is not exactly a nightlife mecca in the summer, let alone in the off-season. But between the Chicken Box, a popular spot for dancing, and the grungier Rose and Crown Pub in town, a night of carousing could be had.

Now in their thirties, many in the group had young families and were not itching for a night on the town. This attendee told Hunter he was not feeling well.

Hunter got in his face and called him a "pussy." It did not come across as a lighthearted jab. He spat the word out. Hunter was sporting stubble, before that look came into style. Between the dinner table and the vehicle, he had donned a dark-colored ski hat. The effect was to make him resemble a burglar from a children's cartoon. The image and the moment stuck with the wedding guest on the receiving end of it. It wasn't that the guest took offense, nor that it was the first time he had seen someone try too hard to get a group of friends to head out on the town. But there was a darkness to it with Hunter.

Hunter's drinking problems continued. The following year, he checked himself into rehab in Antigua. When he returned to Washington, Beau picked him up at the airport and accompanied him to his first Alcoholics Anonymous meeting, in Dupont Circle.[361]

═══════

After marrying, Jim and Sara had a son, Nick, and continued their quest to sustain a high-flying lifestyle. As they navigated financial ups and downs, they found there was no shortage of people with interests at the intersection of business and politics who could be relied upon to help them.

When Joe was crafting his signature 1994 crime bill, he leaned heavily on Tom Scotto, president of the National Association of Police Organizations, the nation's second-largest coalition of law enforcement unions. Scotto made himself a presence in Joe's Washington office, pushing Joe to increase proposed funding as he helped draft the law. Violent crime was surging, and Joe tended to give Scotto what he wanted. "There wasn't one thing when he said, 'No,'" Scotto told the *Washington Post* of the experience.[362]

In 2001, Scotto found himself on the other side of the law when he was named as an unindicted coconspirator in an organized crime scheme to bribe labor leaders.[363] Scotto denied wrongdoing. At the time, the Justice Department described it as the largest securities fraud bust in American history. It ensnared members of all five families of the New York City Mafia, who took part in a scheme to get control of union pension funds and siphon off portions of them for themselves.[364]

Scotto also knew Jimmy. And about a year after the bust, he introduced Jimmy to Anthony Lotito, a New York financial advisor. Jim and Lotito went into business together. They cofounded a private security company, Americore International Security. They also set out to sell financial services to union pension funds governed by the 1947 Taft-Hartley Act.[365]

In 2000, Jim and Sara borrowed $350,000 from Leonard Barrack, a donor to Joe and the former finance chairman of the Democratic National Committee.

Jim talked Barrack into hiring Sara to help his law firm drum up business from local government bodies and pension funds. Jim said he would also help the firm land clients "through his family name and his resemblance to his brother, United States Senator Joseph Biden of Delaware," as Barrack's firm later claimed in a lawsuit after the arrangement went south. The firm alleged that on top of a salary, it had paid Sara a quarter million dollars in fees, and that she had used the firm's money to fund travel to Europe, Hawaii, and Alaska, as well as to boost the Lion Hall Group.

Jim and Sara countersued, and the case settled. They borrowed another $400,000 from Thomas Knox, a donor of Joe's who would go on to run for mayor of Philadelphia.

The couple also sought to sell pension services to labor groups through BBS Benefits Solutions, a firm in which they have been listed as principals.[366]

One senior union official, speaking on the condition of anonymity, described his experience on the receiving end of a Jimmy-and-Sara pitch around this time.

"I get a call from one of Biden's guys. I don't think at this point he was working for Biden anymore," the official recalled. The caller said Joe's brother wanted to stop by and pitch a pension product.

The union official did not deal in-depth with members' pension plans, so he asked an aide who did to sit in on the meeting with Jim and Sara at the union's Washington office. "After explaining to me twenty-three times who his brother was and what a great relationship he has with him," the official recalled, Jim got around to explaining his pension services.

The official ceded the floor to his lieutenant, in order to let him vet the proposal. "He started asking questions and took [Jim] apart," the official recalled. "Apparently it was a bullshit thing."

The official said Sara was more "articulate," and that she tried to defend the product offering.

But the pitch fell flat. Later, the official complained about it to friends in a firefighters union. "I remember them laughing," he recalled. The firefighters told him, " 'They're always doing that.' "[367]

Another business partner of Jim's was Edward Caveney, a Boston insurance broker he had met through Larry Rasky, a Democratic operative and sometime advisor to Joe's campaigns. Jim and Caveney planned to use the Biden family's ties and reputation to sell insurance products to law enforcement groups. At one point, the pair gathered police and fire representatives—with the help of the executive director of the Massachusetts Police Association—inside a luxury box at Fenway Park, home of the Boston Red Sox.

The pair made a bid to sell insurance to Corrections USA, which represents prison guards nationwide. As part of the pitch, the group's executives traveled to Washington in 2007. On the Amtrak ride into the city, Jim introduced the group to Joe, and they met with him again at the Capitol. That night, Hunter joined them for dinner. Jim's political access was an important part of the pitch. "[He] makes sure he tells you his brother is Joe Biden," the group's vice chairman, Roy Pinto, told the investigative outlet ProPublica. " 'We're brothers, we're close.' " That deal, though, did not go through.[368]

Jim had better luck with a tropical land deal. In 2005, he bought an acre of land on Water Island, a five-hundred-acre paradise just south of St. Thomas in the U.S. Virgin Islands. He got an easement from the Virgin Islands territorial government to use an existing driveway to the property, and he split the land into three parcels of roughly equal size. A year after the purchase, he sold one of the parcels for $150,000, the same price he had paid for the entire plot. It was a good deal for Jim, effectively recouping all of his money while keeping most of the land.

The buyer was the lobbyist Scott Green.

Green's relationship with Joe has remained important to his business.

His firm's website features a photo of the two of them together and a testimonial from Joe, saying, "Scott Green was emotionally invested. It wasn't just a job for him; it was an emotional investment."

The purpose of the land deals is not clear: Neither Jim nor Green has built anything on the land.

Joe and Jill had traveled to the Virgin Islands at least once before, in 1994, when Joe had been flown out to address a conference put on by the Aspen Institute, a think tank.[369] In the years following the deal, Joe and his family traveled to the tiny island for holiday getaways. One of the island's roughly one hundred residents told me the Bidens were turned on to Water Island by family friends of theirs from Baltimore.

The Bidens then switched to vacationing on another U.S. Virgin Island, St. Croix. The larger island could better accommodate their traveling entourage, which by then included Secret Service agents.

Green's work, meanwhile, continued to overlap with Joe's. In 2007, Green began lobbying for the Major Cities Chiefs Association, a police group whose priorities included the setting aside of wireless broadband spectrum for use by first responders.

Joe was already a supporter of the cause, which had been recommended by the 9/11 Commission as a way to improve communications in the event of an emergency.

Measures to set aside the spectrum and create the Nationwide Public Safety Broadband Network stalled in the Senate, but as vice president, Joe clinched its passage in 2012. Green's firm, the Lafayette Group, went on to receive contracts worth north of $10 million related to the broadband network, which is now called FirstNet.

Two years before that, in 2010, Jim and Sara took out a $133,000 loan from Green in the form of a mortgage on their remaining Water Island land. In 2013, Green and his wife released the mortgage, and indicated that the loan had been paid off.

Joe's 2020 presidential campaign would not answer questions about the transactions or Joe's relationship with Green. A lawyer for Jim did not provide answers to questions about the transactions, and Green did not respond to my requests for comment.[370]

It can be hard to know what to make of transactions like these in isolation. But the broader pattern was more clear. The Bidens regularly intermingled personal, political, and financial relationships in ways that invited questions about whether the public interest was getting short-changed.

Dynastic Delaware

"Clearly there is something for the eugenists, political scientists, and general critics of Democracy to ponder in dynastic Delaware."

—Prof. Ezra Bowen, 1925

Delaware is a small oddity of a state, and one that has been curiously well suited to maintaining political dynasties.

Its first European settlers were Dutch, followed by the Swedes, who were then displaced by the English. In 1682, the Duke of York granted a lease of land on the Delaware River to William Penn.[371] Penn needed an outlet to the sea for Pennsylvania, his newly founded haven for persecuted Quakers.

The merger of these three lower counties on the Delaware with the rest of the colony never quite took. Within twenty years, the three lower counties had won the right to pass their own laws in an assembly in New Castle, while remaining under the rule of Pennsylvania's governor in Philadelphia.

Meanwhile, Maryland's rulers, the Catholic Calvert family, engaged in a century-long turf battle with the Penns, contended that much of Delaware rightfully belonged to them.

In the 1760s, the Mason-Dixon line was established to settle this border dispute. The line went on to take its place in American history as the demarcation between free states, falling north of the line, and slave states, falling south of the line, hammered out in the Missouri Compromise. But the east–west line does a funny thing when it gets to Delaware, jutting sharply southward to form the state's western border. In other words, Delaware falls *east* of the Mason-Dixon line.

This peculiar position—a slave state, it remained on the side of the Union in the Civil War—placed it largely outside the confines of the North-South conflict that defined the early history of the United States.

In 1787, Delaware became the first state to ratify the Constitution, and for the following two centuries, that arguably remained its primary claim to fame. In many ways, it seems to have been left alone by history altogether, a quiet eddy on the rushing flow of human events.

These placid conditions allowed a single family, the du Ponts, to dominate Delaware's affairs for much of its history. The first du Pont in America, Pierre Samuel du Pont de Nemours, was a French Huguenot who fled Paris toward the end of the French Revolution. Sentenced to the guillotine during the Reign of Terror, he lucked out when Robespierre was captured and executed instead.

He came to America, where he helped broker the Louisiana Purchase.

If the Bidens are tight-knit, Pierre Samuel took kinship to another level. Of his vision for the du Ponts' future, he wrote, "The marriages that I should prefer for our colony would be between the cousins. In that way we should be sure of honesty of soul and purity of blood." Cousin marriage has since been outlawed in much of the country, including in Delaware, but not before Pierre Samuel's descendants were able to honor his wishes at least seven times.[372]

Those descendants became known for their long noses[373] (Steve Carrell had to wear a prosthetic to play John du Pont in the 2015 film *Foxcatcher*).[374] They also went on to amass one of the country's great fortunes and to dominate Delaware's affairs for generations.

Pierre Samuel's son, Éleuthère Irénée du Pont, started E.I. du Pont de Nemours & Company in 1802, setting up shop outside Wilmington. He found the quality of American gunpowder to be poor, and he used the company to bring French manufacturing techniques to the new world.

Over time, DuPont grew into one of the world's largest chemical companies as well as the biggest thing going in Delaware. Political prominence naturally followed, and in a sleepy place like Delaware, there was little to displace the family from its perch.

In 1925, a Prof. Ezra Bowen of Lafayette College in Pennsylvania penned a scholarly article taking stock of the state's remarkable political continuities. In the article, entitled, "Dynastic Delaware," Bowen marveled at the ubiquity of the du Ponts and another Huguenot family, the Bayards, across generations of the state's leaders.

From the first United States Congress through to the eve of the Great Depression, the Bayards, whose roots in Delaware predate English rule, sent six generations of sons to the Senate. The family generally aligned with the Democratic Party, while the du Ponts tended to align with the Republicans.

"The Delaware story reads in large part like a Morse code: Bayard, Bayard, Dupont; Bayard, DuPont, Bayard; DuPont, DuPont, Bayard," Bowen wrote.

"If you live in this smallest state and you have no Bayard or DuPont connection of blood, business, or politics," he warned, "you are a farmer or a shopkeeper, a purveyor to the host."

———

This remained, more or less, the state of affairs when ten-year-old Joey Biden arrived in Delaware in the early 1950s. At the time, Alexis Irénée du Pont Bayard, the living embodiment of Bowen's thesis, was serving as lieutenant governor.

The Bidens had no Bayard or du Pont connections to speak of, and while car salesman was not a common occupation when Bowen published his essay, it is safe to assume the historian would have lumped Joe Sr. in with the shopkeepers.

But Joe's mother instilled in him early the conviction that the Bidens were on par with the du Ponts and all the other blue bloods.

Archmere's campus, the apple of Joe's eye, was set on the estate of John Jakob Raskob, an industrialist and former chairman of the Democratic National Committee. Raskob, a Catholic, had gotten his start as personal secretary to Pierre S. du Pont.[375] Biden later learned that the Irish in Delaware were brought over by the DuPont company as workers.[376] It was for those workers that DuPont donated the land for St. Joseph's on the Brandywine,[377] the Catholic Church where Joe would worship as an adult and bury his eldest son.[378]

By the time the Bidens showed up, DuPont, the giant corporation, was beginning to supplant du Pont the family, whose control of its namesake company gradually dwindled with each passing decade.

When Joe moved from his first Delaware home to the slightly more comfortable environs of nearby Mayfield in 1955, his neighborhood filled up with young professionals employed by DuPont. He came to realize his father's financial precarity as a salesman marked him apart from his neighbors, secure in their status as company men. "The oval will take care of you," they liked to say, an allusion to the conglomerate's corporate logo.[379] Embracing this sort of paternalism, Delawareans nicknamed the company "Uncle Dupie."

As Joe was returning to the state from law school, conditions began to favor change.

In 1968, even sleepy Delaware felt the reverberations of the unrest that was then sweeping the United States and many other countries around the world. That year, in response to the rioting that followed the assassination of Martin Luther King Jr., Gov. Charles Terry, a Democrat, ordered the National Guard out onto the streets of Wilmington.

They stayed for nine months. It was among the harshest crackdowns in the nation, and the second-longest occupation of any American city since the end of the Civil War.[380]

Three years later, in 1971, investigators working under the public interest crusader Ralph Nader had released an eight-hundred-page report titled "The Company State," arguing that Delaware had become, in effect, a private fiefdom of the du Pont family and its corporate behemoth,[381] which at the time owned, among other things, the state's two biggest newspapers, the *Morning News* and the *Evening Journal*.[382]

Discontent with Terry's crackdown and a growing restlessness formed part of the backdrop of Joe's Senate campaign and contributed to the appeal of a fresh-faced, idealistic candidate.

While Joe offered to bring new blood into the ranks of the state's leadership, the du Ponts and their legacy continued to loom over the race, just as they loomed over most things in Delaware.

Boggs, the incumbent, had wanted to retire that year, but Richard Nixon convinced him to run for a third term. Nixon told Boggs that he just had to win, and then he could resign early in his term. Delaware's lone congressman, Pierre Samuel du Pont IV, could be appointed to the seat in order to keep it in Republican hands.[383] Nixon would not get the chance to see this plan through.

In the closing weeks of the campaign, with Joe's coffers running dry, Val set up a meeting for Jimmy and Joe with some wealthy Republican donors at the offices of a wealth management firm in Centerville, a community near the Pennsylvania border with a large number of estates belonging to du Pont heirs.

The group, which included Alfred I. du Pont Dent, asked Joe's thoughts on the capital gains tax. Nixon wanted to lower it, a plan Joe had already publicly opposed. Joe sensed the group was feeling him out, seeing if the young candidate could be induced to soften his position in exchange for some fund-raising help. Instead, Joe reiterated his opposition to Nixon's plan. Jimmy worried that his brother had lost the room.

"Joe, I sure in hell hope you feel that strongly about capital gains," Jimmy fumed on the drive home, "because you just lost the election."

His fears were overblown.[384]

For election night, Val had booked the Gold Ballroom at the Hotel du Pont. The venue was normally the site of Republican election night gatherings, but she had gotten ahead of the opposition, and reserved the room back in June.[385]

The opulent hotel had opened in 1913, when Raskob and his boss, Pierre S. du Pont, decided their growing conglomerate needed its own lodging to put up clients.[386] Sixty years later, the Bidens marked their Delaware political arrival with a party there.

━━━

When Joe arrived in the Senate, per tradition, he carved his name on the inside of his desk. Of the twenty names carved into the desk before Joe's, six were Bayards.[387] Coming from a state like this, there were limits to how far a spirit of change could push concrete reforms.

Joe had run as an idealistic young liberal and a friend of civil rights. He won with the support of Black voters. During his campaign, he called busing "a phony issue which allows the white liberals to sit in suburbia, confident that they are not going to have to live next to a Black." He described the issue, along with amnesty for draft dodgers, as "the kind of things that make great discussions at cocktail parties but do not change the direction of this country."[388] Such rhetoric seemed to imply he felt that busing did not go nearly far enough. He also argued that Nixon was raising the prospect of large-scale busing as a red herring, and strove to make a distinction between de jure segregation, which was imposed by the state, and de facto segregation, which was not. He argued that busing should be used as a remedy only in places with state-mandated segregation.[389]

What Joe called a "phony" issue soon became a thorny issue, and then an explosive one, as busing rose to the top of the national agenda.

At first, he supported the policy. In 1974, the first-term senator cast two votes, one of them decisive, in favor of preserving the power of the courts to impose busing as a remedy for segregation.

In July, two months after that decisive vote, he faced an angry crowd of busing opponents at a school auditorium in a small town near Wilmington.[390] At the time, a federal court was considering a desegregation case against the state board of education, with busing a likely remedy. Later that week, a three-judge panel ordered the state draw up desegregation plans.[391]

As fights over the desegregation of Delaware's schools wound their way through the courts, Biden shifted to become a vocal opponent of busing. In 1977, he introduced a bill along with Delaware's other senator, Republican Bill Roth, that would severely curtail the use of busing and head off the commencement of the practice in Delaware, which was slated for September of that year.[392]

At a hearing on the issue that July, Joe argued that his approach would allow for an "orderly integration of society," and that busing could have disastrous consequences. "Unless we do something about this," he said, "my children are going to grow up in a jungle, the jungle being a racial jungle with tensions having built so high that it is going to explode at some point."[393]

Joe's efforts to curtail busing ultimately failed, but his children were unaffected. He had been sending Beau and Hunter, and would later send Ashley as well, to the Quaker Wilmington Friends School, the private school where Val had been a teacher.[394]

Though Biden and busing both became new facts of life in Delaware, other things remained the same. For one, the du Ponts had not totally vacated the scene. While Nixon's plan to have him appointed to replace Boggs in the Senate went awry, Pierre Samuel du Pont IV, better known as Pete, became governor in 1977.

His most consequential act was the signing of the Financial Center

Development Act in 1981. The law liberalized financial regulation, the cornerstone of a successful bid to draw out-of-state banks into Delaware.

The law began the transformation of the state into a corporate and tax haven, which is what it's best known for now. Corporate entities registered in the state have since come to outnumber its residents. Meanwhile, other states have moved to close the "Delaware loophole," which allows companies to trim their tax bills by registering subsidiaries there, and Delaware's lax approach to enforcement has prompted complaints even from the Cayman Islands, a rival corporate haven.[395]

The du Pont family had pushed for Delaware's original business-friendly corporation law in 1899, and this time was no different. Another du Pont heir, and the governor's cousin, Nathan Hayward III, was instrumental in pushing the 1981 deregulation as the state's acting secretary of community affairs and economic development.[396] So was DuPont's corporate chairman, Irving Shapiro.[397]

Du Pont was prevented by term limits from running for governor again. Republicans, including Ronald Reagan, urged him to challenge Biden for his Senate seat in 1984 instead. Their internal polling showed it would be a close matchup, but the governor passed.[398]

Instead, four years later, the avatars of old Delaware and new both had their turns on the national stage.

Pete du Pont became the first declared presidential candidate of either party when he entered the Republican primary in September 1986, with a kickoff in the jam-packed Gold Ballroom at his family's eponymous hotel. He had planned to depart directly from the campaign kickoff to the airport for his first swing on the campaign trail. But the dramatic departure was foiled when an aide locked du Pont's car keys inside the candidate's minivan, temporarily trapping his luggage and ticket inside.[399]

It was an inauspicious start. (And not, by the way, the last time an American political scion's car problems would cloud their electoral ambitions. In 2014, Herbert Claiborne Pell IV—grandson of the late senator—found his campaign for governor of Rhode Island complicated by revelations he had repeatedly reported his Prius missing to the Providence Police, and that on at least one of those occasions, he later realized he had simply forgotten where he left it.)[400]

His candidacy lasted longer than Joe's, but the du Ponts found that their aristocratic Huguenot brand was a tough sell with Republican primary voters. After finding that his name confused too many Iowans, du Pont's cousin and campaign surrogate, Irenee du Pont May, was reduced to identifying himself as "Ernie."[401] Pete was out of the race after New Hampshire.

In the years that followed du Pont's signing of the deregulation law, Delaware's financial services industry displaced Uncle Dupie at the center of the state's economy. Meanwhile, the Democratic Party began a long run of dominance in state politics, leaving little room for new generations of du Ponts to attain the higher rungs of public office.

As Joe's sons entered adulthood, the circumstances were ripe for the Bidens to plant the seeds of a new political dynasty in the fertile soil of the Delaware River valley.

———

It fell to Beau to carry the mantle of public service forward.

Following the end of hostilities between ethnic Serbs and Albanians in Kosovo in the late 1990s, Beau had worked to train prosecutors and judges in the tiny Balkan state on behalf of the Organization for Security and Co-operation in Europe.[402]

In 2000, he gained notice when he accompanied his father to Return Day, a Delaware tradition in which the state's political class gathers together two days after every statewide election. Beau's appearance at the biennial festivities set off speculation that he was jockeying for a run against the incumbent attorney general, Jane Brady, his father's 1990 Senate opponent, in 2002.[403]

But Beau took a pass on the race that year. He enlisted in the

Delaware National Guard's Judge Advocate General Corps, serving part-time as a military lawyer, instead.

He also went into private practice, at a firm that became Bifferato, Gentilotti & Biden. He wanted to get into complex litigation work, and a family ally was there to help.

The St. Louis–area firm SimmonsCooper made its money in the lucrative practice of asbestos torts. The firm found itself in a natural alliance with Joe, who vocally opposed the creation of an asbestos trust fund in the Senate. The proposal would have hurt torts firms like Simmons-Cooper, which spent millions lobbying for its interests in Washington and became a top source of campaign funds for Joe.

Beau convinced SimmonsCooper to tap his firm as local counsel on the asbestos cases it filed in Delaware.[404] His career as a plaintiff's lawyer proved to be short-lived, though.

By July 2005, the *News Journal* was describing him as "the nearly anointed Democratic nominee" for attorney general in 2006.[405] This time, Beau did run.

Like his father's campaigns, it was a family affair. He conferred frequently with Joe by phone,[406] and his campaign paid over $400,000 to Joe Slade White & Company, the small political consultancy where Val was an executive.[407] Val's daughter, Missy, served as Beau's campaign manager.

In the general election, Beau faced Republican Ferris Wharton. Wharton had earned his stripes in the late '90s prosecuting Thomas Capano, a lawyer from a prominent Delaware family, for the murder of his mistress. It was one of the most sensational trials in the state's history, and Wharton's star turn in it gave him name recognition on par with Beau's.

Supporters of Wharton, then fifty-four, sought to paint the younger Biden, thirty-seven, as too young and inexperienced for the post. At the Republican convention in May, they erupted in chants of "Beau don't know."

The next month, Republicans ran ads calling for an amendment to the state constitution that would require anyone running for attorney general to have practiced law in Delaware for at least five years. It was a thinly veiled jab at Beau, who did not meet that bar.[408]

By the standards of post-Trump-era American politics, these were mild attacks, but by the standards of Delaware and the time, the race was nasty.

Part and parcel with the charge of inexperience came the implication that Beau, whose full name would appear on the ballot as Joseph R. Biden III, was riding his father's coattails.

"Beau struck me as someone who was trying to escape from his dad's shadow," recalled Wharton's campaign manager, Matt Frendewey. "He was extremely self-aware of the allegation that he was not his own man."[409]

(Beau became Delaware's attorney general at the same time that Andrew Cuomo, son of Mario, assumed that office in New York, and the two bonded over their shared dynastic dilemmas.)[410]

Of course, being a Biden in Delaware did come with advantages. The same month that Wharton received the Republican nomination, he looked up from the sidelines of a Memorial Day parade in the city of Newark to see Beau in the thick of things. He was marching with a group of officeholders, and he had his name announced from the reviewing stand, though nonincumbent candidates were supposed to be barred from the event.

In September, Beau showed up at another event from which nonincumbents were barred, a luncheon of the Delaware Volunteer Firemen's Association. The association held so much sway it was sometimes referred to as the state's third political party. When Wharton cried foul over the appearance, Beau told the *News Journal* he had attended as the guest of Larry Mergenthaler, a former president of the group. But Mergenthaler told the paper Beau was there as a guest of Joe's.

"Cheaters never win," fumed the then executive director of the state GOP.[411]

For the most part, Beau remained above the fray, and let his cousin handle the hurly-burly. "Where Beau at least publicly was extremely cautious to be throwing a punch, Missy came from the side of the Biden family where you could tell she's like a staunch defender of her family, and she had no hesitation going on attack," recalled Frendewey, whose job had him sparring in the press with Missy. "She was an extremely aggressive campaign manager. I thought she was impressive."

Rhett Ruggerio, who chaired the Delaware Democratic Party's campaign efforts that year, recalled showing up late to a debate toward the end of the campaign. While Ruggerio stood off to the side near a coat closet, Beau strode up and started to casually chat Ruggerio up about his infant daughter, who had just been born. Feeling the time crunch, Ruggerio interrupted him to say, "You've got to get up there and debate."

"I'm not worried about that," responded Beau, who by then had a young daughter of his own, Natalie, and an infant son, Robert Hunter II. "Back to the baby."[412]

Early in October, news broke that Beau had failed the Delaware Bar Exam three times in the mid-'90s before finally passing in 2001. Republicans tried to seize on the failures to continue painting Beau as a lightweight, but the candidate handled the revelation deftly.

"Never giving up matters," he told the *News Journal*. "As my grand-dad used to say, 'The measure of success is not how many times you get knocked down but how many times you get up.' I got up and did it. You keep plugging away." It might have helped that Beau's bar travails were downright Kennedy-esque. JFK Jr. famously failed the New York Bar Exam twice before passing.

Three weeks before the election, the state chapter of the Fraternal Order of Police met for its annual convention in Ocean City, Maryland. An endorsement in the attorney general's race was on the agenda. As it so happened, Delaware's senior senator turned up to address the convention and assure the assembled police officers that he would fight to secure them funding. Union leaders considered letting him speak ahead of the endorsement vote, but the rank-and-file balked, so his remarks were pushed to after the vote.

Wharton had worked with the police union for decades, but the convention deadlocked, and did not endorse. Beau's campaign greeted the news as a coup, while Wharton's campaign said Joe had ridden to his son's rescue.[413]

The Wharton team was incensed. "It was pretty evident to everyone there that then Senator Biden didn't show up by accident when he had been a senator for thirty years," said Frendewey, explaining that Joe's presence at the convention had not been a regular occurrence over the years. "Up to that point, Beau was really his own man in the race, and this seemed to be a really over-the-top gesture."

Ruggerio said that early in the campaign he considered Beau a "shoo-in," but the race remained uncomfortably close in its closing weeks. "Our polling showed that it was neck and neck," he said.

On Election Day, busloads of union organizers from Philadelphia arrived at the Wilmington riverfront, and from there fanned out to get out the vote for Beau in New Castle County, recalled Charlie Copeland, a former chairman of the Delaware Republican Party. "It was a very impressive sight," said Copeland, a du Pont descendant, "and probably created the margin of victory."

Taking the stage at the Doubletree Hotel in Wilmington that night, Beau acknowledged the role of that familiar Biden family ally in the win. "The women and men of organized labor stepped up and put us over the top," he said, as his father stood by him onstage.[414]

Though Beau won by five points, Copeland said the result was too close for comfort for the family patriarch. "Joe was angry that a Biden could almost lose in Delaware," he said.[415]

But a win was a win, and a new Delaware dynasty was taking root.

Beau took his oath of office on the same massive family Bible that Joe had been using for his Senate swearings-in since 1973.[416]

Two years later, when Barack Obama chose Joe as his running mate, an expectation formed immediately among some Delaware insiders that Beau would inherit his father's Senate seat.

Within days of the pick, one bundler for Joe's 2008 presidential campaign was referring to "his son's role as a future senator" in an email to Anheuser-Busch executives.[417]

But Beau's National Guard unit was called up to Iraq before the election. When Joe vacated his seat, Delaware governor Ruth Ann Minner appointed longtime Biden loyalist Ted Kaufman to temporarily fill it instead.

Speculation soon abounded that Beau would run in the 2010 special election to fill out the seat for the remainder of the term. Congressman Mike Castle, who would be seventy-one on Election Day, was considered the likely Republican nominee. The *News Journal* dubbed the potential match-up "dynasty versus dinosaur."

"It is no secret that I believe my son, Attorney General Beau Biden, would make a great United States senator," Joe said at the time.[418]

But Beau passed on the race. Castle went down in the primary to the Tea Party's choice, Christine O'Donnell. She lost to Democrat Chris Coons in memorable fashion. After video emerged in which she described her youthful experiments in Wiccanism, O'Donnell ran a campaign ad in which she was forced to declare, "I am not a witch."

Truly, it was no longer the du Ponts' Delaware Republican Party.

As the family's mark on the state faded, so did that of its namesake company. The number of Delawareans employed by DuPont fell from an estimated twenty-five thousand employees when Joe was first elected to the Senate to roughly seven thousand by the middle of his second term as vice president.[419]

The company downsized its Delaware presence and restructured to meet the demands of an activist investor and the shareholder-value approach to corporate governance. Environmental advocates shed few tears over the chemical company's waning influence in the state. Among the black marks on its record, the company had produced the toxic pesticide DDT and Agent Orange, the notorious herbicide the U.S. military used in Vietnam.

Joe, though, privately mourned the loss of the corporate paternalism he witnessed in childhood. "He views DuPont as a proxy for a responsible corporate citizen, for a lot of American corporations in the '50s, '60s, and into the '70s," Don Graves, an advisor to Joe during vice presidency and a member of his presidential transition team, told the *Wall Street Journal*. "He felt that over time DuPont and others began shifting away from that framing, because of the focus on quick shareholder returns."[420]

The du Pont name remained ubiquitous, on streets, hospitals, schools, and much else, but the Biden name began to join it on the map. The train station where Joe commenced that first presidential campaign is now named for him, as are a highway rest stop and an environmental training center at a state park on the Delaware Shore.

By all appearances, Beau was destined to make as much of a mark as his father. He cruised to reelection in 2010. That year, the Republicans did not even bother to put up a candidate against the popular incumbent.

The closest Beau came to a scandal was when details emerged about a deal his office had reached with a wealthy father, Robert H. Richards IV, who had pleaded guilty to fourth-degree rape of his three-year-old daughter.

Richards received probation in lieu of jail time, and Delawareans were up in arms over the deal, suspicious that the rich heir had gotten special treatment. Much of the outrage focused on the judge who presided over Richards's sentencing and noted that the wealthy man would "not fare well" in prison.

After two weeks of growing outrage, Beau wrote to the *News Journal* to defend the plea bargain. Richards's daughter had described his crime to child abuse experts at the Alfred I. du Pont Hospital for Children, but there were no third-party witnesses or physical evidence. "This was not a strong case, and a loss at trial was a distinct possibility," he wrote.[421]

Even so, some in the state remained convinced that the Delaware justice system had given Richards special treatment. In large part, their suspicions rested on the fact that the man was related to Delaware royalty. Richards, who also faced accusations of molesting his son, was a great-grandson of the former DuPont president Irénée du Pont I.

The Delaware Way

"...a form of soft corruption, intersecting business and political interests, which has existed in this State for years."

—U.S. Attorney David Weiss, defining "the Delaware Way" in a 2010 court filing

In the spring of 2011, Chris Tigani, a wealthy beer distributor, met up for drinks with a lobbyist in the wood-paneled barroom of the Columbus Inn. The Wilmington restaurant, which boasts a history stretching back to the War of 1812, had been recently renovated thanks to its new owners, Louis Capano Jr. (whose brother Thomas had been prosecuted for murder by Ferris Wharton) and Louis's son, Louis III.[422]

As Tigani recalled the meeting, talk that night turned to the Bidens. They were a natural topic of conversation. Tigani was a bundler for Beau's and Joe's campaigns. The lobbyist had worked for Joe in the Senate.

The family ties ran deep. Both had known the Bidens since childhood and both of their fathers had gone to Archmere with Joe. (Tigani spoke to me on the condition that I not name the lobbyist.)

All this history swirled around the men at the bar as Tigani steered the conversation toward his fund-raising for Joe. Tigani had been reimbursing his employees for their donations to Joe's presidential campaign.

In the pre–*Citizens United* era of campaign finance, this was a not uncommon way for rich bundlers to circumvent individual contribution limits. It was also criminal.

Tigani felt it should have been obvious to the politicians what he was doing. They expected him to gin up big checks overnight, and he was not exactly hiding how he did it. He said he had broached the subject with the lobbyist before, asking how Joe, his sons, and their fund-raising staff could not know what he was up to. "Of course they know," Tigani said the lobbyist had told him. "Of course they know. That's why they call you."

At the bar, Tigani said he elicited the same admission again. The difference was that this time, he was wearing a wire for the FBI.

(The lobbyist wrote to me in an email, "I've known the Bidens my entire life and at no point have I ever been involved in fund-raising at any level nor was I ever in a position to speak about their campaign operations. I know the Vice President as a man of utmost integrity who sets the same high bar for his staff, and I know he never would have tolerated any illegal behavior from supporters or donors." When I pressed the lobbyist with follow-up questions on whether he had discussed the Bidens' fund-raising with Tigani at the Columbus Inn in 2011 or been approached by the FBI about the subject, he did not respond.)[423]

———

Tigani's case was not the first federal inquiry into Delaware's peculiar political culture. The state's old dynasties might have been fading by the late twentieth century, but a new crop of families, of which the Bidens were just the most prominent, stepped in to maintain a pattern of comity upheld by multigenerational alliances.

It was no secret that in Delaware, politics is an insider's game. Its defenders argue that in a state that small—after a century of steady growth, its population still clocks in at under a million people—politics naturally hinges on consensus, long-term relationships, and bipartisan bonhomie. Its detractors see a backwater wracked with cronyism.

The place is so averse to boat-rocking that the state constitution was amended in 1951 to mandate that all five seats on its supreme court be filled by members of the two major parties, with a 3–2 balance at all times (a provision that very arguably violates the U.S. Constitution).[424]

This style is embodied by the tradition of Return Day. On the Thursday after an election, Delawareans gather in the small town of Georgetown, inland from Rehoboth Beach in the southern part of the state. While spectators munch on sandwiches from an ox roast, a town crier in top hat announces election results from the balcony of the Sussex County courthouse. The winning and losing candidates from elections share horse-drawn carriages as they parade through town, and then a hatchet is ceremoniously buried in sand.

The origins of the tradition remain murky,[425] but it dates back at least a century and a half.[426]

More recently, the term "the Delaware Way" has emerged to describe the state's political culture. The earliest written references to the term tend to be pejorative. A *News Journal* columnist wrote of "the Delaware way" in 1981 that "It is best illustrated by the General Assembly's annual Pork-Barreling and Back-Scratching Derby."[427] The concept made the paper again a decade later, when an environmental activist blew the whistle on regulators for meeting in secret to shape toxic emissions regulations. "It's the Delaware way of doing things," the activist complained. "It's the old boy network."[428]

Since then, Joe and other Delaware politicians have appropriated the term to refer to the upside of consensus-based politics. At a Democratic fund-raiser in Dover a month before he entered the 2020 presidential race, Joe suggested Washington could learn something from his home state. "We need a little more of the Delaware way," he said. "We've got to make it more the American way, and it's lost. Our politics has become so mean, so petty, so vicious that we can't govern ourselves, in many cases, even talk to one another. It can't go on like this, folks."[429]

Ted Kaufman, Joe's longtime advisor and the inheritor of his Senate seat, has said of his boss, "He was kind of the person who helped create the Delaware Way."[430]

In the '80s, before the "Delaware Way" label caught on, the Dover bureau of the *News Journal* created a scale from "friendly" to "incestuous" to describe the close, overlapping relationships that ruled public life in the state. Conflicts were so common that, as a rule, the Dover bureau only deigned to write them up if they crossed into "inbred" territory on their rubric (one can guess how they would have rated the du Ponts' cousin marriages).

Politicians in the state did not generally view this state of affairs as a problem. "Only in Delaware are conflicts of interest worn as badges of honor," wrote Celia Cohen in her encyclopedic history of the state's recent political history.[431]

Law enforcement took a less rosy view, and around the 1988 election cycle, Delaware authorities and the Bureau both began sniffing around on rumors of widespread corruption in the state.

Their investigation took a turn when Louis Capano Jr., a developer and the future owner of the Columbus Inn, ran into state attorney general Charles Oberly at a Little League game in Wilmington in 1989. Capano complained that a New Castle County Council member had been shaking him down for political contributions. Oberly sent Capano to the feds, who wired him up. Capano caught the councilman, Democrat Ron Aiello, on tape selling his vote for $100,000 and taking the first installment in cash.

David Weiss, a young lawyer who had been working as assistant U.S. attorney in the Delaware office, was appointed to serve as a special prosecutor in Aiello's case.

The feds were not finished. They then turned to Louis Jr.'s cousin, Mario Capano, who had been swept up in a previous corruption investigation and was willing to play ball. They paired him with an undercover agent, who went by the alias "Joe Edwards." Edwards posed as an investor from Georgia who needed state and local permits for an office complex he wanted to build. This agent posing as a drawling businessman was an outsider to Delaware's tight-knit business and political circles. To break into it, he used Mario as a reference, and it worked.

Edwards hired a lawyer and a disgraced political consultant to help him push the project. An intermediary for the state's transportation secretary, Republican Kermit Justice, solicited $90,000, supposedly so Justice could pay off a loan. When the money arrived, Justice greased the skids on state approvals for the project.

The feds alleged that Justice had also induced John Hynansky, a car dealer and builder whose Winner Automotive Group was among the state's most successful businesses, to invest $84,000 in a coconspirator's real estate project in New Jersey in return for favorable regulatory treatment in Delaware. The transportation secretary had personally intervened on Winner's behalf in a permitting dispute.[432] Hynansky, a German-born émigré of Ukrainian extraction, was not a target in the probe. He said he cooperated fully with investigators and maintained that the investment was a "purely economic decision."

To push the probe further, Edwards also haunted local watering holes—including the Columbus Inn, then under pre-Capano ownership—seeing what other dirty deals came his way. He made a pact with the father of a New Castle County Council member to buy his son's vote. After the cash was passed, more arrests were made.

Operation Newclean, as it was code-named, was a success. Justice hired David Weiss, who had entered private practice after the Aiello prosecution, to represent him. But the former prosecutor was disqualified from the case, which was related to Aiello's,[433] and Justice was convicted.

After his conviction, while he awaited sentencing, members of Delaware's political class flooded the federal judge overseeing his case with scores of letters vouching for his character and seeking a reduced sentence. The state's cozy political culture was on full display, and Judge Sue Robinson did not like what she saw.

"The way things are done in Delaware is through interpersonal relationships," she said from the bench. "The record demonstrates that Mr. Justice worked well within the system, which was particularly susceptible—in my mind, anyway—to the kind of political corruption of which he stands convicted today, and that is of doing a favor in his public role in exchange for money. It therefore is not only Mr. Justice's acts which should and must be condemned in this proceeding, but the political system itself."[434]

One thing the Delaware system's detractors and its defenders can agree on is that it lends itself to political stability.

From 1985 to 2001 the same four people—Joe, fellow Democrat Tom Carper, and Republicans Mike Castle and Bill Roth—held down the four top spots in Delaware's political pecking order: its Senate seats, governorship, and lone House seat. What passed for a shakeup came in 1992, with "the Swap," when the state's term-limited governor, Castle, agreed to trade jobs with its congressman, Carper. The unusual deal, worked out by party leaders, was ratified by voters.

"Only in Delaware would an entire state join in such an open conspiracy," mused Celia Cohen.[435]

In 2000, Carper rocked the boat. Term-limited out of the governorship, the Democrat had the temerity to launch a bona-fide challenge against Roth, the Republican incumbent of thirty years, for his Senate seat. The Delaware Way trumped party loyalty. Joe couldn't bring himself to campaign against his Republican colleague. After Roth lost anyway, Joe told him, "I don't think there was a single Biden that voted a straight ticket."[436]

In 2004, the feds struck again, indicting New Castle County Executive Tom Gordon—a friend and longtime ally of Joe's—and two aides on fraud and racketeering charges, alleging they used county resources to enrich themselves and further their political ambitions.

Central to the indictment were allegations that one of the aides had intervened on behalf of Fieldstone, Hunter's old golf club, to let it build a larger clubhouse than the county had authorized, and that Gordon was later involved in removing documents related to the episode from the public record.[437]

(The golf club's du Pont pedigree concealed a grisly backstory: It was best known to Delawareans as the site of the high-profile arrest[438] of Christopher Moseley in 1998. Moseley's wife was the du Pont heiress who owned the land on which the club was built, and Moseley himself had been instrumental in developing it.[439] Moseley disapproved of the woman his stepson, a du Pont heir, was dating. She had worked as a prostitute.[440] And so Moseley commissioned her murder. The woman was found dead in an air-conditioning duct in a hotel in Las Vegas.[441])

To help the FBI make the case against Gordon and his aide, some of their underlings had worn wires. The prosecutor on the case was Colm Connolly, a George W. Bush appointee, who had led the murder prosecution of Tom Capano alongside Ferris Wharton.[442]

For his defense, Gordon retained the husband-and-wife team of Victoria Toensing and Joe diGenova. For a county-level corruption case, this counted as a high-profile defense team.

DiGenova, a Wilmington native, had led corruption investigations of the administration of Washington mayor Marion Barry as DC's U.S. Attorney during the Reagan administration. Toensing served as deputy assistant attorney general in Reagan's Justice Department. In the '90s, Republicans in the House appointed the couple to serve as co–special counsel on a congressional investigation of the Teamsters. Then they inserted themselves into the middle of the Monica Lewinsky affair, becoming fixtures in the media spectacle surrounding the scandal.

Toensing and diGenova negotiated prosecutors down to lesser charges. Gordon, who maintained the prosecution was politically motivated, got off with a couple of misdemeanor tax charges and a year of probation.

Neither Operation Newclean nor the Gordon case deterred Chris Tigani from playing fast-and-loose with politics and money.

As an heir to his family's beer distributorship, Tigani had grown up immersed in the Delaware Way.

As he took an active role in the family business, NKS Distributors, Tigani learned that working the levers of public power was a vital skill in his heavily regulated industry.

He proved adept at it. In 2003, he successfully lobbied for the legalization of Sunday liquor sales. It did not hurt that state legislators sometimes picked up free booze from Tigani, who would lavish them with tickets to Philadelphia Eagles games. In the summers, NKS would bus lawmakers and assorted hangers-on—some of them decked out in grass skirts and parrothead hats—to Jimmy Buffett concerts.[443]

Tigani and NKS could afford it. So long as he could protect the family business and his stake in it, he was able to maintain a fabulous lifestyle. He purchased a home on four and a half acres in Westover Hills, a neighborhood originally developed to house DuPont executives, at just under $5 million. It was near Joe's own home, in the chateau country outside Wilmington, but Tigani's house was among the grandest in the state. The beer distributor purchased it from Charles Cawley, founder of MBNA bank, who had bought up surrounding land and demolished a nearby house to develop the marquee property.[444] The 24,000-square-foot mansion came with a greenhouse, a tennis court, and a three-bedroom guesthouse, among its amenities.[445]

Tigani grew close with another of the richest men in the state, Hynansky, the car dealer and builder. For a time, the two men co-owned a Learjet plane together.[446]

That arrangement proved short-lived, but private jets remained a part of Tigani's lifestyle. In August 2007, he chartered a flight from Wilmington to Quebec City. On board with him was a lobbyist for the Delaware Alcoholic Beverage Distributors, which Tigani then led. Delaware's governor, Democrat Ruth Ann Minner, was on board with them, en route to a conference of government leaders in the French Canadian city. The beer distributor and the lobbyist used the flight as an opportunity to raise their opposition to a proposed hike on liquor taxes, and the measure was later defeated.[447]

As his political involvement deepened, Tigani became an early bundler for Beau's 2006 attorney general's campaign and then for Joe's second presidential campaign.

———

As with Joe's other runs, family considerations permeated his second presidential bid. Jill had kept Joe from running for the nomination in 2004. When party leaders came to his house in Wilmington to pitch him on that race, she sat seething poolside, until she came up with a memorable way to get her view across. She wrote N-O in big letters on her stomach, and walked through the living room, where they were gathered, in her bikini.[448]

But she was devastated by John Kerry's loss, and a few days before Christmas 2004, she gathered Joe, Val, Ashley, Hunter, Beau, and Ted Kaufman for a family meeting in the library of their Wilmington home. Joe had been openly considering a 2008 run, and so he had an idea of what the meeting was about. After the ordeal of 1987, he was bracing for the family's rejection of the idea, but instead, Jill told him, "I want you to run." The rest of the family shared the sentiment.[449]

When Joe finally entered the race in 2007, the whole clan crisscrossed the country together in a van, campaigning for Joe. Even the grandkids helped spread the word.[450]

Val served as the campaign's national chair, but Jim remained on the periphery. An aide to Joe attributed this to "family tensions" and concerns his involvement could attract unwanted attention. "There were always questions around Jimmy's business dealings—what kind of blowback would there be for the campaign?"[451]

On the occasions when Jim did show up, Joe listened to him. When Joe would go long in his remarks, as he often did, Jimmy would signal him to wrap things up. "He'd be standing in the back of a room telling him to shut the fuck up," another aide recalled of that campaign. "His staff couldn't tell him to do anything, it was only his family. If Jimmy did it, he could get away with it."[452]

The campaign was soon defined by its money woes. In early February, within days of his official entrance into the race, Joe offered his assessment of Obama to a reporter for the *New York Observer*. "I mean, you got the first mainstream African-American who is articulate and bright and clean and a nice-looking guy," he said. "I mean, that's a storybook, man."[453]

The quote came off as racist and condescending, and the national media seized on it. Joe quickly issued an apology but the damage was done. In the lead-up to the race, big-time national fund-raisers who were not sold on Hillary Clinton or John Edwards had been giving Joe a serious look. But the "articulate" remark gave them flashbacks to 1987, and all they could see was the potential liabilities posed by that mouth. "The big national money deserted us," rued Joe's longtime consultant, the late Larry Rasky, in a debrief with Joe's biographer.

Because Jim had been sidelined, he did very little fund-raising. "He came in at the end when we were the most desperate," recounted the aide who described tensions over Jim's role.[454]

Money became the campaign's limiting factor. A former Biden aide involved in fund-raising told me it was "starved for cash" and its finances were "incredibly anemic." Joe's problems were compounded by the fact that he had always been a lousy fund-raiser. He was more like Obama, and less like the Clintons, in that he resented the hand-holding of big donors, and he never really excelled at cultivating them. "He hates having to kiss anyone's ass," the former aide said.[455]

As a result, Joe was left to rely on family loyalists and his Delaware network to keep the ship afloat. That included Tigani. The same month the beer distributor flew to Canada with Minner, he bundled seventeen checks from his employees and their significant others for Joe's campaign. Then he reimbursed the employees using company money, a criminal violation of campaign finance law.

In October, Tigani was one of ten personal guests of the Biden campaign at a primary debate in Philadelphia, where he sat next to Hallie. After the debate, the campaign and its supporters gathered at Smokey Joe's, a dive bar near the campus of Beau's alma mater, the University of Pennsylvania.

That was where, Tigani recalled, Joe asked him if he could pull together $100,000 for billboard ads in Iowa, and Tigani agreed to do it. As the party wound on, he said, Beau and Hunter approached him to confirm he would bundle the money and the brothers then steered him to Dennis Toner, the campaign's finance director.[456]

Toner's Biden ties also spanned generations. His father, Joseph, had served on the New Castle County Council with Joe in the early '70s.[457] Toner himself served as a longtime aide to Joe in the Senate.

Tigani said that in those barroom conversations with the Biden sons and with Toner, he alluded to the money for the billboards coming out of the NKS budget, a sign that the people he was bundling from were merely serving as straw donors.

He said that when he discussed the bundling with Toner, the finance director asked him, "How many people do you have who you can trust?" and that he responded, "All of them."

Toner disputed Tigani's account, and told me in a statement he had no idea his bundler was violating campaign finance laws until he read about it in the newspaper years later.

The former Biden aide involved in fund-raising said that, during this era of campaign finance, it was common for bundlers to find ways to indirectly reimburse donors for their contributions. If the donor and the bundler had a business relationship, for example, the bundler might let the donor pad their next invoice to the bundler in order to make the donor whole, a practice more subtle than Tigani's direct, on-the-books reimbursements. Finance staffers on campaigns were aware in a general sense that this sort of stuff went on, but the former aide said that he never saw any indication that the people involved with Joe's fund-raising in 2007 were aware of any specific straw donor scheme, let alone any indication that they had broken any laws themselves.

Over the course of the fall, Tigani became more engaged with the campaign. He joined in on finance team calls with the campaign staff and close family allies like plaintiffs' lawyer Jeff Cooper of Simmons-Cooper; Philadelphia investor Wayne Kimmel, a childhood friend of Hunter's; Hunter's business partner Eric Schwerin; and Delaware developer Rob Buccini.[458]

The Bidens were betting it all on Iowa. They hoped that a top three showing there would demonstrate to voters in other states he was more than an also-ran and provide a surge of momentum heading into the rest of the early contests.[459] On Thanksgiving, they forewent their near-sacred annual pilgrimage to Nantucket and gathered instead at Bistro Montage, a French restaurant in Des Moines.[460]

A couple of weeks before Christmas, a Biden finance staffer emailed Tigani's assistant at NKS with a list of his employees noting how much money they and their significant others had given to the campaign. Within about twenty-four hours, Tigani scrounged up a half-dozen checks from people listed in the email.

In the end, Tigani bundled just over $70,000 in straw-man donations for the campaign. Most of it came before his conversations at the Smokey Joe's after-party.

It wasn't nearly enough. As the cash-strapped campaign entered the home stretch, Joe personally emailed Tigani: "I know you did a tremendous amount last week, thank you. As we close in on Iowa, we are trying to get any and all contributions still outstanding into our headquarters by COB tomorrow. At your convenience, could you please let me know if you believe you will be able to collect any checks by COB tomorrow. If so, it would go a long way towards helping us increase our media buy in Iowa. I am on the ground here now, and with the cash we can surprise a lot of people.

"Thanks for all the help, I won't forget it," he wrote, signing it, "Joe."

Joe's goal by that time was just to hang on. "We all thought we had a shot at third," Missy said afterward.[461] Instead he came in fifth, earning just under 1 percent of the state delegates awarded. It was over. Jill was crushed.[462] She came to think of Iowa as a "four-letter word."

Joe dropped out, and the race came down to Obama and Hillary Clinton. In his last high-profile political act before his 2009 death, Ted Kennedy endorsed Obama. The Illinois senator, not Joe, was anointed heir to Camelot, and he went on to win the nomination in dramatic fashion.

After his first presidential run failed in spectacular fashion, Joe had undergone twenty years of political rehabilitation before giving it another shot. Now, his second run had failed in mundane fashion. He was sixty-five years old. The race had crystallized his reputation for being long-winded and gaffe prone. By all appearances, his next big act would be retirement, after another Senate term or so.

But, as it turned out, the Bidens weren't done for. In June, Obama called Joe to ask him if he would agree to be vetted for the bottom of the ticket. In short order, Jill, the kids, and Joe's mother talked him into taking the leap for veep.

Obama aides David Plouffe and David Axelrod flew out to Wilmington, where Jill and Beau picked them up at the airport.[463] The Davids met with Joe at Val's house, with the rest of the clan present. As much as anything else, it was the natural affection Joe showed toward his family that sold them on the Delaware senator.[464]

Obama, like most successful presidential candidates in recent memory, was running as an outsider. By now, Joe's image had come full circle from young upstart to totem of the Washington establishment. Joe had the potential both to balance out Obama's inexperience and to undermine his message of change. The potential downsides were illustrated by a report issued earlier in the year by Citizens for Responsibility and Ethics in Washington, a nonpartisan watchdog group, about senators' families profiting off of their positions. Joe figured prominently in the report, titled, "Family Affair," which found he disbursed more campaign money directly to family members—Val and her daughter, Casey—than any other Democrat in the Senate. On account of payments to Hunter's lobbying firm, the report also ranked him among the top five senators funneling money to a relative's employers.

But the Bidens were hardly unique in embracing Washington's culture of nepotistic self-dealing, even if they did so more enthusiastically than most. The sums involved in the report were relatively modest, in the range of five figures, and did not suggest any disqualifying scandal.[465]

In August, Obama called Joe as he sat in the waiting room of a dentist's office where Jill was getting a root canal. The VP job was his. In the ensuing rush of activity, Jill had to borrow a cream-colored suit from Sara to have something to wear to the official announcement the following day in Springfield, Illinois.[466]

Afterward, Obama told Joe that his meager assets made him an attractive pick. "That was one of the easiest vets in the world," he said. "You own nothing."[467]

But after Joe was selected, the Obama campaign's internal research team began to flag issues related to Hunter's lobbying work and his personal problems. When a campaign official raised the issue with Joe, he grew angry. "Keep my family out of this," he said, and that was that.[468]

Contending with the national spotlight was just one of the challenges the Bidens faced in 2008. Joe still had to attend to his duties in the Senate, where he was slow-walking Bush's nomination of Colm Connolly to the federal bench. Senators are afforded great deference in the awarding of federal judgeships in their states, and Joe took months to turn in his blue slip, the form that home state senators use to okay an appointment. When he finally turned it in that July, it was unsigned, an indication that he lacked faith in Connolly, whose nomination floundered and died.[469]

The speculation in Delaware was that Joe was paying Connolly back for the Tom Gordon prosecution and for the vitriolic campaign the Republicans ran against Beau in 2006. Connolly had supported his old colleague Wharton in that race and had ties to some of Beau's more outspoken critics. It later emerged that Joe had not been the only one standing in Connolly's way. In a closed-door session of the Judiciary Committee, diGenova and Toensing had accused him of prosecutorial misconduct in the Gordon case, helping to scuttle his nomination.[470]

Meanwhile, during the Democratic National Convention in Denver that August, Jill learned that her mother, diagnosed with terminal lymphoma, had only weeks to live. In October, Beau's national guard unit was called up to Iraq. On Election Night, as a quarter-million people celebrated Obama's victory in Chicago's Grant Park, Jill held aloft a laptop so that Beau and his unit mates could watch the event over Skype.

Reflecting on the campaign, Jill wrote, "Situations may change, we may change...but one thing stays the same: the Bidens had done this together, as a family."[471]

━━━━

Their Delaware loyalists came right along with them, including Tigani. He remained in the fold for the general election, flying out to St. Louis to attend Joe's vice presidential debate against Alaska governor Sarah Palin as a guest of the campaign. He went on to attend the Inauguration, where he congratulated Joe at a private event for donors.

But Tigani's high-flying run was about to end. A fight with his father over his use of company funds turned into a lawsuit, which dredged up records of his 2007 private jet flight with Governor Minner to Quebec. In the spring of 2010, the story of the undeclared flight landed in the *News Journal*. The paper followed up with an investigation of a favorable deal Tigani had landed, with Minner's blessing, to lease state land for the purpose of building a warehouse.

In the resulting uproar, Beau's office sued Tigani's company, claiming the terms of the land deal were the result of a "scrivener's error," and demanding that the length of the lease be reduced from sixty-six years to five.

Beau was the least of Tigani's problems. One morning that September, Tigani pulled into a Royal Farms gas station near his palatial home to grab a snack. As he returned to his car, he was surprised by agents from the FBI and the Internal Revenue Service, who said they wanted to talk about his relationships with Minner and Joe. Not believing that his campaign contribution reimbursements were criminal, Tigani fessed up to them on the spot, and talked to the agents for hours without a lawyer present.

Not long after, Tigani learned that a grand jury was hearing testimony about the land deal and that he was a target of the investigation. He hired Washington super lawyer Abbe Lowell.

Lowell, who was best known during the Trump years for representing Jared Kushner during Robert Mueller's special counsel's investigation, was not sanguine about Tigani's case. "Chris, normally I'd say, 'Yeah, we want to take your case,'" he told Tigani, "but you already sat down with the FBI and told them everything. I don't even talk to the FBI in court. I don't even say hi to them in court."

Following their initial consultations, Lowell did not take Tigani's case, but he did broker a meeting for the beer distributor with the U.S. attorney, David Weiss—who was back in government a decade-plus after Operation Newclean—and the rest of the feds on the case at their office in Wilmington.

The feds wanted Tigani to record calls and wear a wire to help them root out what they believed was widespread corruption in Delaware politics. Their theory was that the system ran on bribes at the state level and that Delaware's federal officeholders, including Joe, were at least complicit in the whole thing.

Tigani thought the feds were out of their minds. Sure, he was sucking up to the politicians as much as possible: funding campaigns and giving out some football tickets. But that was different from handing over brown bags full of cash in exchange for official actions. That he had not heard of.

The feds' theory might have seemed wild, but it was not without precedent. After all, when Joe first got to Washington, the Justice Department was investigating local corruption in neighboring Maryland. They found a web of illicit payments that extended to the sitting vice president, Spiro Agnew. As a Baltimore County executive and Maryland's governor, Dick Nixon's number two had taken kickbacks from contractors. He resigned in disgrace and pleaded guilty to a felony tax evasion charge.

Besides, Tigani had little in the way of leverage. He had already confessed. So he signed up to become a cooperator. His first outing came in March 2011, when he met with some players in state government at Dover Downs, a horse-racing complex, in the capital. He wore a wire. A female FBI agent came along with him, posing as his girlfriend.

This, and some early initial forays, yielded next to nothing.

Tigani remained fixated on his own predicament. During a get-together, Tigani was commiserating with his lobbyist friend about his bind and his belief that the Bidens and members of their operation knew he had been reimbursing his employees for their campaign contributions. That was when, Tigani recalled, the lobbyist told him that *of course* they knew how Tigani did it.

Tigani was elated. Someone close to the Bidens was saying they were complicit in his straw donor scheme. But the lobbyist was a friend, and the conversation had taken place during a social visit. Tigani had not been wired up. So he lured the lobbyist out to the Columbus Inn, where they rehashed the conversation, this time on tape.

By this time Tigani's troubles, and the existence of a grand jury, had already made the paper, so eliciting more unguarded admissions would be tricky.

In early June, Tigani got Toner on the phone, under the pretense that reporters were asking him about his bundling for Joe's campaign. Tigani tried to get Toner to say he knew all about the straw-man set-up.

Toner found the call bizarre. He suspected Tigani might be recording him. He got off the phone quickly. The next day, the FBI came to Toner's home and told him to expect a grand jury subpoena. He later received one, and testified.

Tigani and his handlers even discussed the possibility of trying to get him in front of Joe with a wire. They didn't think they could set up a meeting. Tigani did not have that kind of pull with Joe at a time when his public scandals made him radioactive. But Joe slipped back into Delaware regularly for this or that dinner or event, and they kept an eye on his schedule. The idea, which would have required clearance from the highest levels of the Justice Department to go forward, never got very far.

The investigation was running out of steam, but Tigani and his handlers tried one last tack. Tigani set up calls with Hynansky, the car dealer with whom he had shared a Learjet.

Hynansky was a rarity in the small, placid world of Wilmington society: a self-made, fabulously wealthy outsider. He was born in Germany after his family fled Ukraine during World War II. He settled in Delaware as a child in the late 1940s, just a few years before Joe came to the state.

He made a fortune selling cars in his new home, and he became a patron of Ukrainian causes as the impoverished nation emerged from

Soviet rule. He even financed the purchase of a property in New York to house a Ukrainian consulate there when the country's government could not buy one itself.[472]

He could be quiet during social outings, but his flamboyant fashion sense spoke for him. The mustachioed mogul made use of a cigarette holder and sometimes wore a cape.

Hynansky was also close with the Bidens. He donated to Joe's campaigns, and Joe made use of a private plane owned by Hynansky's son, Michael. His daughter, Alexandra, was friends with Hunter and Beau growing up. As a senator, Joe attended Alexandra's wedding, where Hynansky accorded him a place of honor, according to another attendee.[473]

Tigani's relationship with Hynansky had deteriorated after they entered into a complex handshake deal involving the Learjet, a Porsche, Hynansky's mansion, and an NKS lease of warehouse space from a Hynansky business. The deal went south and spawned its own legal fight.[474]

Tigani was still able to get Hynansky on the phone for a few calls. But the calls went nowhere, and Tigani's attempted cooperation came to an end.

Days after his first calls with Toner and Hynansky, Tigani pleaded guilty to illegally funneling money to Joe's campaign and to tax evasion charges.

Tigani said he was told later that after his attempted cooperation ended, the FBI went to the lobbyist and played him the tape of their Columbus Inn conversation in a bid to gain his cooperation. But he was told the FBI had little leverage. There was no evidence of wrongdoing on the lobbyist's part.

The lobbyist did not respond when I asked him if he had been approached by the feds. But I obtained a copy of a confidential letter that Weiss and his then deputy, Robert Kravetz, sent to Tigani's probation officer, Walter Matthews, in February 2012, detailing Tigani's attempted cooperation. They wrote that Tigani taped seventeen conversations with six different people, including a "high-level official of the Biden for President campaign," a "prominent Wilmington businessman," and a "former Biden staffer now working as a lobbyist." The lobbyist fits the latter description.

In their letter, the prosecutors wrote that their investigation was hampered by the fact that Tigani's legal troubles were well publicized, and that one of the people taped by Tigani said, "Hi to anyone else who is listening," at the end of a call. (Tigani said it was Toner who said something along these lines during their awkward phone call. Toner said he never said anything like it.)

But Tigani's help "permitted federal agents to compile detailed historical information regarding election offenses and 'soft corruption' in Delaware state government over nearly a decade, which included conduct allegedly committed by federal and state officeholders and/or their campaigns," the prosecutors wrote. "Such information will provide federal agents with a frame of reference for future public corruption investigations in this State."

When Tigani's guilty plea became public, a spokeswoman for Joe quickly released a statement saying he had no knowledge of Tigani's crimes. Kravetz told me the investigation turned up no evidence of wrongdoing by Joe.

Tigani's plea nonetheless sent a shock wave through Delaware politics. Weiss prosecuted only Tigani's donations to Joe's federal campaign, but he referred evidence of Tigani's illegal contributions to Delaware campaigns to Beau's office. Because some of Tigani's straw-man donations had gone to Beau, the young attorney general recused himself and appointed a special counsel, former Supreme Court chief justice Norman Veasey, to investigate.

Veasey had a reputation for probity, but this was Delaware, so he also had ties to many of the people involved, including Joe and Beau. They had received campaign donations from Veasey, whose firm was among the top donors to Joe's recent campaigns.[475]

The state investigation led to new charges for Tigani, who pleaded guilty again in May 2013. A general sense that Tigani was just the tip of the iceberg of something deeper pervaded the state, but specific evidence to back up this feeling proved mostly elusive.

"It's unfortunate you are the only person standing here," Delaware Superior Court judge William Carpenter told Tigani at his sentencing. "It's unfortunate the investigation has not led to others." Maureen Milford of the *News Journal* wrote that Carpenter had voiced "what many in Delaware have been afraid to say publicly."[476]

In the end, Veasey nabbed a couple of other businessmen on small-time campaign finance violations, but he netted no big fish. While he found that nineteen Delaware pols had received illegal straw donations from Tigani, he did not find evidence that they knew what Tigani was doing. He did find that there was "a compelling need to reform the 'pay to play' culture" in Delaware politics.[477]

The whole episode prompted a round of hand-wringing about the Delaware Way. In a sentencing filing in Tigani's case, Weiss defined it as "a form of soft corruption, intersecting business and political interests, which has existed in this State for years."

Joe, though, never stopped holding up the Delaware Way as a positive example of governance that the rest of the country should follow.

Tigani said that ever since the FBI visited the lobbyist, his old friend has, understandably, stopped speaking to him.

Tigani did run into Joe shortly after his release from prison. It was at Founders Day at the Tatnall School, the private school down the road from Joe's house, then attended by both Beau's kids and Tigani's.

Civility, of course, reigned.

Joe shook Tigani's hand with both of his and told him, "Chris, I hope everything's going well with you."

Tigani responded, "Couldn't be better, Mr. Vice President. Couldn't be better."

Joe's Delaware friends, meanwhile, have maintained their overlapping alliances. Obama appointed Toner to the board of governors of the U.S. Postal Service in 2010. Toner went on to cofound the Delaware Board of Trade, a startup stock exchange that was to run on the blockchain, the same technology that underlies Bitcoin. Hynansky invested in the venture.

DBOT pitched Tom Gordon—who had returned as New Castle County executive after an interlude during his legal troubles—on its idea, arguing that the stock exchange would bring jobs to Wilmington.

Gordon oversaw a loan of $3 million of county money to the company in 2015, but the venture floundered.[478] The county went on to investigate Gordon's loan and a 2016 advisory opinion determined that it was made illegally. Gordon did not have the authority to loan the funds.[479]

In 2019, DBOT was acquired by Ideanomics, a company led by the Chinese billionaire Bruno Wu.

In a notable breach of the Delaware Way, Gordon's successor as New Castle County executive, Matt Meyer, said DBOT's founders were "probably criminal" in securing the loan deal, which he called a "scam." Toner sued Meyer for defamation, though it was thrown out in October 2020 because the court determined Meyer was immune from suit.[480] The county eventually recouped its loan principal, but the jobs did not materialize.

Because this was Delaware, the full story of Tigani's work with the FBI did not come out for years. The fact that he was cooperating with the feds was reported at the time his legal saga was unfolding. But the fact that the FBI had probed the fund-raising operation of the sitting vice president, and had Tigani wear a wire to help them do it, remained secret.

I reached out to Tigani while reporting a story about Hynansky at the beginning of 2020, but I did not hear back. He had been in and out of jail and lost his home and his job, so he was hard to track down. Several months later he logged onto Facebook and, finding an old message I had left him, he agreed to talk off the record about Delaware politics. On the call, he mentioned offhandedly that he had worn a wire to investigate Joe's 2008 presidential primary campaign.

A few weeks after that, he agreed to go public with a full account of the investigation. He had already broken the law and gone to jail. He figured he might as well tell his story, even if it meant going against the Delaware Way.

The Bidens Go Global

"Don't bullshit a bullshitter."

—Joe Biden, to Soviet premier Alexei Kosygin, 1979

The former chief compliance officer of Paradigm Global Advisors says he will never forget the day in the summer of 2006 the Bidens showed up at his Midtown Manhattan offices to take control of the business.

The executive recalled that Jim and Hunter showed up with Beau and a couple of large men. The new owners ordered him to fire the firm's president, Stephane Farouze. The large men showed Farouze out of the building.

(At the time, Jim and Anthony Lotito co-owned Americore International Security, a company that employed private security guards. The company also employed a "director of cabaret security,"[481] who oversaw the protection of nightlife establishments.

The chief compliance officer recounted his experience with the Bidens on the condition that his name not appear in print. He cited a fear of retaliation, saying he did not want large men like the ones who came to his office to come knocking on his door.)

Jim had a plan. "Don't worry about investors," he told the executive that day. "We've got people all around the world who want to invest in Joe Biden."

In case the chief compliance officer did not get the picture, Jim painted it more vividly for him: "We've got investors lined up in a line of 747s filled with cash ready to invest in this company."

Beau was then in the middle of his first attorney general's race. His face turned red with anger, the executive recalled. "This is not why we are making this investment," Beau told his uncle. "This can never leave this room. And if you ever say it again, I will have nothing to do with this."

Farouze did not respond to my attempts to contact him. A lawyer for Jim and Hunter said no episode like the one described by their former chief compliance officer ever occurred.[482]

But some things are beyond dispute: While Beau followed in Joe's footsteps, Hunter took after his uncle Jim, becoming a Biden family breadwinner. Hunter and Jim did seek to enlist the family's political allies as investors in Paradigm. Under their ownership, the firm became entangled in legal disputes and financial scandals before quietly winding down. And during their time at the helm of the firm, the Bidens were learning to tap the global demand for business partnerships with the relatives of a powerful American official.

When Jim and Hunter took over Paradigm, Joe was the ranking member on the Senate Foreign Relations Committee. A few months later, when Democrats took the Senate, Joe became the committee's chairman. Val called it, "The best seat in town."[483] The United States was near the height of its global power and prestige. Few people had more say over the running of this globe-spanning empire than Joe did.

———

When thirty-year-old Joe first got to Washington, his Senate seat meant a ticket to see the world. His relatives often came along for the ride. When he was still mourning the deaths of Neilia and Amy, Hubert Humphrey brought Joe along on a delegation to Oxford, England. Then Humphrey, back in his Minnesota Senate seat after serving as Lyndon B. Johnson's vice president, arranged for Jim to fly out and take Joe on a surprise European vacation.[484] Frank got the chance to see Africa.

At first, Joe was more of a tourist on the world stage than an actor upon it. As a freshman senator, he showed up late to a members-only briefing from Henry Kissinger being held by the Foreign Relations Committee, only to have Kissinger complain that no staff were allowed. When he realized his mistake, he apologized to "Senator Bid-den," mispronouncing the name. Joe shot back, "No problem, Secretary Dulles."[485]

Joe aspired to more. He began eyeing a seat on the prestigious and powerful Foreign Relations Committee as soon as he was elected.[486] When he got banking and public works instead, he tried for Foreign Relations again as soon as possible, after the 1974 midterms. The *News Journal* described this ambition as "outlandish" for a first-termer. Joe, who denied it meant he had his eyes set on higher office,[487] got the committee assignment.[488] (Thirty years later, another hotshot young freshman, Barack Obama, successfully landed himself a seat on Foreign Relations. The assignment was interpreted, correctly, as a way to bolster his bona fides for an impending presidential run.)

Cajoling and bonding with world leaders became a part of his job. Channeling, perhaps, Benjamin Franklin in Paris, Joe's style was to bring down-home American bluntness to these diplomatic repartees. In 1979, he led a Senate delegation to Moscow to further the second round of the Strategic Arms Limitation Talks, SALT II. At the Kremlin, he met with the Soviet premier, hardliner Alexei Kosygin. When Kosygin lowballed the number of Soviet tanks deployed in Europe, Joe interjected, "Mr. Kosygin, they have an expression where I come from: Don't bullshit a bullshitter."[489]

Over the decades, he grew into one of the country's most seasoned statesmen. He became ranking member of the committee in 1997 and chaired it during the brief Democratic majority from 2001 to 2003. Then he took the gavel back up after the Democratic rout in the 2006 midterms. This experience and his relationships with leaders around the world were central selling points in his foreign policy–heavy second presidential bid.

In January 2006, before Joe launched that bid, Jim called Lotito for a favor. Hunter needed a new job. Joe was getting ready to run for the Democratic presidential nomination, and his son's work for a Washington lobbying firm would be a problem.

At least that was what Lotito later alleged in court filings. Jim and Hunter denied that a call like that ever took place. One way or another, the three of them decided in early 2006 to get into the hedge fund business.

Owning a hedge fund in New York in the years before the financial crisis was like being a sea captain in eighteenth-century Nantucket or, for that matter, a rock club owner in 1970s Delaware. It was the thing to do.

Hedge funds were originally developed in the mid-twentieth century as vehicles for investments that insulated portfolios from the risks of broader market swings—that is, they were *hedged* against them. They eventually evolved to encompass all sorts of novel investments that were too risky or complex for retail investors to get in on.

They also tended to be too risky and complex for inexperienced investment managers, which was what Jim and Hunter were.

James Park, on the other hand, knew a good deal both about investing and about dealing with powerful families. Park's father had been a Korean military officer and a leader of the Unification Church, the religious movement founded by Sun Myung Moon. Moon was a billionaire Korean industrialist who declared himself the messiah, founded his own church, started the conservative *Washington Times* newspaper, and went to jail in the early 1980s on tax charges.

In the 1960s, following a military coup in Korea, Moon's followers, commonly referred to as "Moonies," enjoyed widespread influence in Korea's affairs. During that era, Park's father moved to Washington to act as a liaison between U.S. and Korean intelligence services. The posting allowed him to establish a Moonie beachhead in the United States.

Later, Moon sent his eldest son, Steve, to live with Park's family there. Steve was a troublesome adolescent, getting into drugs and generally acting out. Park's father dared not discipline the messiah's bratty kid, so instead, whenever Steve acted out, he would spank Park.

Following this ordeal, Park went on to marry Moon's daughter, In Jin. He earned a JD from Harvard Law School and a doctorate in finance from Columbia. In the late '80s and the '90s, as Park set out on a career in finance, hedge funds were emerging as hot investment vehicles. They could be extremely lucrative, but you could also lose a lot of money.

Park had the idea of creating a fund of hedge funds. By spreading investments across a lot of hedge funds, you could lower your risk while still seeing outsize returns. The idea was simple, but James was early in applying it to hedge funds, and Paradigm Global Advisors became a success.

It helped that the firm's labor costs were low. Many of its employees were Moonies who accepted rock-bottom salaries in exchange for the honor of working in close proximity to Moon's son-in-law. About half of its investors were Moonies as well, according to a former executive.

Financial success could not solve Park's personal problems, however. He developed an addiction to cocaine. As his drug use began to complicate his management of Paradigm, Park went looking for a buyer. Lotito connected him with the Bidens.[490]

Jim and Hunter offered to buy the firm out for $21 million. For financing, they leaned on family allies. Larry Rasky, a lobbyist and long-time political advisor to Joe, was going to pitch in a million dollars in financing, though it is not clear if he ever did.

The law firm SimmonsCooper, donors to Joe and business partners to Beau, did provide a million dollars in financing.

Hunter would have his new job, CEO of Paradigm, with a starting salary of $1.2 million. His experience in the financial sector amounted to a few years on the payroll of a credit card issuer.

At Paradigm, Hunter and his uncle found themselves in over their heads. Before the deal was completed, they realized that Paradigm had only a fraction of the assets under management that it purported to, making it far less valuable than they initially believed.

They also discovered that the lawyer they had brought on, at Lotito's urging, to advise them on the acquisition, John Fasciana, had been convicted the year before on a dozen counts of mail and wire fraud.[491] Jim and Hunter backed out of the deal.

The botched acquisition attempt cost them north of a million dollars.[492] To pay back SimmonsCooper, they took out a loan from the lobbyist William Oldaker, Hunter's old boss.

Nephew and uncle still wanted Paradigm, but for a reduced price. They decided to ditch Lotito and make Park a new offer, an $8 million IOU.

Park accepted. Given their lack of relevant experience, Jim and Hunter realized they needed Park's help to keep the business afloat, so he stayed on.

The chief compliance officer said the collaboration was complicated by the fact that Park and Hunter were avid users of cocaine, both during work and after-hours.

The executive said Hunter once offered him the drug, but he declined. "I figured that wasn't right for a compliance officer to be doing drugs," he said.

The executive also said that after work, Park and Hunter would sometimes go to a nearby hotel to do coke and party. He would get notifications that cash had been withdrawn from a company account from an ATM on the route between the two.

The Bidens, though, needed Park to be at the top of his game. Jim talked Park into checking into a rehab center in Florida, the same one to which a judge had sent Frank.[493]

Even so, Paradigm turned out to be an albatross. In January 2007, Lotito sued Jim and Hunter, saying they had improperly gone behind his back to acquire the firm.

Lotito also claimed his former business partners wielded their family's clout as a cudgel. "The Bidens refused to pay the bill, repeatedly citing their political connections and family status as a basis for disclaiming the obligation," his complaint alleged. "The Bidens threatened to use their alleged connections with a former United States Senator to retaliate against counsel for insisting that his bill be paid, claiming that the former senator was prepared to use his influence with a federal judge to disadvantage counsel in a proceeding then pending before that court."

Nephew and uncle denied Lotito's claims, and the case eventually settled, but more problems lay ahead.

The Lotito suit came just as Joe was preparing to announce his second White House bid. At the same time, Hunter and Jim were bringing on Chuck Provini, a veteran of the investment industry, as the firm's new president.[494] Provini told me Jim and Hunter recruited him in part for political reasons. They wanted a non-Biden face atop the troubled firm. "Joe Biden needs to distance himself from this," they told him, "Would you consider the job?"[495]

Jim and Hunter assured Provini that Joe's labor connections would help them land investments from union pension funds. "I was told because of his relationships with the unions that they felt as though it would be favorably looked upon to invest in the fund," Provini told me.

But Provini said that during his tenure, Paradigm was not able to land union pension investments. It did not help that Jim and Hunter were industry novices. "They knew nothing about the hedge fund business," he said. (Provini later sued Paradigm in federal court in New Jersey, alleging it stiffed him out of salary he was owed. The case was settled.)[496]

The chief compliance officer said that his new bosses understood political relationships better than they understood the mechanics of hedge funds.

He recalled one week where a succession of firefighters paraded into the office over the course of a few days and asked to speak with him. They would offer explanations like, "We're friends of Joe, and we want to invest in the fund." The men would drop off modest personal checks. A few thousand dollars here. A few thousand dollars there.

The executive learned that there was a firefighters' convention in town, and Jim had been working the room. "Jim told people they could invest in our hedge fund and that would help Joe," the executive recalled.

Because of legal restrictions on who can invest in hedge funds, and because Paradigm, like most similar firms, insisted that clients fork over minimum investments in the tens or hundreds of thousands of dollars, there was nothing he could do with the checks.

A lawyer for Jim and Hunter said no incident like this ever occurred.

Unable to attract big-time union money, Paradigm's executives searched in vain to find an overseas bank or other foreign buyer to take the business off their hands, including in the banking haven of Switzerland. They struck out.

With Paradigm floundering, they found other ways to seek their fortunes abroad.

Jim began putting together plans for a global influence shop that would offer legal services and lobbying help to deep-pocketed interests from around the world. In the Reagan era, the lobbying firm of Black, Stone, Manafort and Kelly—as in Roger Stone and Paul Manafort—had mainstreamed the business of peddling influence in Washington on behalf of foreign clients.[497]

Jim's new venture was to be a sort of Democratic answer to it. To pull it off, he teamed up with Steve Patterson, the former Mississippi state auditor who had worked for Joe's first presidential campaign and later hooked Jim up with the tort lawyer Dickie Scruggs. A decade before, Patterson had been forced out of his office when he pleaded guilty to lying on official documents to evade a car tax, but the black mark on his record did not deter Jim. Rounding out the founding team was another Scruggs associate, trial lawyer Timothy Balducci.

Patterson, Balducci, and Biden would have connections as far afield as Argentina, Venezuela, and Switzerland. It would also offer legal services. Unlike Patterson and Balducci, Jim was not a lawyer. But his wife, Sara, was, and she was to be a partner in the firm. There was talk of a role for Hunter as well.

On August 10, 2007, as Joe's campaign continued its search for national money, Joe and Jim headed down to Mississippi for a fundraiser, near the campus of Ole Miss. Balducci, Patterson, and Scruggs were among the cohosts.

The firm had not yet launched, but Balducci and Patterson were already counting on their pull with the Bidens, as the FBI agents listening in on their calls soon learned.

While plans for Patterson, Balducci, and Biden were coming together, the FBI was investigating a scheme by Balducci, Patterson, and Scruggs to bribe a judge in a dispute over legal bills. As they eavesdropped on the coconspirators' telephone conversations, they heard a stray reference to the future first family.

At the time, Joe was among the senators pushing legislation that would have provided compensation to Black farmers who had faced discrimination from the Department of Agriculture. An FBI wiretap picked up a conversation between Balducci and Patterson in which they referred to an impending meeting with "the Black farmers."

"We really need to push on the Senate bill," Balducci told Patterson, and "We're gonna meet the Bidens around noon." (After a partial transcript of the call became public, a lawyer for Patterson said he never spoke to Joe about any Black farmers and "never asked Jim Biden to work on anything.")[498]

Around the time of the phone call, Balducci and Patterson were invited up to Washington to be Joe's guests at a dinner for the Congressional Black Caucus's annual September confab. The Mississippians were looking to establish clout in Africa, and hoped the dinner would be an opportunity to strike up talks with a former Clinton administration ambassador to Tanzania.

The former ambassador, Charles Stith, a longtime acquaintance of Jim's, told me that he does not recall any talks about joining the firm.

Plans for the firm soon became moot, anyway. In October, Balducci was arrested. He had left an envelope stuffed with cash on a Mississippi judge's desk. The FBI had it all on videotape, and soon moved to prosecute the other conspirators. When news of the bribery scheme came out, Joe returned the donations he had received from Scruggs, Patterson, and Balducci. The three men went to prison, as did an associate, Joey Langston, another Mississippi lawyer implicated in the scheme.

The extent of Jim's relationship with the men was not documented at length until the journalist Curtis Wilkie published *The Fall of the House of Zeus*, about Scruggs's downfall, in 2010. Wilkie was a longtime *Boston Globe* reporter who had taken a job as a professor at the University of Mississippi. Before all that, he had covered New Castle County Councilman Joe Biden as a cub reporter at the *News Journal*. He had also written the paper's account of Neilia's crashing a local Republican meeting to tape-record the opposition during Joe's first Senate campaign.

Wilkie told me he was startled by the details of Jim's relationship with the Mississippians. "The whole thing was indiscreet at best," he said. Wilkie said that before publication he reached out to the vice president's office to offer to brief Joe personally on his findings. He said he did not receive a response.

While Patterson, Balducci, and Biden blew up on the launch pad, Paradigm continued to sputter along. Hunter, supporting both a family and a substance-abuse habit, was having personal financial problems. At the same time he was acquiring Paradigm, he was buying a $1.6 million Colonial in Spring Valley, a tony neighborhood northwest of Georgetown.[499]

The financial success he found after law school—beginning with his work for MBNA—was rare for a Biden, but it only whetted his appetite for an affluent lifestyle for himself and his family. He longed not just for a bigger house, but for another car and private schooling for his daughters. He found himself locked into an escalating cycle of consumption.[500]

The chief compliance officer said that once, when Hunter found himself short on a mortgage payment, he tried to withdraw $21,000 from Paradigm's coffers to cover it. When the executive balked, Hunter told him, "I'm going to lose my home."

A lawyer for Hunter and Jim said no such episode occurred.

Under financial pressure, Hunter came to identify even more strongly with his uncle Jim, the family's other moneyman. He considered Jim his best friend and admired his knack for taking care of problems. "He gets things done," Hunter later wrote of his uncle.[501] Neither of them, Hunter felt, got the credit they deserved for the financial support they provided to the family.

Then, in the summer of 2008, the slow-rolling crisis that had been roiling global markets reached a head, shaking up both the presidential race and the hedge fund business.

In a September appearance on CNBC's *Squawk Box*, Joe took aim squarely at the hedge fund industry, and its lack of transparency, calling it the root cause of the crisis. "We don't have any regulatory oversight to these guys," he said.[502]

At a campaign rally a few days later at a park in Sterling, Virginia, Joe charged that Republicans had allowed the financial services sector to become the Wild West on their watch. He condemned "the cowboy mentality of the Bush-McCain era."[503]

Meanwhile, Paradigm was embarking on a partnership with Stanford Capital Management, the firm run by Texas financier Allen Stanford. As part of the partnership, Paradigm registered a new fund, "Paradigm Stanford Capital Management Core Alternative Fund," with the Securities and Exchange Commission.

In November, Democrats notched a resounding victory, in no small part because voters felt Barack Obama and Joe Biden would be better custodians of the global financial system than John McCain and Sarah Palin.

For a country reeling from the fallout of the financial crisis, the Inauguration offered a reprieve. Hunter and Kathleen served as honorary cochairs of the event.[504] Beau got temporarily reassigned from Iraq to the Pentagon, and took leave to join his father for the festivities.[505]

On the Sunday before his swearing-in, Joe took his family to Mass at Holy Trinity church in Georgetown, where Jack Kennedy had worshipped the morning of his Inauguration.[506] On Tuesday, Associate Supreme Court Justice John Paul Stevens swore Joe in on the mammoth family Bible.

Enthusiasm for the arrival of the country's first Black president and for the departure of his historically unpopular predecessor ran high. Despite the weather—twenty-eight degrees and windy—an estimated 1.8 million people turned out to see Obama take the oath of office, among the largest crowds the capital had ever seen.[507] The new first family was instantly iconic, and Michelle Obama carved out her place as a fashion icon, starting with the yellow coat and jacket she wore to her husband's swearing-in.[508] Jill held up the second family's end that evening, sporting a strapless red satin dress from the designer Reem Acra. It drew comparisons to a similar get-up the teenage pop star Miley Cyrus wore at a pre-Inauguration concert.[509]

After the party, the reality of the financial crisis set back in.

A few weeks into the Obama-Biden era, Stanford was charged with masterminding a multi-billion-dollar Ponzi scheme. Though it was smaller than Bernie Madoff's scheme, it ranked as one of the largest frauds of all time.

By then, Jim and Hunter had stepped away from the day-to-day operations of Paradigm.[510] Their lawyer said they never personally dealt with Stanford. The lawyer also said that Paradigm had offered to turn over $2.7 million it had received from Stanford's firm to a court-appointed receiver.[511]

More bad news came in April, when the SEC charged another hedge fund business, Ponta Negra, with fraud. Paradigm had rented out some of its office space to Ponta Negra's manager, so the two funds shared a phone number and an address.[512]

The headlines generated by mishaps like these were not helpful to an administration trying to convince the public it was cleaning up Wall Street.

Rocked by the financial crisis, wary of all the bad press, and unable to find a buyer to take the business off their hands, Hunter and Jim decided to unwind Paradigm and give the money back to investors.

The Bidens have long maintained that Joe does not discuss his relatives' business activities with them. That stance has allowed them to invoke their ties to Joe in private, while Joe can say in public their dealings have nothing to do with him. As the Paradigm debacle demonstrated, this arrangement became harder to maintain as scrutiny of Joe grew and his relatives' doings made headlines with growing frequency.

The good news was that the Bidens were hedged. The same unforeseen event that contributed to Paradigm's downfall, the financial crisis, helped propel Joe to the vice presidency, and an even bigger role on the world stage.

Vice Presidential Perks

W hile Joe had always been among the least wealthy members of the Senate, the vice presidency only heightened the contrast between the trappings of his day job and the realities of his home life. Over the years, Joe had borrowed to buy his lakeside house, cosigned on Beau's and Hunter's student loans, and taken out several other loans from financial institutions.[513] He entered the vice presidency with six figures in debt.[514]

Joe's new salary of $227,000[515] would not radically alter his financial situation, but the vice presidency did come with a number of official perks, like living at the Naval Observatory. The lush, seventy-two-acre complex sits on Embassy Row, in a leafy part of the capital north of Georgetown. The vice president's residence, a handsome nine-thousand-square-foot house in the Queen Anne style, boasts a library and sunroom.[516] It included a staff, with their own basement quarters, to attend to the Bidens and prepare their meals in an industrial kitchen that could provide for a small army.[517] Joe and Jill outfitted one room in the residence with bunk beds to facilitate their grandkids' frequent sleepovers,[518] and decorated the walls with the grandkids' art.

There was also a secure hideaway locked behind by a fortified steel door that Joe gabbed about at the first Gridiron Dinner, an elite annual gathering of politicians and DC journalists of the Obama era. The disclosure led to a round of headlines suggesting Joe might have disclosed classified information, a charge his office denied.[519]

For her part, Jill continued to hold down a day job, switching from Delaware Technical Community College to Northern Virginia Community College. In her own, unassuming way, this made Jill a trailblazer. She was the first second lady in U.S. history to work full-time while her husband was in office.[520]

Many of her students, most of whom were foreign-born, showed no sign of recognizing their professor's out-of-classroom importance. Her Secret Service entourage skewed young and blended in with the student population. Once, when an older student whispered to her, "I know who you are, and no one else here does," Jill shot back, "That's right. And we're gonna keep it that way."[521] Another time, she let students who recognized her last name believe that she was Joe's cousin.

In her other life, Dr. Jill held down a six-person staff and a corner office in the Old Executive Office Building,[522] but she and Joe were both determined to maintain some semblance of normalcy.

To keep a lower profile during his return visits to his sleepy home state, Joe ordered that his typical motorcade of fifteen or more vehicles be cut down to two, with the other vehicles trailing by at least a mile. The policy prompted grousing from Secret Service agents who believed it put too much distance between Joe and his military aide carrying the nuclear football. Agents were nonplussed as well by the frequency with which they had to scramble to accommodate impromptu trips to Delaware.

Female agents took exception to one of the vice president's more unconventional personal habits. He took regular skinny-dips at his pool back home in Wilmington.[523] But generally, agents gave Joe and Jill—codenamed "Capri"—high marks for treating members of their detail respectfully.

In the last years of Jean's life, she had moved into a cottage on the grounds of Joe's Wilmington house, where her son could visit with her and share ice cream on a daily basis.[524] After her death in 2010, he began renting it out to the Secret Service for $2,200 a month, the same rate he said he had charged other tenants for the cottage.[525]

Despite all the perks, the taxpayers were only so generous. Jill regularly had to take her laundry back home to do it in Delaware.[526] Joe continued to juggle debts. He took out a mortgage in 2010 and a home equity line of credit the following year, then refinanced them in 2013 at lower rates.[527]

An awkward dynamic, meanwhile, hung over Joe's relationship with the president. While Joe was the senior partner in terms of age and experience, Obama was his boss, and commanded a global following larger than that of any celebrity or rival world leader, one that could border on the messianic. He had chosen Biden in part because of the pitch that the sexagenarian Delaware senator, after two failed presidential bids, had no political future of his own to tend to.

Back in 2005, when Obama first arrived in the Senate, he sought Joe out in his office for a get-to-know-you chat. Joe suggested they find a time to catch up at greater length over dinner at a nearby Italian joint. "Nothing fancy," Joe explained.

"We can go to a nice place," the freshman senator responded. "I can afford it."

That response, Joe wrote in his second memoir, "rang in my ears as a strange comment, bordering on arrogant." Joe later came to chalk it up to a misunderstanding: Obama must have assumed that Joe was well-off and was merely condescending to him.[528]

A few weeks into the new administration, Obama held his first primetime news conference as president. Toward the end, Major Garrett of CBS asked about a speech Joe had given a few days earlier in which the new vice president referred to an Oval Office conversation with his boss on an unspecified policy issue. In the speech, Joe had said he and Obama concluded they had a 30 percent chance of screwing up their handling of the issue, but he had not said what the issue was. Garrett wanted to know what this issue was that the new administration was prepared to flub.

The president laughed. "You know, I don't remember exactly what Joe was referring to," Obama said, prompting guffaws from the press corps, which shared an appreciation for Joe's long-winded speeches and verbal stumbles. The president lifted his hands from the podium in a little shrug and added, "Not surprisingly."[529]

Moments like this did not pass unnoticed. Hunter gave Obama's inner circle a wide berth, wary, he groused, of finding himself "play-ing golf with the President or one of his aides and look[ing] at my phone and see[ing] another headline that reads, 'President makes joke about Biden.'"[530] After the end of the administration, Joe let slip that Obama had never had him over to his residence in the East Wing.[531]

For Joe and Jill, there was a silver lining to this imbalance. While the Obamas chafed at the insular bubble imposed by the presidency, the Bidens managed to eat out, go to the movies, and generally hit the town with a minimum of hiccups.[532] When the Obamas tried to get out, traveling to New York for dinner and a Broadway show, the disruption caused by their date night became a microscandal of its own.

Awkwardness aside, Obama valued Joe's counsel, giving him an expansive portfolio that included starring roles in the administration's relationship with Capitol Hill and its foreign policy.

(Bob Gates, who succeeded Donald Rumsfeld as secretary of defense and stayed on for much of Obama's first term, memorably panned Joe's handling of the latter portfolio. "He has been wrong," Gates wrote in his memoir, "on nearly every major foreign policy and national security issue over the past four decades.")[533]

Joe's role in foreign policy permitted him and Jill more opportu-nity than ever to show their grandkids the world. The kids divided the globe into spheres of influence, with each claiming first dibs on trips to different world regions.[534] They tagged along to a state dinner in China, a meeting with King Abdullah II of Jordan, and a tour of Korea's Demilitarized Zone.

Joe, making good on his father's dinner table exhortations to mind the lessons of the Holocaust, took Finnegan to Dachau, a notorious concentration camp in Bavaria. It was a rite of passage that Joe had overseen for Ashley, Beau, and her father, Hunter, during his time in the Senate.[535] In another eye-opening field trip, fourteen-year-old Finnegan accompanied Jill to a hospital for rape victims in the war-torn Democratic Republic of the Congo.[536]

On the road, grave expeditions like these were balanced out by occasional moments of levity. Ahead of a trip to California, Jill arrived early at Joint Base Andrews in Maryland and embarked on an empty Air Force Two. In a move that probably was a first, and likely will be a last, for a second lady of the United States, she then scrunched herself into an empty overhead bin. When the flight began to fill up and an unsuspecting staffer opened the bin, he was greeted by Jill, tumbling out and shouting, "Boo!" provoking him to shriek with fright.[537]

For the Bidens, the vice presidency also came with a slew of unofficial perks. Joe's elevated profile meant Hunter had to give up his lobbying job. While Paradigm had failed, there was no shortage of opportunities for the son of a popular, empowered vice president.

A few days before Obama announced Joe as his running mate, Hunter's lobbying partner, Eric Schwerin, registered a new business, Seneca Global Advisors.[538]

Hunter was a cofounder of the consulting firm, which shared its name with a first-century A.D. Roman statesman who wielded influence over the emperor Nero. Seneca is also the name of one of the Finger Lakes in upstate New York, the region from which Neilia hailed. Other businesses registered by Hunter have used the name Skaneateles, the lake on which his mother grew up, and Owasco, another nearby Finger Lake.

At Seneca, Hunter no longer worked as a registered lobbyist, but Schwerin continued to lobby for some of their old clients under the auspices of the new firm.[539] Among the services the firm offered was help expanding into foreign markets.[540]

Soon, Seneca entered into a joint venture with Chris Heinz, son of Theresa Heinz Kerry and stepson of John Kerry, who succeeded Joe as chairman of the Senate Foreign Relations Committee when Joe became vice president. At the time, Heinz was running Rosemont Capital, a private equity firm named for the Heinz family farm outside of Pittsburgh.

Heinz and Hunter had met at least once before, in the hallway of a hotel in Des Moines in January 2004,[541] as Heinz's stepfather was clinching the Iowa caucuses. Years earlier they had overlapped at Yale, when Hunter was in law school and Heinz was an undergraduate.

The joint venture was brokered by Heinz's business partner Devon Archer, who had played midfield for Yale's lacrosse team and had been Heinz's roommate when the two were undergrads.[542]

In June 2009, they registered Rosemont Seneca Partners in Delaware, one of several entities with variations of the Rosemont Seneca name formed during this period.

They went on to team up with James Bulger, the son of Billy Bulger, a former president of the Massachusetts Senate, to create Rosemont Seneca Thornton.[543] Unfortunately for James, he shared a name with his uncle, James "Whitey" Bulger, the notorious Boston mobster, who for years evaded one of the world's most extensive manhunts and was found guilty of involvement in eleven murders, among other crimes. There was no evidence that Billy was complicit in Whitey's crimes, but his brother's infamy had pushed Billy out of public life in Massachusetts. Rather than pursue a career in politics, his son James worked in international investment, helping firms navigate the Chinese business landscape at his advisory firm, the Thornton Group.

Hunter later took on another job. In the spring of 2013, he was commissioned to the Navy Reserve as a public affairs officer. It was a plum gig, and he had to get two special waivers to land it. One was for his high school cocaine arrest, and the other was for his age. Joe swore him in at a private ceremony at the White House.

But when Hunter showed up for duty in Norfolk, Virginia, that June, he was given a drug test, which came back positive for cocaine. In a letter, Hunter told the Navy that he did not know how cocaine got into his system, and claimed that he believed a cigarette he had bummed from two South African men outside a bar had been laced with the drug.

A superior officer who drilled with Hunter that summer described him as humble and said he was well-liked by his fellow officers. When the superior officer sat down with Hunter in Norfolk, he told the new ensign that he would be treated just like anybody else. Hunter, who by that time knew he had failed his drug test, responded, "I wouldn't have it any other way."[544]

The Navy gave him the boot in early 2014. Hunter has made conflicting statements about the episode. When news of it broke later that year, he seemed to take responsibility for the drug use, saying, "I deeply regret and am embarrassed that my actions led to my administrative discharge." But in 2019, he repeated his story about a drug-laced cigarette to the *New Yorker*.[545] Then, in his 2021 memoir, he acknowledged returning to rehab after the incident.[546]

Over time, it became clear the Rosemont Seneca partnership was a mismatch. Heinz's family had already made its fortune, in foodstuffs like ketchup, and so he had little appetite for financial or reputational risk. Hunter and Archer, on the other hand, were hungry for lucrative deals.

In 2013, Rosemont Seneca and Thornton Group agreed to a partnership with two Chinese investment firms, Bohai and Harvest. They announced plans to raise $1.5 billion for a spree of private equity investments. One of Bohai's main backers is the state-owned Bank of China.[547] BHR Partners, as the venture was called, essentially put Hunter into business with China's government, though his lawyer has said he initially came on as an unpaid advisor and did not take a stake in the business until 2017.

In December 2013, Joe traveled to East Asia and brought Hunter's daughter Finnegan along with him. In Tokyo, Hunter joined up with his father and daughter and hitched a ride on Air Force Two to Beijing. Hunter invited Jonathan Li, the head of Bohai, to the hotel where Joe was staying and introduced his father to his business partner there.[548]

In 2015, their firm, BHR Partners, teamed up with a state-owned defense conglomerate, Aviation Industry Corporation of China, to acquire a U.S. auto-parts maker.[549] The acquisition target, Michigan-based Henniges Automotive, was a leader in technologies that reduce vibration inside a vehicle.[550] Such technologies have military applications, and the deal required approval from the Committee on Foreign Investment in the United States, which consists of representatives from across the executive branch and vets deals for national security concerns.

CFIUS rubber-stamped the deal. That outcome was hardly unusual during the latter years of the Obama administration, when the committee approved 96 percent of all Chinese acquisitions it reviewed.[551]

A newcomer to the family also learned the benefits of being a Biden. In 2010, the year Ashley earned her master's degree in social work from Penn, Beau and Hunter introduced her to Howard Krein. Krein was a genial doctor from Philadelphia in his midforties, whom the Biden brothers had met at a fund-raiser for Obama and Joe.[552] A Philly native, he practiced head-and-neck surgery, as well as plastic surgery—both cosmetic procedures, like Botox injection, and reconstructive ones—at Thomas Jefferson University Hospitals.[553]

Krein had also been involved with OrganizedWisdom, a business run by his siblings and a family friend that billed itself as a health-centric, online social network.[554] Not long after Krein met Ashley,

OrganizedWisdom began a transformation into StartUp Health, a medically oriented venture capital firm. Krein served as its chief medical officer.

The launch of StartUp Health, which was initially described as a "strategic initiative" of OrganizedWisdom, got a big boost from the Obama administration.

In June 2011, Steven Krein and cofounder Unity Stoakes traveled to Washington to unveil StartUp Health at the Health Data Initiative Forum, put on by the Department of Health and Human Services. Press coverage of StartUp Health gave the vague impression that it was part of the administration's entrepreneurship initiative, called StartUp America.

On a phone call, Howard Krein mentioned to Joe that his brother, Steven, and Stoakes were in town. So, the day before their announcement, Joe arranged for Steven Krein and Stoakes to meet with him and Obama in the Oval Office. Steven told Obama that his administration's technology-forward approach to health policy was leading to a "treasure trove" of new opportunities for entrepreneurs.

"The President loved it," Steven Krein recalled afterward, "and it became a talking point for him."[555]

The next day, Steven Krein and Stoakes appeared at the HHS conference as guests of Todd Park, then chief technology officer at HHS.

Before Steven Krein took the stage to unveil the initiative, the Obama administration's CTO, Aneesh Chopra, gave him a rock star's welcome.

"As you've heard all day today, this health-and-wellness movement is most certainly a new market opportunity. I am really excited to announce today, in the spirit of the president's StartUp America Partnership and collaboration, the next formal announcement that will come to you," Chopra said. "And to make that announcement, please welcome to the stage Steve Krein from New York City, who is going to make a big deal on a big opportunity. Make us all successful in health care. Come on, man!"

Spokespeople for Park and Joe both said that Joe was not involved in arranging the conference appearance.[556]

In June 2012, Ashley and Krein were married at St. Joseph on the Brandywine.[557]

———

The Obama years were more difficult for Jim's daughter, Caroline. She was pretty, and this provided her the self-confidence to speak publicly as a surrogate for her uncle's campaigns.[558] But after graduating with a bachelor's degree from Georgetown in 2012, Caroline decided to get plastic surgery to address a vascular malformation beneath her right eye that created a minor imperfection.

When Joe became vice president, he had asked Kevin O'Connor, an army doctor dispatched to the White House during the Bush years, to stay on as his attending physician.[559] He and Joe became close, and O'Connor became a regular source of medical advice and referrals for members of the Biden clan.[560]

In early 2013, Jim asked O'Connor for a referral, and the physician pointed him to a plastic surgeon in New York.[561] That May, she went under the knife, but the doctor allegedly botched the procedure, and Caroline became self-conscious about the results.

Caroline sued, and her case offered insight into some of the pitfalls of growing up Biden. "Being from a political family, and having a famous last name, and all of that business, people assumed that I have access to good medical care," she explained in a deposition.

After the procedure, her problems continued. In April 2015, she borrowed someone else's credit card with permission to use it for a purchase of a few hundred dollars at C.O. Bigelow Apothecary, a posh pharmacy in Greenwich Village. Then she used the card to secretly open a line of credit at the store, and over the following months she racked up over $100,000 in unauthorized purchases. When she was caught, she pleaded guilty and got off with probation and community service.[562]

Caroline's older brother, Jamie, on the other hand, made the most of the Obama years. After Georgetown, he enrolled in Fordham Law School, but soon abandoned the pursuit for a more Bohemian lifestyle.

With shoulder-length hair and the hint of a beard, he cultivated a look you might call caveman chic and split his time between disc jockeying at nightclubs and playing guitar in a rock band called Bloody Social. He also split his time between a loft apartment in lower Manhattan and a charming Dutch Colonial–style country house[563] in the Catskills, just outside Woodstock.

His wife, the model Amy Bracco, purchased the house in 2011,[564] three years before they were married at a nearby resort, with Joe in attendance. Jamie built a recording studio in a barn on the property.

He rounded out this fabulous lifestyle with frequent trips to the Hamptons to spin discs at the Surf Lodge, a waterfront party destination in Montauk.[565]

Jamie and Caroline's father, meanwhile, remained busy as ever with entrepreneurial ventures. In the fall of 2010, Jim embarked on a stint at HillStone International, a subsidiary of Hill International, a construction firm headquartered in the Philadelphia area. The gig came with an equity interest in the subsidiary.[566] Among Jim's partners was real estate executive Kevin Justice. Justice was hoping to employ a new method for building low-cost housing that involved spraying concrete.

A former Marine lieutenant, Justice had played baseball and football at Wilmington Friends School while Beau and Hunter were at Archmere.[567] He was also the son of Kermit Justice, the former Delaware secretary of transportation who went down in Operation Newclean.[568]

Three weeks before Jim's role with HillStone was announced, Justice and another HillStone executive, Bruce Prolow, visited the vice president's office in the early afternoon, spending a little over an hour inside the White House complex.[569] Prolow told me that HillStone did not come up at the meeting. "Kevin's known President Biden since childhood," he said. "No business was discussed. It was a social visit."

Hill had large contracts in the Middle East, which came with serious geopolitical risk. Not long after Jim took the job, the Arab Spring began to sweep the region. As unrest boiled over into full-fledged civil war in Libya, Hill had to stop work on an expansion of Tripoli's Al-Fateh University[570] and evacuate more than two hundred people from the country.

The company's stock slumped. But a few months later, in June 2011, Jim's subsidiary, HillStone International, landed contracts worth an estimated $1.5 billion to build houses in Iraq, pending final sign-offs from the governments involved. Hill's stock jumped more than 50 percent on news of the massive new deal.[571]

The contract came via TRAC Development Group, a Korean firm, which in turn was being paid by the Iraqi government.

At the time, Joe had oversight of the American occupation of Iraq. Though he became a critic of George W. Bush's handling of Iraq, he had voted in the Senate to give Bush the authority to invade.

A few months after HillStone landed the contract, in October, Jim donned a tux and his wife, Sara, a sleek black gown to attend a state dinner at the White House with the South Korean president, Lee Myung-bak.[572]

Two executives involved in the Iraq deal said Jim was not involved in landing it. "We just didn't include him, to protect the project," said one of them. "We didn't want any publicity."

Even so, Jim's value was obvious in a part of the world where little distinction is made between powerful leaders and their relatives. Joe was the face of American power in much of the Middle East, and Jim shared not just a name but a strong family resemblance with Joe. If you squint, you could confuse one brother for the other.

According to a Washington area businessman who worked with Hill, Jim traveled with Hill executives to Saudi Arabia and then Libya in early 2012 as part of ongoing disputes over unpaid bills. The person said the Saudis resolved the dispute by offering Hill more business. In March 2012, Hill announced two new contracts with one of its existing clients in the country for $6.7 million.[573] In July, it announced a contract worth $3.8 million from the country's General Authority of Civil Aviation.[574] In October, it announced contracts from the Ministry of Health worth $34 million.[575] Neither Jim nor a lawyer who has acted as a spokesman for him responded to a question about the alleged business trip.

That same month, Fox Business published an article about Jim and the HillStone Iraq contract.

Reporter Charlie Gasparino wrote that in a closed-door meeting with investors, Hill's president, David Richter, explained the fortunes of Jim's subsidiary by pointing to the benefits of having "the brother of the vice president as a partner."

The company's employees, according to Gasparino, had pointed to its Obama administration connections in conversations with outside stock analysts. The employees argued that the firm had access to top administration officials, and that the Iraq contract would ultimately come through, despite delays.

Richter told Gasparino that while the Obama administration did help Hill win the Iraq contract, neither the Biden name nor Jim's relationship to his older brother had been a factor. "It's just the opposite," he said. "We have to be careful not to use his name because people might not like his brother Joe Biden. So it's not likely to get you a job, but cost you a job."

Instead, Richter said Jim's value was in understanding the nexus between business and government. He also cited another Biden family strength, describing Jim as a "good salesman."

The story, which published just a couple weeks before Obama stood for reelection, did not draw a response from the administration.[576]

But the Washington-area businessman who worked with Hill said Jim confided to him afterward about the fallout from the article. Joe had "woodshedded" him—a DC term that originates with a dressing-down Ronald Reagan gave to a young economist who had embarrassed his administration—after the HillStone news broke. He said Joe had chewed him out during an encounter in Lafayette Square, across Pennsylvania Avenue from the White House. Neither Jim nor the White House responded to questions about the alleged encounter.

For all the headaches the deal caused, the big Iraq payday did not materialize. As delays dragged on, Jim and his partners descended into infighting, and HillStone's role in the contract was ultimately canceled.[577]

If the episode upset Joe, Jim found a way to make it up to his brother.

In late 2013, Jim and Sara plopped down $2.5 million for a luxury vacation home in South Florida. Situated on five acres on Keewaydin Island off the state's west coast, the four-thousand-square-foot house came with six bedrooms and seven bathrooms, a guesthouse, and a private dock.

Within days of the purchase, Joe came down for a holiday stay at the new house, which was nicknamed "the Biden Bungalow."[578]

The getaway was marred by a leak in a cistern that deprived the property of running water, a harbinger of the costly repairs the house would soon require. Jim and Sara struggled to afford the renovations. They had bought the house despite falling behind on their federal tax payments to the tune of $589,000, according to a lien filed by the IRS.

———

After Joe's Florida respite, it was back to the world stage. In late February, a popular revolt ousted Ukraine's Russia-aligned president, Viktor Yanukovych. Vladimir Putin responded immediately, orchestrating a campaign of pro-Russian agitation in eastern Ukraine that resulted several weeks later in the invasion and annexation of Ukraine's Crimean Peninsula. Obama delegated the crisis to Joe. Ukraine's fate was largely in his hands.

At the same time, Hunter's business ventures were leading him to Ukraine, too. Early in 2014, Archer had entered into talks about joining the board of Burisma, a Ukrainian energy company in serious need of an image makeover. The firm had prospered in recent years because it had won valuable licenses for natural gas extraction from Ukraine's Ministry of Ecology and Natural Resources. But there was a problem. Burisma's owner, Mykola Zlochevsky, had been Ukraine's minister of ecology and natural resources when the licenses were awarded. The ouster of Yanukovych presented a serious threat to Zlochevsky's business. How would Ukraine's new government handle the awarding of licenses by a Yanukovych minister to his own company?

Archer agreed to take a position on Burisma's board and worked to recruit Hunter to join him. On April 16, Archer and his son, who was working at the time on a White House–related school assignment, visited Joe at the White House. Hunter and Archer have said that Burisma did not come up during the visit.[579] Two days later, Hunter was appointed to Burisma's board.[580]

He was tasked with helping Burisma clean up its corporate governance and paid roughly $1 million a year to do it. The easy money allowed Hunter to feed his worsening drug addiction.[581]

Taking the job also meant that Joe would be lecturing stakeholders in the country about cleaning up its culture of corruption while his son worked for an oligarch who himself was under suspicion of serious corruption.

George Kent, a career diplomat who served as the State Department's deputy chief of mission in Kiev and as a top anticorruption official during this period, has described Zlochevsky as a "poster child for corrupt behavior."[582]

Publicly, the White House deflected questions about the propriety of the role. "Hunter Biden is a private citizen and a lawyer," a Biden spokeswoman said at the time. "The vice president does not endorse any particular company and has no involvement with this company."[583]

Behind the scenes, Joe's aides were troubled by the arrangement, but they did not raise the issue with him because they feared being yelled at or hurting Joe's feelings.[584] According to Hunter, his father called him and told him, "I hope you know what you're doing."[585]

The Burisma appointment and its fallout precipitated Heinz's break from Hunter and Archer. News coverage pointed out Archer's ties to the family of Obama's secretary of state.

Heinz has said through a spokesman that he cut ties with Hunter and Archer on account of their Burisma work because it showed a "lack of judgment."[586]

A year after the Ukraine crisis broke out, Jim and Sara recorded a loan of $400,000 in the form of a mortgage on their primary residence in Pennsylvania. The money came from 1018 PL LLC, a corporation registered in Delaware the day before.[587]

A month later, they got another $500,000 mortgage on the Biden Bungalow from the same corporate entity. At the time the loans were made, there was no public indication of who was behind 1018 PL LLC. Several years later, a mortgage release was filed for the Biden Bungalow that revealed the entity was controlled by Hynansky.

In the years before the annexation, Hynansky had contacts with the administration. Back in 2009, Joe had acknowledged him during a speech in Kiev. "My very good friend, John Hynansky, a very prominent businessman from Delaware, is here," he said. "I had breakfast with him the other day."[588]

A few months after that speech, the Overseas Private Investment Corporation, a federal government agency that oversees foreign development lending, approved a $2.5 million loan to Hynansky's business, Winner Automotive Group.[589] In 2012, OPIC authorized up to $20 million to help Winner expand its dealership facilities in Ukraine to sell Porsches, Land Rovers, and Jaguars.[590] Hyansky did not respond to queries.

A spokesman for Jim and Sara told me Hynansky is a "longtime friend of the Bidens" and that the couple had paid him an above-market interest rate of 6 percent on the loans.

The loans did not end the couple's financial problems. The IRS filed a $30,000 lien against the Florida house in 2014, and a contractor slapped another $75,000 lien against the house for unpaid bills.[591]

Hunter's work with Burisma, meanwhile, presented complications for Joe. In December 2015, Joe gave a speech to Ukraine's parliament, the Rada, in which he implored the country's leaders to gird themselves for "a historic battle against corruption."

"The only thing worse than having no hope at all," he said, "is having hopes rise and see them dashed repeatedly on the shoals of corruption."[592]

Three days before the speech, a communications aide, Kate Bedingfield, emailed another Biden aide, Michael Carpenter, to address how Joe should handle any questions about Zlochevsky's alleged corruption. She advised that Joe respond, "I'm not going to get into naming names or accusing individuals."[593]

As part of its efforts to improve its image in Washington, Burisma also hired Blue Star Strategies, a political advisory firm. In February 2016, Blue Star's CEO, Karen Tramontano—a former deputy chief of staff to Bill Clinton—invoked Hunter's name as she sought a meeting with the State Department officials. The following month, Tramontano met with Undersecretary of State Catherine Novelli to argue that Burisma was not corrupt, and again invoked Hunter's name.[594] It is not clear whether Blue Star's work for Burisma met the legal bar for registering as a foreign agent with the Justice Department, and the firm did not file a registration.[595]

———

When Joe became Obama's running mate, his sister did not take any position with the general election campaign, though she remained an informal confidante.[596] During the administration, Val, who sometimes referred to herself as "vice sister,"[597] was an in-demand speaker for paid engagements.

In May 2013, she traveled to Baku, the capital of Azerbaijan, an oil-rich nation on the Caspian Sea. She was there to speak on women's rights at a conference ostensibly organized by a Houston-based nonprofit. Former Obama aides Jim Messina, Robert Gibbs, and David Plouffe also attended the event,[598] along with members of Congress from both parties. Some of the lawmakers received gifts, including fine rugs. The trip prompted an investigation by the Office of Congressional Ethics, which found that the ultimate source of funding for the conference was Azerbaijan's state oil company. At the time, the company had been currying favor in Washington. It was working on a natural gas pipeline in partnership with an Iranian state oil company, and successfully seeking sanctions exemptions for the project.[599] As a private citizen, Val was not bound by the same rules that restricted the lawmakers.

Val did briefly take a formal role with the administration in 2016, when Obama appointed her an alternative representative to the United Nations General Assembly.[600]

Val's younger daughter, Casey, spent the first two years of the administration at the Treasury Department, where she worked as the special assistant to the senior coordinator for China. She then moved to the private sector, taking a job at Revolution Growth, a Washington-area venture capital firm, before decamping to Seattle and taking an executive position at Starbucks.[601]

Val's older daughter, Missy, spent the early years of the Obama administration working as deputy chief of staff at the Department of Energy and then as chief of staff to the deputy secretary at the Commerce Department. In 2012, she moved over to the private sector, taking a job as a director for public affairs and diplomatic relations at Coca-Cola.

Coke's new tie to the second family came at a time when its relationship with the first family was fraught.

When she arrived at the White House, Michelle Obama made healthy eating and lifestyles her signature project, with a focus on childhood obesity.

The initiative created a dilemma for soda companies. Public health experts have long pointed to the adverse health effects of sugary drinks.[602] At first, the first lady's healthy lifestyle message included calls to drink less soda and to post calorie counts on soda fountains.[603]

This all threatened to become a real problem for the industry, with proposals bubbling up for federal and state soda taxes. Citing Michelle Obama's efforts, the *New York Times* food writer Mark Bittman asked, in February 2010, "Is soda the new tobacco?"[604] That question hung over the industry for years.

When Missy joined Coke in mid-2012, Mike Bloomberg, then New York City's mayor, was launching his "war on soda," calling for a ban on sugary drinks in containers larger than sixteen ounces.

The first lady signaled her support for Bloomberg's effort, which ultimately failed.[605]

Jill struck a different note. In late May 2013, she and Joe traveled to South America for official visits. In Rio de Janeiro, Jill visited a program run by Coca-Cola that provided job training to young people.

On June 3, days after their return, Missy went to the White House complex for a meeting with Harley Feldbaum, director of Global Health, Food Security and Development at the National Security Council at the Old Executive Office Building.[606] Feldbaum told me he does not recall the meeting, but he considers it unlikely that it dealt with Jill's visit to the Coca-Cola program, because, he said, the visit seems to fall outside the issues in his portfolio.[607]

Two days later, Jill published a post about the trip to the official White House blog, and Coke earned a glowing review. "I met with students from the Coletivo Varejo program, part of Coca-Cola Brazil's Coletivo CSR platform, through which Coca-Cola integrates its supply chain in order to transform the lives of thousands of people by boosting self-esteem and generating income," Jill recounted. "Programs like Coca-Cola's Coletivo go into communities and work with young people where they live. They provide skills and training, not so people can out-grow or leave, but so they can better the community and themselves."[608] A spokeswoman for Coca-Cola said that Missy no longer works for the company and referred all questions to her. Neither Missy nor a spokes-man for Jill responded to questions about the visit.

At the time, the soda companies were pumping tens of millions of dollars into a yearslong lobbying blitz. Rather than pushers of the new tobacco, they preferred to be seen as socially responsible, all-American brands.[609] Conservative media, meanwhile, was savaging the first lady's healthy living initiatives, painting them as a threat to personal liberty.

In September 2013, Michelle's anti-soda efforts became less explicit. She launched a "drink up" campaign to encourage Americans to drink more water. Many public health experts were baffled, saying available research did not support the conclusion that drinking more water, on its own, would improve public health.[610] "It's not so much what FLOTUS said as what she didn't say," noted Rene Lynch in the *Los Angeles Times*. "Mainly, that Americans should drink more water and less soda, which is the message that some in the health community wish the first lady had delivered."[611] A spokeswoman for Michelle Obama did not respond to a question about whether the former first lady ever felt pressured to dial back her calls for reduced soda consumption.

Occasionally, Missy attended public events with Joe. She accompa-nied him at his induction to the Irish America Hall of Fame just after St. Patrick's Day in 2013. In his prefatory remarks, Joe gave his niece a shout-out. "Stand up, baby," he said, prompting the audience to applaud. Then Joe turned to Donald Keough, a former CEO and chairman of Coke, who was then still on the company's board.[612] "She represents Coca-Cola in New York. I just want you to know that," he said. "So take damn good care of her, or Aunt Gertie will be back."[613]

In April 2014, ahead of the upcoming World Cup in Brazil, Joe trekked over to Foggy Bottom to join Kerry for an unveiling of the World

Cup trophy. The trophy tour was sponsored by Coca-Cola. At the State Department event, the vice president and the secretary of state stood in front of a Coke-branded backdrop and pulled off a covering to reveal the golden trophy, which sat atop a Coke-branded pedestal; then they applauded, while cameras snapped all around them.[614] Missy was among the corporate representatives standing by. "Although my plans are not yet final, I want you to know I intend to go to the games. I'm looking at my niece, Missy Owens, who works for Coca-Cola, to get me a good seat if I go," Joe joked. "I'm not so sure we can handle it, but Missy, maybe you'll be able to help me out."[615] (He did attend the U.S.-Ghana match on Brazil's east coast two months later. Neither Missy nor the White House responded to a question about whether Missy had facilitated Joe's appearance at the event.)

When Joe bumped into the company's chairman and CEO, Muhtar Kent, at Davos in 2016, he had a question for him: "You taking care of my niece?"[616] A couple of months later, Missy, along with her father, Jack, scored an invitation to attend a White House state dinner for Canadian prime minister Justin Trudeau.[617]

Despite soda's troubles on the homefront, the rest of the world continued to offer new market opportunities.

During Obama's first term, the administration made a "Pivot to Asia" a cornerstone of its foreign policy, focusing on the Pacific in order to counter China's rise. A big part of the pivot was a rapprochement with Burma, also known as Myanmar. The country had been ruled for decades by a military junta, its economy choked off from the world by Western sanctions. It was a "hermit state," the most insular country in the world, other than North Korea. Like North Korea, its lifeline to the rest of the world ran through Beijing, and the United States wanted to change that. In exchange for promises on human rights and democratic reform (some of which have since been forgotten, and others of which were never observed), the U.S. agreed to ease sanctions on Burma in a bid to tug the country into its sphere of influence.

U.S. and European business interests formed a beachhead in Yangon, the country's largest city and former capital. Coke was the tip of the spear of the Western expansion into the country.

I traveled to Burma in June 2013 on a journalism fellowship to cover the early stages of this opening. At that time, Burma was still, by and large, untouched in recent decades by Western influence. In some places, like the city of Muse on the Chinese border, most residents had never seen an American in person. But Coke was already widely available, and its branding was highly visible at roadside food joints. The company had been shipping its products into the country for the better part of a year and opened a bottling plant in the south of the country that month.[618]

With Burma opened up, there were only two countries left on Earth outside the reach of the Coca-Cola Company. One was North Korea. The other was Cuba.

Soon, Cuba inched closer to being within reach. In late 2014, the Obama administration restored diplomatic relations with its island neighbor. Early the next year, Coke executive Rafael Fernández Quirós expressed the company's hope that "in the future, hopefully not too distant, things will change and we'll be able to re-establish our presence on the island."[619]

In the waning months of the Obama era, the administration made a final push to normalize relations with Cuba. In October 2016, Jill traveled to Havana and the island's Camaguey province at the head of a U.S. government delegation.

Her itinerary called for her to meet with "government officials and engage with a diverse range of Cubans on topics related to culture, education, and health," according to a White House statement.[620] Along with representatives of the State Department, she was accompanied by Ashley and by Missy. Neither Missy nor a spokesman for Jill responded to questions about whether Missy's position at Coke played any role in her participation in the trip.

Among American firms, Coke was far from alone in its eagerness to get into the embargoed Cuban market. But only Coke got a director of public affairs and diplomatic relations inside a White House delegation to Havana.

———————

While serving as Obama's number two, Joe never fully gave up his hopes of reaching the top spot, even as his eldest son began nurturing presidential ambitions of his own.

In 2009, Joe spent his first Independence Day as vice president in Baghdad. In the morning, he and Jill attended a naturalization ceremony for soldiers on the site of one of Saddam Hussein's old palaces.[621] Later in the day, Joe visited with Beau's unit and remarked on the new purpose to which the U.S. had put the late dictator's home. "That S.O.B. is rolling over in his grave right now," he said.[622]

In the fall, Beau's unit returned to Delaware, where Joe greeted them with a welcome-home ceremony in Dover.

Beau went back to his day job as the state attorney general and surprised the state's political observers by passing on the chance to run for his father's old Senate seat in 2010. Instead, he won an easy reelection as Delaware attorney general over an independent challenger.

In 2012, at the Democratic National Convention in Charlotte, North Carolina, Beau put his father's name in for the vice presidential nomination as Joe looked on, his eyes welling up with tears.

At the end of that year, after the Obama-Biden ticket won again, Beau and Hunter took stock of Beau's career prospects. Democrat Jack Markell had just won a second term as Delaware governor, meaning that he would be term-limited in 2016, and there would be a wide-open race for the seat. The brothers thought Beau could win it. After that, he could set his eyes on the presidency.[623]

Beau was popular with voters. He performed high-profile military service. He had the Biden name. He was handsome. He was still young. But in 2010, Beau suffered a scare reminiscent of his father's aneurysm, and around the same age. One day that spring, he had woken up with stroke-like symptoms, unable to move the right side of his body, and was taken to the hospital. Within hours he had recovered.

Beau went back to work. Sometimes, though, on long runs he would get dizzy or start hearing strange sounds that he knew were coming from inside his head. He wondered if his time in Iraq had left him with post-traumatic stress syndrome.[624]

Meanwhile, after Obama won reelection, Joe began maneuvering for a possible presidential run of his own. He did not immediately begin to make pilgrimages to Iowa, but on the eve of Obama's second inauguration, he did the next best thing, stopping off at the Iowa State Society Inauguration Ball.

Addressing the attendees, he made a Freudian gaffe, saying "I'm proud to be president of the United States." The party-goers cheered. Beau, standing by, interrupted Joe's remarks to clarify that his father had meant *vice* president.[625]

The next day, Joe took his oath of office for his second term at the Naval Observatory. Jill, Hunter, Ashley, and much of the rest of the clan were on hand. Also present were bigwigs from early nominating states, including Maggie Hassan, governor of New Hampshire, and Dick Harpootlian, chairman of the Democratic Party in South Carolina.[626]

That evening Joe hosted a couple hundred prominent Democrats at the Naval Observatory to revel in their victory. Obama's former chief of staff and Chicago's then-mayor Rahm Emanuel, NAACP president Ben Jealous, and Planned Parenthood president Cecile Richards were just some of the big names on hand.

The event left many who attended with the strong impression that Joe was maneuvering for a third presidential bid. One Democrat close to the administration said at the time that the teetotaler vice president was "intoxicated by the idea" of a third go at the presidency.[627]

Frank

"I've never made a dime from any association with my brother Joey, and it's just wrong to imply otherwise. Just wrong."

—Frank Biden, phone call with author, October 2019

In the years following the San Diego car accident, Frank had mostly laid low. After his brother secured the vice presidency, he took on a larger public profile. He became a front man for Mavericks in Education, a for-profit charter school company, and served at times as the company's lobbyist in Florida and as its president.

Frank had gotten involved with Mavericks after a chance run-in with Mark Rodberg in 2009 at a Starbucks in Palm Beach Gardens.[628] Rodberg was a developer who owned several restaurants.[629] He pitched Frank on his latest venture: for-profit charter schools where kids who struggle in traditional learning environments could sit in rows of cubicles and take classes on a computer.

Frank, recalling his own school-age struggles with a stutter, signed on to become a pitchman. He was in exalted company. Mavericks' last celebrity pitchman had been the Miami Heat's star shooting guard, Dwyane Wade.

In the Biden family tradition of sales, Frank traveled around Florida, sometimes by private jet, to build political support for the schools. "I give you my word of honor on my family name that this system is sustainable," he declared at a school board meeting in Palm Beach County in February 2011.[630]

He also became a face of the business at events like school openings and graduations, where he made frequent reference to his vice presidential brother. In meetings, Frank would sometimes wear cuff links bearing the presidential seal.[631]

Mavericks expanded rapidly, opening new locations around Florida. By the fall of 2014, it had taken in $70 million in state funding.

It also became mired in allegations of malfeasance. A mother at one school complained that Mavericks staff forced her child to apply for a state meal subsidy that the family was not eligible for. The complaint prompted state and federal investigations.

The U.S. Department of Education found that Mavericks engaged in "questionable, possible fraudulent, activities" related to meal subsidies, and referred their findings to Florida authorities. Investigations released by Florida's auditor general found that Mavericks was getting state funding for students who were not actually enrolled.[632]

Even without findings of malfeasance, the politics of charter schools are complicated. Republicans have generally been more supportive of the charter school movement than Democrats, who have more often aligned with public school teachers' unions against the movement. The technocratic Obama administration, though, embraced charter schools.

When Tom Sutterfield, a pro–charter school Republican, ran for school council in Palm Beach in 2014, Frank endorsed him. Then he did one better. In October, Joe came to Broward County to campaign for Charlie Crist, the Democratic gubernatorial candidate. Sutterfield met with Joe backstage at one of the stops and the two posed for a photograph.

In the closing weeks of the campaign, Sutterfield raised eyebrows in Palm Beach with mailers that included this photo with Joe. The mailer advertised that Sutterfield had been "endorsed by Frank Biden."[633]

Sutterfield, who ended up losing the race, told me that Frank arranged the backstage meeting with Joe. Frank told me he had nothing to do with arranging the meeting and that he had never seen the photo of his brother and Sutterfield. "Does Tom have a photo with Joe?" he asked me.[634]

While Frank was working to bolster Sutterfield's campaign, two former officials at a school that had been run by Mavericks were busy scrutinizing the school's finances.

Susan Latvala and Lara Shane were administrators at New Alternative Education High School in Pinellas County, a charter school near Tampa on Florida's west coast. Since 2009, the school had contracted with Mavericks in Education to run its operations.[635]

In 2012, the local board in Pinellas decided to terminate its relationship with Mavericks over changes it made to its curriculum that meant students would not graduate with real high school diplomas.[636] When the local administrators informed Mavericks of their decision, Frank came out to meet with them, and told them they would be "stupid" to sever ties. Frank was wearing his presidential cuff links, but the administrators were not swayed.

After the breakup, Latvala and Shane began sifting through the school's financial records. They allegedly found evidence that Mavericks was engaged in a fraud more sweeping and elaborate than the ones previously investigated.

In 2014, the women filed a whistleblower lawsuit in federal court against Frank, other Mavericks leaders, and several Mavericks-related corporate entities. Their complaint, which was initially filed under seal, alleged that Mavericks had defrauded the U.S. Department of Education, the Federal Communications Commission, the Florida Department of Education, and local school boards out of tens of millions of dollars.

The complaint alleged that in addition to inflating enrollment, Mavericks reported false payroll figures and charged school boards for maintenance services it did not provide; drew up fake checks to receive state reimbursement for expenses that it never incurred; diverted federal grant money for unauthorized purposes; used a web of corporate entities to lease land to school boards at inflated prices; and used a web of non-profits to improperly shield itself from tax liability.

After filing the suit, Shane and Latvala met with state and federal prosecutors to go over their findings. The authorities had the option of taking up the case themselves, but in March 2015, the U.S. Department of Justice and the Florida Department of Legal Affairs both declined to intervene in the case, which was then unsealed. The women decided not to litigate the claims themselves and abandoned the case.[637]

One person who worked with Mavericks said they were not sure how much Frank knew about the alleged frauds taking place because he seemed unfamiliar with the mechanics of running a charter school. "But," the person said, "he was president of the company, and they paid him well. In my mind, he's accountable."[638]

When I asked Frank about Mavericks' alleged failings in July 2019, he stood by the business. "My involvement with Mavericks was motivated by a desire to provide educational opportunities for high school dropouts and marginalized kids to obtain an accredited high school diploma," he wrote in an email. "We did that. Check the record."[639]

———

While Joe was in the Senate, Frank had spent time in Nicaragua, working with Hand in Hand Ministries, a charity with operations in the United States and Central America.

He maintained his ties to Latin America during the Obama years. He pivoted from charity work to entrepreneurial ventures as Joe took a leading role in the administration's policy toward Latin America.

For years, Frank worked on developing a large golf course, casino, and resort complex called the Guanacaste Country Club near the border with Nicaragua.[640]

In early 2014, Frank unveiled the Sun Costa Rica initiative to power the proposed resort with a solar energy plant.[641] He served as president of Sun Fund Americas, the holding company behind the project.

In June of that year, Joe traveled to Colombia and the Dominican Republic,[642] where he announced the Caribbean Energy Security Initiative, which provided U.S. government financing for energy projects in the region.[643]

As part of the initiative, the Overseas Private Investment Corporation, the same federal agency that made loans to Hynansky's car dealership in Ukraine, provided $47 million in financing for a twenty-megawatt solar farm in Clarendon, Jamaica.[644]

A few months later, Frank's company, Sun Fund Americas, announced it had signed a power purchase agreement for a twenty-megawatt solar project in Jamaica. When I asked Frank whether that project in Jamaica was in fact the one in Clarendon, and whether his brother's role in regional energy policy helped him land the deal, he did not answer directly. Instead, he wrote back, "I never developed ANY solar projects in CR," meaning Costa Rica, where Sun Fund Americas was headquartered. "Check your facts." When I reiterated that I was asking about the project in Jamaica, he did not respond.

———

Down in Florida, Frank struck up a close relationship with Joe Abruzzo, a Democratic state legislator from Palm Beach County. Frank, a constituent, would make use of Abruzzo's office during his lobbying trips to Tallahassee, leaving his bag in Abruzzo's office or kicking his feet up there to take a rest.

Abruzzo, who was elected to the state House in 2008, and moved up to the Senate four years later, sat on the Senate subcommittee that oversaw education funding. The two have maintained that Frank never lobbied Abruzzo, but emails that were made public under Florida's open records law call that into question. The emails, which first surfaced in an unrelated news report, show another lobbyist, Nancy Ann Texeira, emailing with Abruzzo's staff to set up a meeting with the state senator on a charter school funding for herself and Frank in April 2013.

By that time, Abruzzo and Frank were teaming up on another project. Victoria McCullough, the heiress of an oil empire and an animal rights activist, was on a quest to ban the slaughter of horses for meat.

McCullough lived on a large estate in Palm Beach County, complete with luxury horse stables lined with white columns and topped with a mansard roof. A lover of horses, she devoted part of her fortune to rescuing thousands of them, buying the unwanted animals before they could be sent to the slaughterhouse.[645]

McCullough comes across as friendly and sometimes flighty in conversation, but she knows how to work the levers of power, a skill that she put to the test in the fight over horse slaughter.

Banning horse slaughter might sound uncontroversial, but it was the subject of years of political fighting. While it is not common in the United States, horse meat is eaten regularly in cultures as far afield as Japan, Russia, and other parts of Europe. In the United States, ranchers, who want to get rid of horses that have outlived their useful working lives, long opposed a ban.

When Abruzzo, still shy of thirty, first ran for the state House, McCullough supported him. After he was elected, Abruzzo was instrumental in pushing through a landmark law that made it a felony to slaughter horses. The law was named after McCullough.

After her success in Florida, McCullough wanted a federal ban, and she again enlisted Abruzzo to help her.

She also called on Frank. Over decades, as she dealt with the regulatory challenges of her family's private oil company, Chesapeake Petroleum, McCullough had gotten to know Joe's Senate staff. She also became fond of Frank, whom she sometimes refers to by his full name, "Francis." Later, she formed a relationship with Beau, and became a supporter of his Beau Biden Foundation for the Protection of Children.

Through Frank and her other Biden world connections, McCullough landed a meeting for herself and Abruzzo with Joe at the Naval Observatory in 2011.

The meeting was initially slated to last just thirty minutes. Joe was preparing for travel. But as the duo made their case, Joe, who had supported similar attempts at banning horse slaughter in the past, waved off the minders trying to move his day along. The meeting went on for hours, as they hashed out strategy. Joe and Abruzzo settled on defunding the Department of Agriculture's inspections of horse-slaughter facilities as a promising approach to enacting a de facto ban.

But the issue languished for years. By the spring of 2013, the USDA was starting to approve new horse slaughterhouses, creating a renewed sense of urgency around the issue. That May, Abruzzo registered as a federal lobbyist in order to help McCullough push the horse-meat ban through Congress.[646]

The defunding proposal made its way into the proposed budget released by the White House, but the issue was fiercely contested on the Hill, where it did not fall neatly along partisan lines.

"This issue, I kid you not, caused more problems in Congress than you could imagine," Tom Rooney, a former Republican congressman from Florida and a supporter of McCullough's measure, told me.

McCullough was able to get the language into the draft omnibus budget bill, which came up for a vote in January 2014. "We inserted this into the Omnibus privately, secretly, basically under the radar so opposition wasn't there," she later explained.

But one big obstacle to victory remained. Senate Minority Leader Mitch McConnell was sympathetic to ranchers who opposed restrictions on horse slaughter.

Abruzzo went to Frank to enlist more help from his older brother. Joe agreed to raise the issue with McConnell.

McCullough accompanied Joe to the minority leader's office. "This is going to take just a few minutes. This is a very good man," Joe told her, before he went inside to hammer out a deal. "We've differed our whole careers, but we have a friendship and a respect for each other, and we've had twenty-seven years in the Senate together."

"Good luck," McCullough told him. She sat out in the hall on a bench. After about fifteen minutes, Joe returned, and flashed his trademark smile. The measure would become law.

In April, McCullough traveled to the American Equine Summit, a group for horse lovers, to explain how she had engineered the triumph. At the gathering in Chatham, in upstate New York, she lavished praise on Joe, crediting him as the measure's indispensable patron.

The horse enthusiasts were also treated to a video message from Frank and Abruzzo. They had shot it outside, from seats overlooking a tree-lined intersection in Tallahassee. Frank, besuited, with a pocket square, passed along a greeting from Joe. He cited his family tie to upstate New York via Neilia, and lavished praise on McCullough.

"We have a special place in our heart in the Biden family for Victoria," he said. "Joe and I wish we were with you, but we're with you in spirit."

"Joe felt strongly about this issue," he said. "The president felt strongly about this issue."

Abruzzo credited the "great advocacy and work from Frank and Joe" for the measure's passage, and described the final clinching of the ban as it faced a vote in Congress.

"I turned also to Frank and said, 'We may need a little help from the vice president and the administration talking to some senators,'" Abruzzo recounted. "And when Frank and the vice president and Chair [Debbie] Wasserman Schultz jumped in, by the morning sunrise, after Victoria's advocacy as well, we had no opposition and a voice vote and a passage of appropriations."

"My brother's long-term relationships in the Senate proved to be the final nail in the coffin to be able to pull this thing forward," Frank explained.

Years later, I came across the Equine Summit video and made calls to Frank, Abruzzo, and McCullough to ask them about it. I got a variety of shifting, sometimes conflicting answers about how they interacted with each other and with the levers of the federal government.

In an initial phone call, Frank told me that he had not helped Abruzzo push the horse measure through Congress, but that Abruzzo did regularly consult with him for advice in general. "He turned to me to help him and support him in scores of things, and had up until that point, asked me for advice on lots of different issues and continues to."

Did that mean Abruzzo had asked him for advice on pushing the horse measure? "No," Frank said. "No. He was a facile state senator and didn't need my advice in terms of legislative procedure."

In another call, later the same day, he said he was not even aware of how the measure became law. "I don't even know whether it was through Congress or not through Congress," he said.

Frank was reluctant to discuss the details of what exactly he did regarding the horse measure, and when. "You're not going to catch me on a date and a time," he said.

Eventually, Frank provided a version of events more consistent with the video he had recorded in 2014, in which he did help Abruzzo push the measure through Congress. "I advised him on tactics," Frank said. "I was not the mechanic fixing the engine. I was the old salt standing close by the young guy's ear."

Frank said he did not get paid for his help on the horse measure, but that there would have been nothing wrong with it if he did. "I would have been happy, happy to have been offered the job and to be paid for it," he said.

When I spoke with McCullough, she said that after the horse-slaughter victory, in 2015, she had hired Frank for work related to Chesapeake Petroleum. "Frank Biden is very close to me," she said. "He worked for me."

At the time, she said, the company was considering branching out into government contracting, and she valued Frank's knowledge of Washington, not to mention the influence of his family.

"The Bidens were very important and very helpful, and I needed someone that knew the agencies as well as he did," she explained.

When I asked Abruzzo about this, he told me that McCullough misremembered what had happened, and that actually he, Abruzzo, had done the work she described, not Frank. He said Frank only received payment years later for work that happened after Joe left office. He told me he would call McCullough to "refresh her memory."

McCullough then called me back and said, "Frank was never working for us." She said Frank was often helpful to her, but that he was not paid for his trouble.

"I could consult with him," she explained. "I mean, you could call up Frank Biden at any moment to consult with him, if you're me."[647]

(Frank's finances have been complicated by the fact that he still had the judgment from the wrongful death suit hanging over his head. In 2019, the holder of the judgment went after Frank for $275,000 in Alachua County, Florida, court. The judgment holder sought to garnish a bank account and slap a lien on Frank's Range Rover SUV. The judge also granted her attorney's fees. It is unclear how much of the judgment the plaintiff, who declined to speak to me, has collected from Frank. Frank told me the matter has now been settled.)

A LinkedIn profile for Frank supports McCullough's original version of events: It lists Frank as a "member director" of the Delmarva Group, a consulting business set up by Abruzzo, starting in 2015.

In 2016, during the final year of Joe's vice presidency, the Delmarva Group, on behalf of Chesapeake, hired Cassidy and Associates to lobby Congress in a bid to get contracts from the Department of Defense. The lobbying effort did not pan out.[648]

When CNBC asked Abruzzo about this in 2021, he maintained that Frank was not involved, and that the business was not even formed until after Joe had left office. "Frank Biden and I began planning the business in 2015 and had discussions through 2016," he said. "The structural for-mation and Frank's formal involvement began in 2017."

Delmarva Group's corporate registration, filed with the state of Florida, shows that it was formed in May 2015.[649]

On its face, the story Frank offered on video was a straightforward, feel-good one about the Biden brothers stepping up for animal rights. Scratch beneath the surface, though, and there is a more complicated story—obscured by a whirl of contradictory statements and evidence—about Frank's ties to a federal lobbyist and a wealthy patron and an effort to win defense contracts for an oil company.

No evidence has emerged that Joe aided those efforts, and he has offered general assurances that he maintained an "absolute wall" between government business and his relatives' private interests during the Obama administration.[650] Frank has offered assurances, too. "I've never made a dime from any association with my brother Joey, and it's just wrong to imply otherwise," he told me, when I came calling about the horse meat. "Just wrong."

Dynasty Deferred

In the summer of 2013, the Bidens' political ambitions took a backseat to more important concerns.

Someone at Joe's house, where Beau was temporarily staying, called 911 to report a "possible stroke." The call was quickly canceled, and the Bidens deflected local press questions about the incident.[651] Two weeks later, in mid-August, Beau became incapacitated during a summer vacation with his family and Hunter's on the shores of Lake Michigan.[652]

This time, he was rushed to the hospital, and doctors in Chicago found a brain tumor. The clan sprang into action. Krein and O'Connor scrambled to find Beau the best care. Beau flew down to MD Anderson Cancer Center, the renowned research and treatment center attached to the University of Texas in Houston. Val packed into her car and drove one hundred miles south to a yacht club near Rehoboth Beach to stand in for Beau at a fund-raiser.[653]

In Texas, the prognosis was not good. Beau seemed to have glioblastoma, a particularly pernicious type of brain cancer. O'Connor called it "the monster." Fewer than 10 percent of patients survive five years past a diagnosis. Most succumb much earlier.[654]

The vice president's office released a statement acknowledging Beau's health scare and his visit to MD Anderson,[655] but the family kept the severity of Beau's illness to themselves. Even within the clan, Beau put on a brave face, fully confiding only in Hunter.[656]

After the diagnosis was confirmed, Beau kept up his public duties. But as the disease worked its course, reality increasingly set in. In April 2014, he announced he would not seek reelection in November. He said he would focus instead on running for governor of Delaware in 2016.[657]

Joe confided in Obama at one of their weekly standing lunches that Beau might have to step down before his term ended, losing his salary in the process. Joe and Jill were contemplating taking another mortgage out on their house to support him. Obama told Joe to forget about a second mortgage. "I'll give you the money," Obama said, taking his vice president by the shoulders. "I have it. You can pay me back whenever."[658]

Joe had not let go of his presidential ambitions. At Thanksgiving, the family made its annual pilgrimage to Nantucket. Joe expected his sons to resist his interest in a third White House run, but to his surprise, both urged him to pursue it during a kitchen table conversation. Beau, who did not want to be the reason his father abandoned a lifelong dream, told him that running was his "duty."[659]

In February 2015, Joe traveled to Des Moines to tout the administration's education policies. A week later, he gathered with aides Mike Donilon and Steve Richetti, as well as Beau and Hunter, for an evening meeting at the Naval Observatory. They were there to discuss a memo Donilon had put together outlining the case for Joe's viability as a presidential candidate. Beau's AG term had ended, and his deterioration, both physical and mental, was becoming more apparent. After the meeting, Hunter told his father that now that cancer had dashed Beau's presidential aspirations, it was up to Joe to keep shouldering the family's political ambitions. "It has to be you, Dad," he said.[660]

Around this time, Kent, the State Department official, brought his concerns about Hunter's arrangement with Burisma to the vice president's office, but he was told that Joe did not have "bandwidth" to deal with the issue on account of Beau's cancer.[661]

In mid-May, Beau entered Walter Reed Medical Center, the military's flagship hospital outside of Washington. On May 30, he died.

It seemed that all of Delaware mourned him. Flags around the state flew at half-mast. On the Thursday following his death, his body lay in honor at the Capitol in Dover. It seemed, too, that most of Delaware felt some intimate connection to the Bidens' saga. In Dover that day, one man, a few years older than Joe, told me he had volunteered on the 1972 campaign and had watched Beau, in his hospital bed, up close at Joe's first swearing-in.

Another mourner, Rosemary Williams, a retired command sergeant, had worked with Beau during their stints in the Delaware National Guard. She said guard members felt like they had lost a loved one. "We're a family," she told me. "There's a void there."[662]

The next day, thousands gathered in Wilmington for the wake. Rain fell as Beau's coffin, draped in an American flag, was carried into St. Anthony of Padua's church. Outside, Anita DiSimplico and Henry Alisa, a pair of septuagenarian siblings, told me their family and the Bidens had been showing up for each other for decades. Their mother had hosted a spaghetti dinner fund-raiser for Joe in 1972. After he became a national figure, Joe still made it to their mother's surprise seventy-fifth birthday party and later attended her funeral to pay his respects.[663]

At Beau's funeral the next day, Obama delivered a eulogy. "Rather than use his childhood trauma as justification for a life of self-pity or self-centeredness," Obama said of Beau, "that very young boy made a very grown-up decision: He would live a life of meaning. He would live a life for others. He would ask God for broader shoulders." The president recited the story about Beau's refusal to get out of a speeding ticket on account of the cop's fondness for Joe. The moral, Obama explained, was that "Beau didn't trade on his name."

———

As Joe grieved, he was left to grapple with the question of whether he would enter the presidential race. Hillary Clinton had already announced. Obama did not play favorites in public, but his preference was no secret. "I knew a number of the president's former staffers, and even a few current ones, were putting a finger on the scale for Clinton," Joe wrote in his second memoir. "The president was convinced I could not beat Hillary, and he worried that a long primary fight would split the party."[664] Joe had been a loyal vice president to Obama, but, according to former defense secretary Leon Panetta, he "oftentimes felt that that loyalty was not being rewarded."[665]

In the run-up to the decision Hunter and Val were open to letting Joe make up his own mind, but Jill, especially, was resistant.[666] There were other reasons not to jump into a presidential race in his midseventies. Joe was a well-liked figure, and polls showed he would be viable, but Hillary Clinton was the de facto front-runner. Running risked the possibility that the final act of his public life would come as an underwhelming primary loser, rather than a successful, two-term vice president.

After months of flirting with a run, Joe took a pass. In an emotional Rose Garden speech that October, he announced his decision. "I couldn't do this if the family wasn't ready," he said. "The good news is the family has reached that point, but as I've said many times, my family has suffered loss, and—and I—I hope there would come a time—and I've said this to many other families—that, sooner rather than later, when—when you think of your loved one, it brings a smile to your lips before it brings a tear to your eyes."

In the speech, Joe announced he would devote much of his energy over his remaining time in office to what he described as a "moon shot" effort to accelerate cancer research and cure the disease.

In his State of the Union Address the following January, Obama formally announced the Cancer Moonshot initiative, and its leader. "I'm putting Joe in charge of Mission Control," he said.

Three days later, Joe traveled to the University of Pennsylvania's Abramson Cancer Center for the official launch event. Krein accompanied him.[667]

It seemed that wherever Joe went to promote the moonshot, the chief medical officer of StartUp Health was right alongside him. A few days after the Penn kickoff, Joe jetted off to Davos to talk up the initiative. Krein was there with him.[668] In the spring, Hunter and Krein both accompanied Joe to the Vatican, for a conference on regenerative medicine, where the three men hobnobbed with Pope Francis.[669]

Over time, the line between the administration's public health initiative and the private investment initiatives of Joe's son-in-law grew blurry.

In its marketing materials, StartUp Health took to describing Krein as a White House advisor on the initiative.[670] (When I sent Joe's 2020 campaign a list of questions related to StartUp Health, including whether the White House advisor description was accurate, a campaign spokesman responded to some of the questions, but not that one.)

In October, the Cleveland Clinic's Medical Innovation Summit landed Joe as its keynote speaker. Krein's brother scored the speaking slot immediately before the vice president. In his speech, Joe gave his son-in-law a shout-out, describing him as "the leading surgeon... in the Delaware Valley."[671]

StartUp Health used the occasion to announce that it was launching a "cancer moonshot" of its own, along with nine other health-related moonshots.

The firm issued a press release that featured a photo of Joe speaking at the summit in front of a backdrop plastered with the words "cancer moonshot."

Readers of the release could be forgiven for assuming the vice president was endorsing a venture capital firm's new investment funds. It was titled, "StartUp Health Announces 10 Health Moonshots with Global Army of Health Transformers to Improve Health of Everyone in the World" and subtitled, "StartUp Health and Vice President Joe Biden Kick Off 2016 Medical Innovation Summit at Cleveland Clinic."

The release begins, "Today, StartUp Health, its global army of Health Transformers, and Vice President of the United States Joe Biden kicked off the 14th annual Cleveland Clinic Medical Innovation Summit, sharing an urgent message with nearly 2,000 health leaders, CEOs, and entrepreneurs."

It goes on to quote a passage from Joe's speech in which he said, "The Moonshot is all of us who understand the urgency and need to reimagine the cancer fight for the 21st century. It's the spirit of discovery that defines this country. And it gives me every confidence that we are going to make enormous progress."

The release does not make any distinction between StartUp Health's cancer moonshot and the Obama administration's.[672]

A year after Beau's death, Joe traveled to Ireland. He brought along Ashley, Jim, Sara, Val, Missy, and several grandchildren. Ahead of the six-day trip, he shared the documentation he had collected of his family history with the Irish genealogists Helen Moss and Fiona Fitzsimons. On the morning of the twenty-second, the pair presented their findings to the family at the residence of the American ambassador.

Joe told the Irish genealogists that the idea for a big family trip to Ireland had originally been Beau's. He had suggested it following the death of Joe's mother. Now that Joe had lost Beau, too, he was finally doing the trip, in remembrance of both of them.

The Bidens traveled the island to great fanfare, with thousands lining the streets to wish them well.[673]

Fitzsimons accompanied the family on their travels. She told me that before the trip, she let a White House staffer know that she had uncovered local folklore about some of Joe's Finnegan ancestors and their interactions with "the wee people," also known as leprechauns. The White House staffer said the whimsical tales held no interest, but while riding around with Val and Sara, she found they wanted to hear all about them. "They're people's people," Fitzsimons concluded of the family.

She watched as Joe balanced his packed public schedule with the personal aspects of the trip. "It was actually quite a clever thing to do," she said. "He gave the journalists and people who turned out to meet them their due, and he spent time, real time, talking and meeting and saying hi to everybody, but he did that to try to carve out a little private space for the family."

Toward the end of the journey, on Saturday evening, they stopped near an old graveyard in Templetown in County Louth, where some of Joe's ancestors were buried. Fitzsimons and the rest of the traveling entourage were asked to stay away, as the Bidens proceeded to have a moment to themselves in the graveyard.

Fitzsimons sensed that for Joe, the trip was about more than just a family outing and some politicking. "Everybody just looked at it as he was just coming back to reconnect with his roots," she said. "He was looking for continuity. I think he was looking for a sense of purpose."

In November 2016, Donald Trump shocked the world by defeating Hillary Clinton.

The upset provided Joe a measure of vindication.

While the president liked to analyze data and expeditiously plot a course of action, Joe would wax about how a given proposal might affect regular Scrantonians. The slick technocrats around Obama rolled their eyes at this style.[674] Now, their chosen successor had lost Pennsylvania, Wisconsin, and Michigan, and Democrats were voicing rueful what-ifs about Biden's never-launched candidacy.

The following January, a week before Donald Trump's inauguration, Joe made one of his last public appearances as vice president in San Francisco at the StartUp Health festival, an annual confab put on by Krein's firm on the outskirts of the J.P. Morgan Healthcare Conference. Joe delivered his remarks behind a podium bearing the vice presidential seal and in front of a screen covered in StartUp Health's logos.[675]

Back in Washington later that week, Obama surprised Joe by awarding him the Presidential Medal of Freedom. In an emotional ceremony, Obama quoted some of the pearls of Biden family wisdom that Joe had inherited from his parents, including Joe Sr.'s ultimate lesson: "When you get knocked down, Joey, get up. Get up. Get up." Joe fought a losing battle to hold back tears.

After the handover of power, Joe and Jill returned to Delaware to great fanfare. They traveled by Amtrak back home to Wilmington, where supporters feted him at a welcome home rally on the Wilmington waterfront near the train station. In rare public remarks, Val set the stage for the couple's postadministration public life and wrote the entire state into the social contract of the extended Biden clan. "We in Delaware are going to be right there with them as they continue to walk along this path," she said. "Because we've always had their back, because they've always had us in their hearts."[676]

A few days later, Joe and Jill unveiled the Biden Foundation to further the projects they prioritized in public life. In June, they launched another nonprofit project, the Biden Cancer Initiative, with Krein serving on the board, alongside various luminaries.

Joe also jumped into the river of power. He launched the Penn Biden Center for Diplomacy and Global Engagement at the University of Pennsylvania, finally getting into the Ivy League himself, just as he had made sure his children did.

In the years after Joe left the vice presidency, Frank continued his entrepreneurial ventures, including a partnership with a Maryland company that provides substance abuse treatment.[677]

Missy remained with Coca-Cola, though her trip to Havana did not pay off. Trump's surprise victory was propelled in part by hardline anti-Castro Cuban Americans in south Florida. Once in office, the new president reversed Obama's opening to the island nation, dashing American companies' hopes of entering the market.

Missy's name began appearing on the company's list of in-house lobbyists in its disclosures beginning in the fourth quarter of 2017.[678] In Washington, she lobbied on environmental issues, according to Coke's lobbying disclosures.[679]

For Veterans Day that year, Jill, in her capacity as the Biden Foundation's honorary cochair, traveled to Atlanta to participate in Coke's Veterans Employee Appreciation Day. There, the company doled out $1 million to veterans causes.

The Biden Foundation published a post about Jill's visit. "Coca-Cola has committed to go the extra mile," it said, "for service members, veterans, and their families."[680]

———

As medical research became central to Joe's public initiatives, his brother Jim ventured into the health care sector.

He teamed up with Joey Langston—one of the Mississippians jailed for the botched attempt to bribe a judge—following Langston's release from prison.

In August 2015, they registered Earthcare Trina Health LLC in Nevada. The Nevada corporation listed Langston as one of its managers. Another manager was JBB SR. Inc., a Delaware corporation registered to Jim's home address that lists the firm of Joe's former law partner Melvin Monzack as its registered agent.

The name of the corporation refers to two separate businesses in which Jim was involved, Earthcare International and Trina Health.

According to its website, Earthcare International sells both agricultural and medical products. "Our team of scientists have created revolutionary patented products that provide solutions to drastically improve our environment," its website says. "We have gone beyond the land and water and now also provide solutions to one of the worst diseases that continues to grow in amazingly rapid rates—Infections, Diabetes and More. The technology we bring will change the quality of life for most patients suffering from diabetes and infectious viruses."

Like Earthcare, Trina Health made sweeping claims about its products. The company was founded by G. Ford Gilbert, a Sacramento attorney whose daughter, Trina, suffered from diabetes as a girl. Gilbert claimed to have developed a revolutionary approach to diabetes treatment that mimicked the function of the pancreas, delivering insulin in small bursts over several hours, rather than all at once. The medical establishment, regulators, and insurers were skeptical. But Ford touted miraculous results, and his business grew rapidly on the strength of those promises. Trina Health clinics sprouted up around the country, drawing in patients who hoped to find a better way to relieve their suffering.

Langston served as president of Trina Health of Booneville, a clinic in his Mississippi hometown.[681]

The exact nature of Jim's involvement with Trina is not clear, and he did not respond to a question about it. In a business bio recovered from Hunter's laptop, Jim described himself as a partner in Trina Health. Shad Ellison, a businessman who was in talks to raise capital for Trina clinics, told ProPublica that Jim "was going to have a big bite of the apple."[682]

But Trina failed to take off. As questions about the efficacy of Trina's treatment method mounted, the company met its downfall in Alabama.

Because Trina's treatments were unproven, Blue Cross Blue Shield of Alabama did not reimburse for them. In 2015, the insurer discovered that a Trina clinic in the state had been submitting the wrong billing code and receiving reimbursements anyway. When Blue Cross moved to cut off Trina from reimbursements, Gilbert sprang into action, trying to push a law through the state legislature that would force the insurer to cover his treatment.

Gilbert had political clout to draw on. He had brought Alabama's House majority leader, Republican Micky Hammon, in on the business. As Gilbert made his legislative push in 2016, Trina Health made a $2,000 payment to Hammon.[683] Gilbert also allegedly told a bank that Trina would cover an outstanding debt of close to a quarter million dollars owed by the majority leader.[684]

Despite Gilbert's pull with Hammon and his relationships with other Republicans in the state, he failed to make Blue Cross budge. Then, federal law enforcement stepped in.

In September 2017, Hammon pleaded guilty to unrelated mail fraud. Six months later, a grand jury indicted Gilbert on bribery and fraud charges. A former chairman of the Alabama Republican Party was indicted along with him. Gilbert pleaded guilty to conspiring to bribe Hammon and was sent to jail.[685]

Once again, a bribery scandal had derailed Jim's plans with his Mississippi allies. This time, Langston did not go to jail. Neither he nor Jim were implicated in the Trina scheme, but the debacle added to the growing list of scandal-plagued ventures involving Bidens that were unbecoming for a family of their stature.

Jim soon moved on to another venture, which encountered its own legal problems.

In 2017, Langston introduced him to Grant White, the founder of Americore Health.[686] A Canadian with a background in investment banking, White was moving aggressively to expand the business, which operated rural hospitals.

In much of the country, those hospitals have long struggled to remain viable, and their troubles have made it harder for rural residents to access adequate health care. Americore sought to make the hospitals more profitable by capitalizing on the underlying value of the real estate on which they sat. Because Medicare allows rural providers to bill more for lab tests, Americore also sought to increase the number of lab tests it performed at its hospitals.

Jim had teamed up with Michael Lewitt, a fund manager, and Amer Rustom, a Florida-based entrepreneur, to make big health care investments. The group found Americore's model promising. Jim said he could land the company large capital infusions from deep-pocketed foreign investors and help the firm make valuable connections in the United States. "He could get us in front of the unions. He could get us in front of certain people in government. He could get us in front of the right people," recalled Tom Pritchard, a former Americore executive, of Jim's pitch.

It was not an empty boast. In September 2017, Jim brought White to a golf and tennis tournament followed by a silent auction at the Wilmington Country Club. At the event, a fund-raiser for the Beau Biden Foundation, Jim introduced White to Joe.[687] The event featured a surprise appearance by Obama,[688] whom White briefly met as well.[689]

Jim began to set up shop in a corner office on the second floor of Americore's headquarters in Fort Lauderdale, Florida. He filled the office with photos of himself, Joe, Obama, and foreign dignitaries. "It was like a little museum and shrine to him and his brother and Obama," Pritchard recalled. Jim had business cards printed up identifying him as a "principal" of Americore, though he has denied he was ever a principal at the company. Former Americore executives said he planned to become a principal, but parted ways with the company before he could be made one.

In legal filings and interviews, Jim's business contacts have described his efforts to pitch his services and broker health care deals. Jim and his partners have denied wrongdoing, and Jim has denied the allegations that he invoked his family's influence in business settings. A spokesman for Jim described some of the allegations as "pure fantasy." But the general picture presented by these health care executives, one in which Jim pitched his family's political power as giving him a leg up in business ventures, was consistent with the pattern of allegations that emerged around the rock club, the hedge fund firm, and the abortive international lobbying shop.

In January 2018, Jim traveled to Pineville, Kentucky, home of a hospital operated by Americore. There, he met with Michael Frey, the president of Diverse Medical Management, a company that specializes in substance-abuse treatment and elder care.

Americore was interested in making a big investment. As Frey presented his firm's approach, which had the potential to garner contracts for court-ordered rehab, Jim allegedly blurted out, "My brother needs to have you in every court system in America."

Executives at Americore were under the impression that the money to make investments in companies like Diverse Medical Management were going to come via a capital infusion of hundreds of millions of dollars. They believed Jim would land the investments on the strength of his brother's global influence.

But the promised infusion kept getting delayed. It became a running joke at Americore headquarters that the money was always coming in two months.

Jim helped Americore land a bridge loan meant to hold it over until the larger infusion arrived. Then he allegedly had Americore transfer several hundred thousand dollars to him personally in the form of a loan.[690]

One person who discussed the alleged loan with Jim said he needed the money for repairs to his Florida vacation home, the Biden Bungalow.[691]

Jim and Sara had put the house on the market for $6 million in 2016, but it did not sell. In the late summer of 2017, Hurricane Irma had ravaged south Florida, wrecking the Biden Bungalow in the process. The insurance claim was in the seven figures. Around the time Jim was allegedly getting a loan from Americore, he and Sara were in the process of selling the house to a couple of local south Florida architects. The couple got $1.35 million for it, roughly half of what they had paid for it a few years earlier.[692]

From the perspective of Americore's executives, a few hundred grand for a loan would look like chump change when the Middle Eastern money arrived. But it never did. "It was all smoke and mirrors," Pritchard told me. Jim's relationship with Americore soon broke down. In the spring, his office in Fort Lauderdale was packed up and emptied out.

According to one version of events, Jim and his partners discovered that White had misrepresented the soundness of the business and that he had secretly taken out high-interest loans that would cripple it with debt. So they cut ties.

According to a competing version, White was spending freely because Jim and his partners kept promising a massive cash infusion was imminent. When the money did not show up as expected, he was forced to take out the high-interest loans to keep the business afloat.

Either way, financial mismanagement hobbled the company's operations. Pritchard said that Jim stepped away from the company because he did not want its financial problems to complicate Joe's impending presidential run. He said that Lewitt, whose fund retained a stake in Americore, asked to review corporate documents and organizational charts to ensure Jim's name was not on them.

After Jim left Americore, Lewitt and their partners continued to pursue investments in Diverse Medical Management and another firm, Azzam Medical Services.

In early September, Diverse Medical Management's general counsel, Mitchell Cohen, had dinner with Jim near Philadelphia. Jim allegedly told him that Joe's influence at the Department of Veterans Affairs could help DMM get contracts from the VA.

Jim allegedly made similar promises to Mohannad Azzam of Azzam Medical Services, telling him that Joe's influence with VA, and with labor unions, would help the business expand.[693]

In another call, Jim allegedly told Azzam that Joe would feature DMM's unique approach to psychiatric care in his impending presidential campaign.

Jim and his partners also set their eyes on Integrate Oral Care, a Florida-based firm whose products included a medical-grade oral rinse used by cancer patients. In a November phone call, Jim allegedly told Integrate executives that the Biden Cancer Initiative would promote their product.[694]

Jim and his partners still hoped that the planned investment binge would be financed with money from the Middle East. One potential investor Jim was courting was the Qatar Investment Authority. It was an opportune time for a Biden to strike a deal with the gas-rich nation's sovereign wealth fund. In 2017, Qatar's Arab Gulf neighbors had banded together to blockade the tiny country. The coalition cited a number of grievances, including Qatar's cozy relationship with Iran. Qatar scrambled desperately to shore up its political support in the West. As part of that effort, it made investments in politically connected businesses in the United States and Europe.

Jim also sought financing in Turkey.

He and his partners courted Dogan Holding, one of the country's largest corporate conglomerates.[695] The company's leadership was familiar with Joe. In August 2016, a few weeks after a failed coup attempt by Turkey's military, the then vice president had flown to Ankara to meet with Turkish president Recep Tayyip Erdoğan. While there, Joe also met with Mehmet Ali Yalçındağ,[696] a Dogan executive whose wife and father-in-law have served as top Dogan executives themselves. Yalçındağ is best known in the U.S. for spearheading Dogan's partnership with the Trump Organization on Trump Towers Istanbul, and chairing a Turkish state-sponsored trade group in Washington.

In 2019, Jim and Sara traveled to Turkey, where they were hosted by Ekim Alptekin, chairman of the Turkey-U.S. Business Council. Alptekin has said he arranged meetings for Jim and Sara during their trip.[697]

Like Yalçındağ, Alptekin is better known for his Trump world connections. His name came up in Robert Mueller's investigation of foreign influence in the Trump administration on account of his relationship with Trump's first national security advisor, Michael Flynn. Alptekin had paid Flynn's company half a million dollars as part of a campaign to undermine the standing of Fethullah Gülen, a Muslim cleric and enemy of Erdoğan's.

At the time of Jim and Sara's trip, a grand jury in Virginia had just indicted Alptekin on charges that he broke lobbying rules and lied to the FBI about his involvement with Flynn

Despite the couple's efforts, the promised overseas funding did not arrive. In anticipation of a big investment, Frey had been spending money to grow DMM, but as the weeks ticked by without the promised infusion arrivng, he began to worry that he would not be able to make payroll. He told Jim he feared that the company's stretched finances could land it in hot water with Medicare.

Lewitt then texted Frey to reassure him. "Don't worry," he wrote. "Every time someone threatens to sue you you're with us now nobody is gonna touch you."

Frey assumed this meant that DMM was "protected" on account of its Biden ties.[698]

But the relationship soured. Diverse Medical Management and Azzam Medical Services eventually sued Jim and his partners. They alleged that Jim and company had never really intended to make a large investment. Instead, they claimed the promises of investment were a bait and switch designed to string the companies along. They claimed that Jim and his partners wanted to steal their business models while encouraging them to spend more money, which would drive them into insolvency and allow the defendants to take control of the company.

As evidence, they cited a text message that Jim had sent Frey, apparently by accident, in which he wrote: "We can wrap [Americore] into Frey's entity further diluting the both in the process? After we take control of both. Just a thought. We must have complete control, too many moving pieces."

Jim and his codefendants denied the claims and countersued. The case was eventually settled.

Americore's problems, on the other hand, only got worse. Back in 2017, before Jim's falling-out, the company had acquired a hospital in Ellwood City, Pennsylvania, north of Pittsburgh. In pitching local authorities on Americore, White had repeatedly invoked Jim's family name to bolster the company's credibility. The city allowed the acquisition to move forward.[699]

But the hospital soon encountered severe financial problems. It stopped paying workers in late 2018. The problems were so disruptive that local authorities opened a criminal investigation of the hospital's finances early the following year.[700]

By the end of 2019, the hospital had shut down, leaving a gap in medical care in the area. "Our town is suffering," Anthony Court, Ellwood City's mayor, told me. "We should have never been put in this position in the first place."

It is not clear whether Jim's alleged offers of help from his brother and his family's cancer initiative were empty boasts. But the Biden name did help convince people in a small Pennsylvania town to trust Americore, and the results were disastrous.

In the two years following the end of the Obama administration, Joe earned $15.6 million, mostly from book-related income and giving about four dozen speeches, for which he charged as much as $234,000 an appearance, and enjoyed the luxury perks of the high-end speaking circuit. He gave about $1.25 million to charity.[701]

His speaking appearances tended to be on college campuses, but he sometimes showed up at confabs for the moneyed elite, like the Milken Institute Global Conference. In May 2017, he spoke at financier Anthony Scaramucci's SkyBridge Alternatives Conference, a few months before Scaramucci's memorable ten-day stint as Trump's White House communications director.[702]

He and Jill began renting a twelve-thousand-square-foot mansion in northern Virginia, complete with a gym and sauna, from Washington-area businessman Mark Ein, on undisclosed terms.[703] Fulfilling a long-time promise to Jill, Joe also bought a vacation house for $2.7 million. Above the front door, he placed a sign reading, "A promise kept."[704]

The house is in Rehoboth Beach, a resort town for the great

American middle. Joe has frequented the area since childhood. In town, Jill is known as a regular at Browseabout Books, and Joe likes the ice cream stands that dot the main drag.

At DiFebo's, an Italian restaurant favored by the Bidens, the host described them as friendly, and said they had posed for photos with staff. At Something Comfortable, an intimate apparel store, a sales associate said Joe and Jill had dropped in to shop a few years earlier. It is the sort of activity a more uptight political couple would avoid doing in public.[705] Joe even posed for a photo with a staffer, which the store posted on its Facebook page.[706]

Not long after buying the house, Joe hosted a *Vanity Fair* correspondent there. Reflecting on his life, Joe expressed an unusual regret. "I should have raised one Republican kid," he mused. The statement puzzled his interviewer. Joe clarified that he wished one of his children had struck it rich.[707]

The Notorious R.H.B.

"7, this rule is so underrated
Keep your family and business completely separated
Money and blood don't mix"

—The Notorious B.I.G., "Ten Crack Commandments"

Robert Hunter Biden had been living on the edge for years. In the wake of Beau's death, he unraveled completely. His marriage fell apart. His life became a blur of drugs and booze and women. His nights saw him partying with small-time criminals. His days had him doing business with the white-collar variety. Until finally the FBI and IRS turned their focus to Hunter himself.

On the drive home from Beau's funeral, he had mused to Kathleen about getting into politics himself, now that his older brother was no longer alive to carry the Biden dynasty forward.[708] But given Hunter's lifestyle, the idea of running for office was, well, a pipe dream.

As Hunter's substance abuse continued, Kathleen kicked him out of their house. For a time, he lived at Jim's home in Pennsylvania while he underwent rehab at Penn.[709]

He began staying overnight at the home in Wilmington that Hallie had shared with Beau. He helped Hallie take care of their two children, telling them bedtime stories and accompanying the family to church. In his memoir, Hunter writes that he was trying to re-create the dynamic that developed after his mother's death, when Val and Jim moved in to look after him and his brother. He writes, also, that during this period he slept apart from Hallie, in the den.[710]

He moved into the Holm, a new apartment building just east of Logan Circle in Washington. He drank constantly. Joe, still in office, checked in with Hunter by phone several times a day.[711] At one point, Joe shed most of his Secret Service detail and slipped into the Holm to pay Hunter a visit. "You need help," Joe told him. Hunter soon flew off for another round of detox in California.[712]

It did not work, and Hunter's addictions increasingly interfered with his other duties in life. At one point, he traveled to Amman to advocate for Syrian refugees as part of his work for the board of the United Nations' World Food Programme. He recalled being consumed by thoughts of drinking there, even as he sat face-to-face with Jordan's King Abdullah II.[713]

Back in Washington, Hunter reconnected with Bicycles, the homeless woman who had first sold him crack as an undergrad. She became his steady dealer, and moved in with him.[714] As securing access to crack increasingly ruled his life, Hunter kept chasing a different kind of big score.

Though Heinz had cut ties with them, Hunter and Archer made plans to create a financial empire. They wanted to resurrect Burnham and Company, a remnant of the old Drexel Burnham Lambert investment bank. To do it, they teamed up with, among others, financier Jon Burnham, who still ran investment businesses under the Burnham name.

To most Americans, Drexel Burnham is best known for its stunning collapse in the early '90s and the imprisonment of a top executive, "junk bond king" Michael Milken, for securities and tax crimes.

This made the Burnham brand a curious choice, especially for the scion of a prominent political family. But to the firm's would-be revivers, it was a storied investment house, and Milken was a genius worth emulating.

Teneo, a high-powered Washington consultancy, helped the team behind the Burnham revamp put together a presentation for investors.[715] The presentation listed Hunter as the vice chairman of Burnham & Co. and the CEO of Burnham Advisors, a firm that was acquired by Burnham Financial in 2014.[716]

The revamped Burnham had roughly one hundred employees working on Fifty-Seventh Street, a block away from Trump Tower. Hunter kept an office there.[717]

Another financier, Jason Galanis, who had fallen afoul of securities regulators earlier in his career, got involved with the business. Galanis masterminded a plan to use bonds issued by the Oglala Sioux, a Native American tribe, to help facilitate the creation of the new financial conglomerate, which was to be called Burnham Financial Group.[718]

"This is pure genius a lá Mikey Milken!! The Native American Bonds!!" one participant in the scheme emailed Galanis, copying Archer.[719]

When others involved in Burnham raised concerns about Galanis's checkered past, Archer reassured them by pointing to Hunter's involvement in the business.[720]

But in May 2016, the feds arrested Archer, Galanis, and several of their associates. They were charged with defrauding the Oglala Sioux out of $60 million. The conspirators had pocketed most of the proceeds from the bond issuance, rather than investing them on behalf of the tribe.[721]

In October, Hunter, who was not accused of wrongdoing in the bond scheme, set out on what he described as a "crack-fueled, cross-country odyssey." His goal was to reach Sedona, Arizona, a desert mecca for new age hippie types, and try once more to get clean. This time he would have the help of a healer who—having been christened thus by a shaman—went by the name "Puma St. Angel."

The odyssey hit several snags. At one point, Hunter abandoned his cross-country flight during a connection at LAX and sunk into a week of debauchery in Los Angeles. After that, while driving east on I-10, near

Joshua Tree National Park, he fell asleep behind the wheel, and his rental car jumped a median at eighty miles per hour. He landed on the westbound side of the highway, facing oncoming traffic.

Hunter was lucky. He emerged unscathed, though his car was totaled. A tow truck brought him to a new rental car, which he dropped off in Prescott, Arizona.[722] In his haste, he left behind a crack pipe, a Delaware attorney general's badge, and a Secret Service calling card. A Hertz employee, coming across this bizarre array of objects, called the police, who investigated but did not file charges.[723]

It was only after his stay in Sedona that Hunter says his relationship with Beau's widow, Hallie, became a romantic one. In early March 2017, the *New York Post*'s gossip column, Page Six, broke the news of the relationship. Hunter leaned on his father to come out in support of the unorthodox coupling. Joe obliged, telling Page Six, "We are all lucky that Hunter and Hallie found each other." The story made the couple a tabloid sensation.

Not long afterward, they moved to Annapolis with Hallie's children to escape the judgmental gaze of Wilmington society.[724]

Kathleen, who was seeking a divorce, had her say when she alleged in a court filing that Hunter had wasted their money by "spending extravagantly on his own interests (including drugs, alcohol, prostitutes, strip clubs and gifts for women with whom he has sexual relations), while leaving the family with no funds to pay legitimate bills." She also revealed that Hunter had come into possession of a large diamond, pegging its value at roughly $80,000.[725]

Hunter told the *New Yorker* that he did not keep the 2.8-carat diamond, but instead gave it away to unnamed associates.[726] It had been a gift from a Chinese oil tycoon.

———

Ye Jianming had risen from obscure origins in southern China to build a thriving oil conglomerate, CEFC China Energy, and become a globe-trotting dealmaker. The fresh-faced magnate had bought up what seemed like half of Prague[727] and had once lavished a gift on the late North Korean dictator Kim Jong Il.[728] As he sought to build inroads in the United States, Ye cultivated the Bidens. He started courting Hunter during the latter years of the Obama administration, and their plans to go into business together picked up after Joe left office in 2017.

They discussed partnering on energy projects, which often require political clout and regulatory approvals, as well as investing in real estate in New York, through a business called Hudson West. Together, they explored plans to invest in a liquified natural gas project on Louisiana's Gulf Coast. Jim also got involved with Hunter's plans with the Chinese businessmen.[729]

At the beginning of May, Joe flew out to Los Angeles, too. He was in town for the Milken Conference, where he was slated to discuss his cancer initiative onstage with the now-reformed and rehabilitated Michael Milken. (After prison, Drexel Burnham's junk bond king had reinvented himself as a philanthropist and thought leader, and his eponymous annual conference had grown into a Davos-like gathering of the global elite.)

The night before his appearance, Joe met with Hunter, Jim, and Tony Bobulinski, another partner in the planned LNG venture, according to Bobulinksi, who said that in the course of their conversation, Joe showed familiarity with his relatives' business plans.[730]

Also in May, Hunter met with Ye in Miami.[731] On May 13, another partner in the venture emailed Hunter, Bobulinski, and a fourth partner, outlining their plans for compensation. The partner wrote of "a provisional agreement that the equity will be distributed as follows." The breakdown indicated that "H" and the three other partners would get 20 percent each, along with 10 for "Jim" and, finally, "10 held by H for the big guy?"[732]

The email seemed to indicate that Hunter planned to hold 10 percent of the venture on behalf of Joe.

Hunter has not disputed the authenticity of the email, and a person with independent access to Hunter's emails confirmed its authenticity to me. The email's recipient, Bobulinski, later came forward to state publicly that the email was authentic and that it did in fact indicate plans for Hunter to hold equity on Joe's behalf.

A spokesman for Joe has said he never considered getting involved with a relative's business or had anyone hold a stake in a venture on his behalf.[733] Asked about Bobulinski's account, a White House spokesman pointed me to public statements by James Gilliar, the author of "10 held by H for the big guy?" email. Gilliar has said that Joe was not involved in any discussions related to the planned venture and that it generated no revenue.

Two days after the email was sent, SinoHawk Holdings LLC was registered in Delaware[734] as part of the planned venture.

A week after that, another entity related to the venture was registered in Delaware. It was called GK Temujin LLC.[735] Temujin is not a reference to the Finger Lakes, but is instead the birth name of Genghis Khan.

Soon, payments totaling about $5 million began to flow from a CEFC-affiliated entity in Hong Kong to a Hudson West entity and then onto Owasco, Hunter's law firm. The payments were described as consulting fees. From Owasco, $1.3 million flowed to Jim's Lion Hall Group. The memo line for one payment from Owasco read "HW3," an apparent reference to Hudson West III.

According to a report issued later by Republicans on the Senate Homeland Security and Finance committees, when Lion Hall Group's bank contacted Sara to inquire about the payments, she told them that the firm provides consulting services and was supporting Owasco's work for a foreign client. According to the report, Sara declined to provide more information or corroborating documents, and the bank shut down the account.[736] Neither James nor Sara responded to questions about the payments.

The LNG venture was still steaming ahead in September when news broke that CEFC was going to take a $9 billion stake in Rosneft, Russia's state oil company. The deal had wide-ranging geopolitical implications, including the strengthening of energy cooperation between Vladimir Putin's government and the Chinese Communist Party.[737]

A few days later, the *Financial Times* published an investigation of CEFC's ties to Chinese military intelligence through a hawkish Chinese think tank. The paper reported that "CEFC is no ordinary private company."[738]

A few days after that, Hunter emailed the management of his new office building in Washington, the House of Sweden. The building, a boxy, modern structure on the Georgetown waterfront, is owned and operated by the Swedish government, and houses the country's embassy as well as Iceland's.

Hunter instructed the building manager to have keys to the office made up for both of his parents, for Jim, and for Gongwen Dong, an associate of Ye's. He also requested that the office sign show that it housed two entities: the Biden Foundation and "Hudson West (CEFC US)." But Hunter did not last long at the House of Sweden.

His correspondence with building management provides a vivid illustration of the ways in which his out-of-control private life threatened to spill over into a public liability. In this case, he accused a Swedish government agency of racism and threatened legal action against it, while invoking both the Obama family and his own.

On September 18, the building manager emailed Hunter and his business partners. She chided them for violating the building's security policies by having guests enter the building after-hours through a back door, bypassing security at the main entrance. The email reminded them that security was important because the building houses both the Swedish and Icelandic embassies.

Among the visitors Hunter had let in this way was Alexis Lunden Roberts, a former basketball star at Arkansas State University and current graduate student at George Washington University, who was paying her way through school by working as a stripper. Another visitor Hunter let in this way was a woman matching the description of Bicycles, who is Black.

Three days after receiving the reprimand, Hunter wrote back. "If [a Sweden House employee] has an issue with the race or dress of my visitors I think we should all sit down and discuss with an attorney present."

He described Roberts as "my youngest daughter's basketball mentor," and wrote that "she worked out with Maisy and Sasha Obama when they played in rec league together. Maisy, my daughter continues to pursue a NCAA Div. One team and Lunden continues to help." Hunter then attached a headshot of Roberts and a short bio detailing her college basketball career.

Turning to the subject of Bicycles, Hunter reiterated his charge of bigotry and his threat to call in his lawyers, appending a description of DC's local antidiscrimination laws.[739]

He mockingly suggested that a building staffer was afraid of Bicycles. "She has stayed in MY parents home," he wrote. "She has been to the White House with me and she has met my entire family."

He terminated his office lease not long after.

In the months that followed Hunter's exchange with the House of Sweden staff, Roberts became pregnant. She later sued Hunter for paternity. Hunter initially denied ever having sex with Roberts, but a paternity test established that he was in fact the father of the child. The paternity case attracted the attention of the tabloids and of Republican operatives, but it settled before it could devolve into a full-fledged campaign sideshow. Roberts gets a single sentence in Hunter's memoir, in which he writes that he challenged her paternity claims because "I had no recollection of our encounter."[740]

But the emails to the House of Sweden came in September 2017, and the child was born the following August, suggesting that, at a minimum,

Hunter's relationship with Roberts lasted a few months, rather than encompassing a single, forgotten encounter.

As a deal with Ye seemed to be reaching fruition, Jim had begun telling his contacts at Americore Health that a big influx of capital would come from Hunter's Chinese connections.[741]

But his hopes for a Chinese windfall had him on edge. While his new age nephew practiced yoga, old-school Jim managed the stress by hitting the gym. He was right to be nervous. Signs were growing that federal authorities were investigating Ye's right-hand man, Patrick Ho. That summer, Hunter has said, Ye hired him to serve as Ho's lawyer.

In November, Ho met the fate that has befallen all too many of his and Hunter's business partners. He was arrested by the feds. They charged him with violating the Foreign Corrupt Practices Act by passing bribes to high-ranking government officials in Chad and Uganda in exchange for oil rights.

When the FBI arrested him, Ho placed his first call to Jim.[742] Hudson West went on to wire Hunter's law firm, Owasco, $1 million, earmarked for Ho's representation.[743] Ho eventually got three years in prison for bribery and money laundering.[744]

Over the following winter, Ye dropped off the map. He was reportedly detained by Chinese authorities, and ceased to be seen in public.[745] Hunter's big Chinese score had gone up in smoke.

No proof has emerged that Ye and his associates intended their dealings with Hunter and Jim as anything other than normal business activity. But Ho's bribery conviction, Ye's disappearance, CEFC's reported ties to Chinese military intelligence, Sara's refusal to provide the bank with more information about the payments to Lion Hall Group, the alleged plans to cut Joe covertly into the deal, and Hunter's wayward lifestyle add up to a troubling picture. It would be reasonable to suspect that Ye and his associates intended to use their contacts with Jim and Hunter to either gather intelligence, compromise Joe or his relatives, gain influence over Joe, use their association with the family to deflect government scrutiny of their activities, or some combination of these ulterior motives. Hunter has addressed some of his interactions with CEFC in 2019 interviews with the *New Yorker* and denied wrongdoing, but neither he, Jim, Sara, nor Joe have come forward to offer full accountings of what happened.

———

By the spring of 2018, Hunter's relationship with Hallie was on the rocks, and he returned to LA. He camped out at the Chateau Marmont, a legendary old-Hollywood hotel on Sunset Boulevard. There, he cooked his own crack en suite and resumed his marathon parties with a motley crew of strippers and friends he described as "Samoan gangsters."[746]

Though he had not been implicated in the Sioux tribal bond scheme, he did figure in Archer's trial, which commenced that spring in the Southern District of New York. The presiding judge was Ronnie Abrams, an Obama nominee and a trustee at Dalton, one of the nation's most prestigious private schools.[747]

On the day the trial began, Abrams called a sidebar with the lawyers for both sides. "I also want to make a disclosure, and that is that I have met Hunter Biden," she said. "He was a couple of years behind me at Yale, and we have a mutual friend in common. I haven't seen him in years. I don't know him well at all."

Hunter's name came up repeatedly in the weeks that followed, as Archer's defense sought to cast his relationship with the vice president's son as a testament to Archer's high character. One witness testified to seeing Hunter at Burnham's offices in New York.[748]

The jury did not buy it, and it convicted Archer along with several coconspirators. Then in November 2018, Abrams overturned his conviction, saying she was not convinced of Archer's guilt. The other convictions stood.

This was great news for Archer. It turned out to be bad news for Hunter.

The prosecutors, after some grumbling about Abrams—they had not forgotten her disclosure about meeting Hunter—turned back to Archer's case. Their purpose was determining whether, and how, to appeal Abrams's ruling. But they also began to scrutinize apparently unrelated foreign payments to Hunter that had surfaced in bank records during the course of the prosecution. Prosecutors thought they showed signs of possible money laundering.

They soon learned that the investigation centered in Delaware was well ahead of them, and the higher-ups at SDNY showed little interest in the matter, so the prosecutors on the tribal bond case dropped their Hunter inquiry.

By that time, Hunter had already set off alarm bells across the federal government.

After coming across payments made by Hunter to an overseas website in the course of an ongoing investigation, the IRS criminal division began to look at whether he was paying taxes on all of his income. Wire transfers from CEFC and Burisma-related entities to entities related to Hunter had also triggered a series of Suspicious Activities Reports. Financial institutions are required to file the reports to the Financial Crimes Enforcement Network, a part of the Treasury Department, if they suspect clients might be engaging in money laundering or fraud.[749]

Hunter's and Jim's dealings with CEFC had aroused counterintelligence concerns inside the FBI, as had payments Hunter apparently made to eastern European women.

The FBI had Hunter under surveillance. Investigators were aware of his many "non–white collar" transgressions, but they remained focused on potential money laundering, FARA violations, tax violations, and counterintelligence concerns.

In the fall of 2018, when Hunter returned to Delaware, and Hallie threw out his gun, the FBI was already watching.

The timing, a few months before Joe launched his third presidential run, was not great.

Hallie was the founder and cochair of the board of directors of the Beau Biden Foundation for the Protection of Children.[750] Joe had led the Obama administration's gun control efforts in the wake of the Sandy Hook Elementary School shooting. The gun had gone missing right across the street from a high school, and there was concern that a student might have found it.

While Hunter had indicated on the purchase application that he did not use illegal drugs, he remained a crack user during this period, as his memoir later made clear. Lying on the forms is a felony, though the law is almost never enforced.

After he was called to the scene by police, Hunter said he used the gun for target practice and that he believed Hallie disposed of it because she feared he would kill himself. When a police officer asked Hunter whether the gun had been used in a crime he grew angry.

Gone were the concerns Hunter expressed about discrimination during his correspondence with the House of Sweden. As he was being questioned, two Hispanic employees of Jannsen's walked by. Hunter expressed the view that the store had a lot of "shady" people working for it. When a police officer asked Hunter whether he was referring to the two men, he responded, "Yea, prolly illegal," according to the police report.

When the officer asked Hunter whether he had called Joe about the episode before he came to Jannsen's, Hunter said, "I have never called my dad for anything."

In the hours following the incident, Secret Service agents showed up at the store where Hunter had purchased the gun. They tried and failed to get the paperwork he had filled out to make the purchase. Then the ATF got involved. But within days the gun was returned by the elderly man known to search the grocery store's trash bins for recyclables. No charges were filed, and a public spectacle was averted.[751]

Hunter escaped to Massachusetts for his ketamine therapy, flight lesson, and skiing.

When he disappeared from Newburyport the following winter, he went to Connecticut for several more weeks of binges in the company of drug dealers and prostitutes.[752]

As Joe considered a third presidential bid, the toll it would take on his relatives, especially Hunter, weighed heavily on him. It almost caused him to remain on the sidelines, but Hunter and the rest of the Bidens argued that the ordeal would be worthwhile.[753] A few weeks before the campaign launch, Jill lured Hunter back to Wilmington. When he arrived, the Bidens had gathered for an intervention. Hunter was not having it. "I don't know what else to do," Joe told him. "I'm so scared. Tell me what to do."

"Don't ever ambush me like this again," Hunter responded, storming out. Joe caught up with him in the driveway and embraced him in a bear hug. Hunter agreed to go to a nearby rehab facility. Instead, he snuck back to Los Angeles.

In Hunter's retelling of events, he flew to Los Angeles in March and remained there through May.[754] According to John Paul Mac Isaac, the owner of the Mac Shop in Wilmington, Hunter dropped off computer equipment for repair in Wilmington in April.

Either way, Hunter was in LA in May, engaging in more debauchery, when some strangers tried to chat him up poolside at his hotel. Hunter ignored them, but the next day, he engaged. Over the course of their conversation, they suggested Hunter meet their friend Melissa.

Melissa Cohen was a pretty, young, aspiring documentarian from South Africa. She spoke five languages. Hunter told her he loved her on their first date. Her eyes reminded him of Beau's. She told him she loved him, too.

They were married within a week in the presence of an officiant and the man who had introduced them. The Bidens were not there for the ceremony, or even aware that Hunter had a new girlfriend. Right before the ceremony, he called Joe, then a few weeks into his campaign, to break the news.

"Honey," Joe told him, with near infinite patience. "I knew that when you found love again, I'd get you back."

At long last, Hunter felt ready to straighten out his life for good.[755] It might have been too late.

The Plot Against the Bidens

"I'm the real whistleblower. If I get killed now, you won't get the rest of the story."

—Rudy Giuliani, phone call with author, September 2019

R udy Giuliani smelled blood.

His client, the president, was staring down a special counsel's investigation that threatened to implicate him in Russia's 2016 election interference. So Giuliani had been snooping around eastern Europe. He wanted to muddy the waters by implicating Ukraine's pro-Western government in election meddling of its own.

During the campaign, officials at Ukraine's embassy in Washington reportedly had informal contacts with a Democratic activist and with reporters digging on Trump's connections to Russia. Meanwhile, various Ukrainian actors had a hand in investigating and publicizing the so-called black ledger,[756] a handwritten accounting document that purported to show off-the-books payments to Trump's campaign chairman, Paul Manafort, from his consulting clients in Ukraine's pro-Russia Party of Regions.[757] (The black ledger helped force Manafort's ouster from his campaign post, and he later went to jail for crimes related to his work in Ukraine.) These were meager ingredients with which to gin up a narrative of Ukrainian election interference on par with the extensive, top-down operations that Putin fielded in 2016 to benefit Trump. It did not stop Giuliani, Trump, or the Russians from trying.

But when Giuliani started hearing tales about the Bidens, he sensed a new opportunity to score points for his client and to advance his own interests in Ukraine.

Like Hunter, Giuliani was going through a personal unmooring. His third wife, Judith, had filed for divorce, and he was drinking more, noticeably so. He would hold court at the Grand Havana Room, a high-end cigar bar in the Kushner-owned skyscraper at 666 Fifth Avenue in New York or stop by Shelly's, a smoke-filled cigar bar by the White House, and make off-color cracks about Hillary Clinton. His public statements had been getting sloppier, too, like when he admitted during an appearance on *Hannity* that Trump had known about his fixer Michael Cohen's hush payments to the porn star Stormy Daniels, something Trump had been trying to deny.[758]

But the former mob prosecutor still had a nose for mischief, and he sensed the making of a scandal in Hunter's activities in Ukraine. The Bidens weren't in Delaware anymore. They were in the middle of a geopolitical minefield, and their enemies knew it.

In the decades since Joe had first traveled to the Soviet Union as a young senator, the old Cold War had ended, and a new one taken shape.

The poles of this conflict were still Moscow and Washington, but instead of pitting communism against capitalism, this one pitted the liberal, democratic, cosmopolitan values espoused by the Washington establishment against a Putin regime that fancies itself the standard-bearer of Western civilization and a patriarchal form of Christianity.

Roughly speaking, the Washington establishment and its Western European allies have aligned with opposition groups inside Russia and its allies; governments on the Russian periphery that are wary of Putin; and, in some countries, civil society groups backed by the liberal financier George Soros.[759] Putin's regime has aligned with loyal oligarchs, satellite regimes, Russian organized crime bosses, and increasingly, the forces of right-wing populism emerging within the Western democracies. Underlying this ideological conflict is a good old-fashioned geopolitical one, with control of lots of natural resources at stake.

Over the past decade, flashpoints in the conflict have included corruption in Ukraine's natural gas sector, Russia's 2016 election interference, and Giuliani's quest to dig up dirt on the Bidens.

In these episodes, a relatively small group of well-connected figures kept reappearing, among them Manafort, and Dmitri Firtash, a Russia-aligned Ukrainian businessman who allegedly had ties to Semion Mogilevich, the boss of bosses of the Russian underworld, though Firtash denied this.

Joe had been a player in the Washington-Moscow conflict longer than any of them. By the time of his third presidential run, he was among the senior-most American foreign policy figures still standing, rivaling Kissinger in his longevity on the world stage.

In 2011, Joe had met with Putin, then the prime minister, at the Kremlin, to discuss NATO's deployment of missile defense systems, the central bone of contention in the conflict at that time. As Hunter's daughter Finnegan waited just outside his office door, Putin invited Joe to admire the ornate room. Joe retorted, "It's amazing what capitalism will do, isn't it?"[760]

While Joe rubbed Putin's nose in America's victory in the last cold war, it would not be long before his son risked becoming collateral damage in the new one.

The story being peddled to Giuliani was this: Joe, as vice president, had engineered the firing of Ukraine's prosecutor general, Viktor Shokin, because Shokin was investigating Burisma and Zlochevsky. Zlochevsky, who was paying Hunter lots of money, wanted Shokin gone, so Joe made it so.

Joe had in fact played a central role in forcing Ukraine's government to fire Shokin, threatening to withhold U.S. aid if he was not sacked. In 2018, he recounted the episode at an event hosted by the

Council on Foreign Relations. Joe said he told Ukraine's then president, Petro Poroshenko, "If the prosecutor is not fired, you're not getting the money."

"Well, son of a bitch," Biden related. "He got fired."

But there was a problem with the claim that Joe did this to help Hunter's benefactor. Getting rid of Shokin was consistent with U.S. policy.

Shokin was seen as standing in the way of Western anticorruption efforts. Allies like the EU and the World Bank wanted him gone, too. Part of the rap against Shokin, in fact, was that he was suspected of dragging his feet in an investigation of Zlochevsky.[761] Exactly what was going on inside Ukraine remains murky, though. A few weeks before Joe forced Shokin's ouster, the Ukrainian arm of the Russian news service Interfax reported that Shokin's office had just seized Zlochevsky's property as part of an illicit enrichment investigation.[762]

Meanwhile, Shokin's replacement, Yuriy Lutsenko, was also widely seen as corrupt himself.[763]

After Trump's election, officials in Poroshenko's government and their allies, who had chafed at the U.S. government's anticorruption efforts in their country, hoped those efforts would end. When the efforts continued, they concluded that Soros, who was among the backers of a prominent anticorruption group in Kiev, and Marie Yovanovitch, a career diplomat serving as the U.S. ambassador to Ukraine, were to blame.[764]

As Lev Parnas and Igor Fruman made inroads with Republicans in the United States, they pushed for Yovanovitch to be fired and derided her as a member of "this Soros cartel."[765] The pair facilitated Giuliani's contacts with Shokin and Lutsenko, the Ukrainian prosecutors claiming the Bidens' actions were corrupt.

Giuliani began pushing his story about the Bidens to news outlets. At the same time, he pursued his own business interests in Ukraine. This included potential consulting deals from Lutsenko and the Ukrainian government, though he has said the deals did not come to fruition.[766]

Giuliani had other collaborators, including diGenova and Toensing, the husband-and-wife legal team that had defended New County Castle executive Tom Gordon. The couple was now representing Firtash, the Ukrainian businessman. He was holed up in Vienna fighting extradition to the United States, where he faced bribery charges.

DiGenova and Toensing were also the lawyers for John Solomon, a conservative journalist. A month before Joe entered the race, Solomon began publishing a series of opinion columns for a Washington publication, the *Hill*. The columns echoed the line that Giuliani and his collaborators were pushing on the Bidens and Yovanovitch. The *Hill* later conducted a review of the columns that identified several problems, including failures to disclose relevant facts about some of his sources, like his relationship to diGenova and Toensing.[767] Solomon later left the *Hill* and continued to pursue this line of inquiry independently. He was the first to obtain documentation from the State Department showing that Blue Star Strategies had invoked Hunter's name with department officials.[768]

But Giuliani and company had the president's attention. In May, Trump recalled Yovanovitch from her post. That month, Trump also aired the corruption claim about Joe, Shokin, and Burisma in an interview with Fox News.[769]

Hunter generally kept a low profile, but in July he joined his new wife, his daughter Finnegan, and his father for a fund-raiser in Los Angeles. He also attended some of the primary debates and offered advice to his father's campaign.[770]

In late August, in response to a question from *Politico*'s Marc Caputo, Joe told a gaggle of reporters in unequivocal terms that he had nothing to do with his relatives' private dealings.

"I have never discussed, with my son or my brother or with anyone else, anything having to do with their businesses. Period," he declared. "And what I will do is the same thing we did in our administration. There will be an absolute wall between personal and private [business interests] and the government. There wasn't any hint of scandal at all when we were there. And I'm going to propose the same kind of strict, strict rules. That's why I never talked with my son or my brother or anyone else, even distant family, about their business interests. Period."[771]

That same day, *Politico* reported that Trump was holding up $250 million in military aid meant for Ukraine, causing bipartisan concern on Capitol Hill.[772]

The rest of the story soon trickled out. A whistleblower on the National Security Council revealed that Trump had pressured Ukraine's new president to publicly announce an investigation of the Bidens at the same time he was blocking the military aid.

Trump had done exactly what he was accusing Joe of doing, only with Trump, the case that he had improper motives was far more convincing. Watergate has long been cited as proof of the adage that the cover-up is often worse than the crime. Now, Ukraine-gate raised the prospect of an *investigation* that was worse than the alleged crime.

But the country's new president, Volodymyr Zelensky, did not announce an investigation. Instead, the FBI arrested Parnas and Fruman, charging them with campaign finance violations. Democrats in the House impeached Trump.

The plot against the Bidens was blowing up.

———

Giuliani was undeterred, and he continued to push his version of events. "I'm the real whistleblower," he told me in September, as Democrats moved toward impeachment. "If I get killed now, you won't get the rest of the story."

He claimed that payments to Hunter took a circuitous route through banks in Latvia and Cyprus that was indicative of money laundering.[773]

The report issued a year later by Senate Republicans detailed payments similar to the ones Giuliani described, though the report said it was unclear whether some of the payments were connected to each other,[774] as Giuliani claimed they were. Though the Republicans' report does not make this explicit, its findings were based on Suspicious Activity Reports from the Treasury Department, according to one person familiar with the internal workings of the Senate investigation and a second person who has viewed the underlying Suspicious Activity Reports. (Unbeknownst to the public at the time, at least some of the payments to Hunter described in the Senate report were among those that have attracted scrutiny from prosecutors in the Southern District of New York and investigators in Delaware. These federal authorities also suspected Hunter might have been involved in money laundering, though prosecutors in New York abandoned this line of inquiry after learning of the investigation of Hunter underway in Delaware.[775] That investigation, which has reportedly shifted away from a focus on money laundering,[776] remains ongoing as of June 2021.)

But in the fall of 2019, Giuliani said he was unable to provide documentation of his claims, which remained vague. He was long on bluster and short on hard, convincing evidence that Hunter had committed a crime, let alone that Joe was complicit in one.

News soon leaked Giuliani himself was under investigation, as prosecutors in the Southern District of New York sought to determine whether his Ukraine-related activities violated foreign lobbying laws.[777]

This did not deter Rudy, either. In December, he traveled to Ukraine, where he participated in a television program about his claims being produced by One America News, a small cable outlet with a political tilt to the right of Fox News. During the trip, he met with Andriy Derkach, a Ukrainian parliamentarian. The Treasury Department later sanctioned Derkach, saying he had "close connections with Russian intelligence services."[778] (The Office of the Director of National Intelligence went on to conclude that Putin's government had used proxies to promote "misleading or unsubstantiated allegations against President Biden," including by helping to produce the One America News documentary, in order to boost Trump's reelection effort.[779])

As Giuliani went about digging for dirt on the Bidens, Attorney General Bill Barr set up a side channel for the former New York mayor to provide Biden-related material to the U.S. attorney's office in Pittsburgh. In January, Giuliani and his lawyer, Bob Costello, traveled to Pittsburgh, where they met with the U.S. attorney there, Scott Brady.

In Delaware, Giuliani's antics were causing headaches. The preexisting investigation there was led by David Weiss, the veteran prosecutor who had been involved in Operation Newclean, overseen Chris Tigani's attempted cooperation, and taken a dim view of the Delaware Way.

Investigators in Delaware worried that Giuliani's material could taint their case. It did not help that Brady's office pressed them to take overt actions, the sorts of steps that would make the existence of the Hunter investigation public. The Justice Department has long had an informal rule against publicizing politically explosive investigations during campaign season, and Weiss's office was forced to fend off these overtures from Pittsburgh.[780]

(Also in January, FBI agents from the Pittsburgh office raided the Americore Health facility in Ellwood City, Pennsylvania, and left with boxes of documents, as part of a separate investigation of the hospital operator. Many of the allegations of malfeasance at Americore appear to be unrelated to Jim, and it is unclear whether he is a focus of that investigation, but FBI agents on the case later sought information about Jim from at least one witness.)

Meanwhile, the subject of Hunter and Burisma remained a sensitive one for Joe. While campaigning in Iowa, he snapped at a voter who accused him of sending his son to work for Burisma as a way of selling access. "You're a damn liar, man," Joe shot back. "That's not true and no one has ever said that. No one has proved that."

At the beginning of February, he placed fourth in the Iowa caucuses, a result he called a "gut punch." The next week, he came in fifth in New Hampshire. In between Iowa and New Hampshire, the Republican Senate acquitted Trump. After winning in New Hampshire, Vermont senator Bernie Sanders overtook Joe as the clear front-runner in national polls.

Regardless of whether the president's attacks had any purchase with Democratic voters, Joe's campaign was on the rocks. He had been knocked down before in life, by Neilia's car accident, the Kinnock debacle, his aneurysm, his 2007 primary flameout, and Beau's death. Each time, he had obeyed his father's admonition to *get back up*. This time, at age seventy-seven, it seemed he was finally down for the count.

Then at the end of February, he won the South Carolina primary by an overwhelming margin, thanks to strong support from Black voters. His moribund campaign snapped suddenly back to life. He received a wave of endorsements from other Democratic candidates and wrestled the nomination away from Sanders in a matter of weeks.

The Bidens were back. Val, for the first time, did not have a top position on her brother's campaign. But she remained a confidante. She, Jill, and Ashley were also in-demand surrogates. After the arrival of the novel coronavirus shut down the country and upended the campaign, Ashley's husband informally advised the campaign on pandemic response, even as StartUp Health launched a COVID-focused investment fund. Jim and Frank generally stayed away from the campaign. One union official told me they complained to a campaign advisor about a business approach from a Biden relative, and the advisor responded by saying the campaign planned to warn Jim, Frank, and Hunter not to intermingle their ventures with political activities. At one point, Joe personally admonished Frank about pursuing business dealings that could cause a scandal. "For Christ's sake," Joe reportedly told him. "Watch yourself."[781]

It was Hunter, though, with his combination of dubious business dealings and tortured personal life, who caught the imagination of Joe's antagonists on the right.

There were other knocks against Joe. At the outset of his campaign, some women said they felt Joe's habit of touching people during interpersonal interactions and otherwise invading their space made them feel uncomfortable. Joe apologized. During the primary, his vote to authorize the Iraq war and his records on race and criminal justice came under intense scrutiny. California senator Kamala Harris enjoyed a brief bump in the polls after she went after Joe for his record on busing during a debate. (Jill and Val were incensed by Harris's attack, but Joe was more ready to forgive. He went on to choose Harris as his running mate, citing a bond she had formed with Beau when both were state attorneys general.) A former Senate staffer, Tara Reade, accused Joe of sexually assaulting her in the early '90s, a charge Joe denied. Evidence came to light that Reade's mother had called into *Larry King Live* on CNN in 1993 and asked for advice about what her daughter could do, other than go to the press, to address an unspecified work issue with an unnamed senator.[782] And some people who knew Reade confirmed that in the past she had privately told them of misconduct by Joe.[783] But reporters digging into Reade's allegations found inconsistencies in them, while some people who knew her described her as unreliable.[784] The story faded away, in part because no other allegations emerged, while more than a dozen women had already accused Trump of sexual assault or other misconduct.[785]

For his part, Trump strived to paint Joe as old and "sleepy." But above all, he fixated on Hunter.

In their focus on Joe's son, Trump and Giuliani were onto something. There was a real FBI investigation into Hunter's activities. Career prosecutors in multiple U.S. attorney's offices suspected possible money laundering and had scrutinized payments similar to the ones Giuliani was attempting to raise a fuss about. But he and Trump were not credible messengers. Their parallel efforts amounted to a sloppy and compromised smear campaign.

There was also the issue of hypocrisy. The president's business dealings and personal conduct had generated their own enormous scandals, and he, unlike Hunter, was on the ballot. This did not stop Trump from indulging an instinct for assailing his opponents in deeply personal terms. So, on top of "Lock Her Up," and "Little Marco," he added a new catchphrase to the lexicon of American political insults: "Where's Hunter?"

The "Laptop from Hell"

F ive days before the vote, the millennial heirs of what Hillary Clinton once called the "vast right-wing conspiracy"—a loose confederation of Republicans dedicated to finding dirt on, and propagating negative stories about, their political enemies—gathered around a long table in Steve Bannon's Capitol Hill town house. For the past two weeks, the hottest item in American politics had been a cache of files that had allegedly come from Hunter's laptop. The group had gathered to copy the files onto thumb drives, disseminate it online, and generally bask in the Bidens' misfortune.

In the basement of the building formerly known as the "Breitbart Embassy"—it lost that moniker after Bannon parted ways with the far-right outlet in 2018—spirits were running high. Harlan Hill, a pro-Trump political consultant, regaled those present with his experience the night before at the Trump Hotel, where he had spotted Attorney General Bill Barr. Unaware that the DOJ already was investigating Hunter, Hill had approached Barr and berated him for failing to investigate Hunter.

The senior figure in the room, Jack Maxey, a cohost of Bannon's *War Room* podcast, tracked a false internet rumor that Hunter had died of a drug overdose in Los Angeles and talked excitedly of the hints of corruption he saw in the emails.

Jack Posobiec, a former Navy intelligence officer and a correspondent for the far-right One America News—which had accompanied Giuliani to Ukraine to publicize his attacks on the Bidens—was there, too.[786] For Posobiec, this scenario was a familiar one. When Emmanuel Macron's hacked emails first surfaced online on the eve of France's 2017 presidential election, he gained notice as an early and prolific disseminator of the material. He was even identified as the first person to use the hashtag #MacronLeaks on Twitter.[787] That leak, like this one, had raised suspicions of Russian hacking, though Russia's government denied any involvement.

The leak had failed to stop Macron, but to the diehards in Bannon's basement, this felt more like a repeat of 2016. Then, Trump had pulled off his improbable upset following another last-minute leak and an announcement that the FBI had reopened an investigation of Hillary Clinton's email use.

The saga of Hunter's laptop had burst into view two weeks earlier, with a front-page story in the *New York Post*. The story might have counted as an October Surprise, if something like it had not been so widely anticipated.

Memories of 2016 remained fresh. In the closing weeks of that campaign, emails stolen by Russian hackers from Clinton campaign chairman John Podesta leaked out, causing a media frenzy.

Now, Trump was trailing in the polls and hundreds of thousands of Americans had died of COVID-19. Fewer than four in ten Americans approved of his handling of the pandemic.[788] Just as he had been four years earlier, Trump was in dire need of a distraction that could shake up the race and deflect attention from the coronavirus.

He and his allies had made clear that even after impeachment, they viewed Hunter and Burisma as one of their best lines of attack against Joe. Nine months before the *Post*'s story dropped, a cybersecurity firm in California concluded that Russian military hackers had breached

Burisma's email systems, raising the prospect the intruders were fishing for dirt on the Bidens.[789] Over the summer, one think tank, the Aspen Institute, even ran a simulation of a scenario in which material from Burisma that seemed to implicate Joe and Hunter leaked in the run-up to Election Day, along with news of a grand jury investigation of the Bidens.[790]

Then, on the second Wednesday of October, the *Post* published its first story based on files that purportedly came from Hunter's laptop. They included an April 2015 email from a Burisma advisor thanking Hunter for arranging a meeting with Joe. The vague email was not exactly a bombshell. But, if it was genuine, it undermined Joe's insistent claims that he remained totally insulated from his relatives' business dealings in general and threatened to renew scrutiny of Hunter's relationship with Burisma in particular.

The story ran with several photos of the Bidens that were part of the cache, including one of Hunter with what looked like a crack pipe in his mouth. The *Post* also published a December 2019 Delaware grand jury subpoena for a laptop and a hard drive.

The article provided an account of how the emails had wound their way into the newspaper's possession: Someone had dropped off a laptop at a computer repair shop in April 2019 but never picked it up. The store owner later provided a copy of the laptop's contents to Giuliani's lawyer. Then Bannon, the former chief White House strategist, who was now working with Giuliani as an outside supporter of Trump's, told the *Post* about the cache of data. A few weeks later, the *Post* went to print.

There were plenty of reasons to be wary of the story.

The existence of a grand jury in Delaware investigating Hunter's activities was still secret at the time the story published. It was already known, on the other hand, that Giuliani's efforts to dig up Burisma-related dirt on the Bidens had led him to make contact with the alleged Russian agent Andriy Derkach. Bannon was a self-described "propagandist" who had recently been indicted for alleged fraud stemming from an unrelated scheme to crowdfund a private wall along the U.S.-Mexico border. The *Post* is owned by Trump's friend Rupert Murdoch and is a corporate cousin to the unabashedly pro-Trump Fox News.

Reporters quickly identified the repair store owner as Mac Isaac, and tracked him down at the Mac Shop in Wilmington, where he revealed that he was legally blind and so unable to positively identify his customer.[791] He said the emails were not stolen because the repair agreement stipulated that the laptop became his property when its owner did not pick it up after ninety days.[792]

The Biden campaign said that a search of Joe's official schedules showed no meetings with the Burisma advisor. Neither the campaign nor Hunter disputed the authenticity of the emails, or that Hunter had left behind a laptop at a repair shop.

Nonetheless, in the hours after the story published, Facebook took steps to prevent it from spreading on its platform. Twitter blocked it entirely, citing its policy on hacked materials and the inclusion of people's private contact information in the documents published with the article.[793] The company suspended the *Post*'s Twitter account and even prevented users from sharing links to the story in private messages. (Jack Dorsey, Twitter's cofounder and CEO, later described the platform's heavy-handed response as a "mistake" in congressional testimony.[794])

Bannon envisioned the story as the opening salvo in a barrage of embarrassing disclosures, not just about Hunter's business dealings but also about his personal life, that would continue through to Election Day. He was particularly enamored of racy images that allegedly showed Hunter and Hallie. He considered the images his "pièce de résistance," not so much for the effect they would have on voters but for the effect they would have on Joe. Bannon thought they would "break" him psychologically. He expected the *Post* to publish images from it over the weekend, but the paper never did.[795]

The next day, the *Post* did publish a story based on emails related to the abortive deal with the Chinese oil company CEFC. It included the May 2017 email from one of Hunter's business partners showing a "provisional agreement" that 10 percent of their CEFC-related venture would be "held by H for the big guy?"

But reports emerged that the FBI was investigating the emails as potential Russian disinformation[796] and that some reporters at the *Post* doubted the paper's story was solid.[797]

Meanwhile, allegations against the Bidens kept mounting.

In the wake of the *Post* story, the conservative muckraker Peter Schweizer jumped into the fray. Schweizer's allegations of malfeasance at the Clinton Foundation had been the subject of extensive controversy in 2016. He had gone on to feature the Burisma episode and other Biden family dealings in his more recent books. In the far-right outlet Breitbart News, he revealed that he had an email cache of his own. He published emails obtained from Bevan Cooney, a coconspirator in the Oglala Sioux bond scheme who had arranged from prison to give Schweizer access to his Gmail account. (Earlier that month, the Second Circuit Court of Appeals had reinstated Archer's fraud conviction in that case.) The emails purported to show associates of Hunter arranging a White House meeting for Chinese investors.[798]

Next came Tony Bobulinski, Hunter and Jim's former partner on the abortive CEFC deal, and the recipient of the "held by H for the big guy?" email published by the *Post*. On the eve of the second presidential debate, Bobulinski issued a statement saying the email was genuine, and that it did in fact refer to Hunter holding 10 percent of the equity in the venture on behalf of Joe. He also said that he had come to realize that their would-be Chinese business partners viewed the venture "as a political or influence investment."[799]

Bobulinski, a Navy veteran turned investor, had previously donated only to a couple of Democrats in federal races,[800] but now he was working with Trump-aligned operatives to publicize his claims.[801]

He said he was motivated to speak out after reading the report on Hunter's activities by Senate Republicans. His planned venture with

Hunter and Jim had sputtered out, but the report revealed that Hunter received other CEFC-related payments without his knowledge. Bobulinski said he felt betrayed by the revelation. He told the *Wall Street Journal* he also felt motivated by a desire to correct Joe's claim to have "never" discussed his relatives' business dealings.

Bobulinski recounted meeting with Jim, Hunter, and Joe in May 2017 in Los Angeles, where they discussed the CEFC venture. Bobulinski said Joe was "plainly familiar" with the venture "at least at a high level."

Bobulinski's story, about meeting with Joe and discussing the venture in broad terms, did contradict Joe's claim about never discussing his relatives' business ventures.

Rather than reiterate the blanket claim, Joe's campaign responded to Bobulinski's story with a more narrowly worded statement that "Joe Biden has never even considered being involved in business with his family, nor in any overseas business whatsoever. He has never held stock in any such business arrangements nor has any family member or any other person ever held stock for him."[802]

On October 22, Bobulinski attended the second and final presidential debate in Nashville, Tennessee, as a guest of Trump's campaign. In a statement there, he said that people involved with the CEFC deal told him that Jim and Hunter were "paranoid" about Joe's involvement being discovered, and that "it was made clear" to him never to put Joe's name in writing.[803]

This cascade of allegations was dramatic, but it was not clear if they were credible, or exactly what they amounted to if true. It was also unclear whether a focus on the dealings of Joe's relatives was an effective strategy at a time when the country remained in the throes of a deadly pandemic.

At their first debate, in late September, Trump had raised Hunter's drug use and his Navy discharge. "My son, like a lot of people at home, had a drug problem," Joe had responded. "He's overtaking it. He's fixed it. He's worked on it. And I'm proud of him. I'm proud of my son." The response won Joe praise for destigmatizing addiction.[804]

At the second debate, Trump's attacks on Hunter were difficult to follow. His knack for branding, at least, remained intact. He urged voters to have a look at "the Laptop from Hell."

In response, Joe panned the leaked emails as "a Russian plant," citing analysis by former intelligence officials. He called Giuliani a "Russian pawn."

After the debate, Bobulinski gave more interviews. He said that the last thing Joe told him outside the Milken Conference had been, "Keep an eye on my son and brother and look out for my family." He recounted a scene from a dinner in New York, in which Hunter berated one of his Chinese business partners, yelling, "You owe my family tens of millions of dollars, why haven't you paid?"[805]

He suggested to Fox News host Tucker Carlson that an extra 10 percent of equity allegedly set aside for Jim following the "for the big guy?" email represented the cut of the deal intended for Joe, but said he had no direct evidence for this. Neither Jim nor lawyers for Hunter responded to questions about the alleged plans to hold equity on behalf of Joe.

Bobulinski told the Sinclair Broadcast Group, the right-leaning operator of local news stations, that days after going public, he was interviewed for several hours by FBI agents, as part of an investigation of Hunter. Sinclair was weeks ahead of mainstream outlets in reporting on the existence of the investigation.[806]

Before the election, I asked Bobulinski for interviews and for help tracking down documents that might corroborate his claims. He emailed me his prepared public statement but did not cooperate further. After the election, I continued seeking information from him, but he expressed anger that I had not already published articles related to the claims.

Bobulinski burst onto the scene in the closing weeks of a presidential campaign, working with the Bidens' opponents to make damaging claims about them, and appeared reluctant to speak to outlets that were not right-of-center or owned by Murdoch. These are all reasons to be cautious of his accounts. But he was in fact working with Jim and Hunter on a planned venture with Ye and company. And his chief claims are not particularly outlandish: that an obvious interpretation of the "for the big guy?" email is in fact the correct one; that Joe was broadly familiar with a big business deal his son and brother were working on; that the Chinese businessmen looking to deal with Hunter and Jim were interested in currying influence with a powerful family. What is not clear is that Bobulinski's account, taken at face value, seriously implicates Joe.

———

While the allegations flew, the Bidens hunkered down. Fox News sent a news crew to Jim's new house on the Eastern Shore of Maryland, where they shouted questions about "the China deal" and "Tony B" at him. Jim, dressed casually in a quarter zip sweatshirt and a white ball cap, entered the house without offering responses.[807]

In mainstream media outlets, the reception to the leaks and allegations was skeptical and muted. The case being made was incomplete, and its messengers were too flawed. It did not help that Bannon and Giuliani initially resisted making the files widely available to journalists, a stance that did little to allay suspicions of the files or help their story gain traction.[808]

As Election Day grew near, the laptop's contents began trickling out to a wider circle. From the people working with Bannon, I obtained a large portion of the hundreds of thousands of files contained on the laptop. The cache contains emails, calendar entries, text messages, notes, and media files.

The files include sexually explicit photos and videos; an audio recording that appears to be of Hunter complaining to an unidentified woman that a *New York Times* reporter has called him to ask about his relationship with Patrick Ho, whom Hunter refers to as "the fucking spy chief of China"; emails about Hunter's taxes; correspondence from 2014 in which Hunter describes a desire to arrange high-paying legal jobs for his father and brother, in part to pay for Beau's cancer treatment; and text messages that appear to be from Joe, expressing support, such as, "Good morning my beautiful son. I miss you and love you. Dad."[809]

It also includes Hunter's correspondence with Tucker Carlson, who prominently featured the laptop story on his show. The Fox News host has mentioned on air that he and Hunter used to be neighbors, that he knew Hunter well, and considers him "a totally good guy" who happens to benefit from a corrupt system.[810]

In one email from several years ago, Carlson thanks Hunter for writing a letter to Georgetown on behalf of one of Carlson's younger relatives, around the time the relative would have been applying to college. Lawyers for Hunter did not respond to questions about the Georgetown letter. Asked to confirm the authenticity of the email—and that of another email chain in which Hunter asks Carlson for a personal favor—Carlson did not answer directly. Instead, he offered what appeared to be a series of sarcastic jabs at journalists who were quick to dismiss Hunter's laptop as fake. "Wait. Isn't this Russian disinformation? And you're falling for it?" Carlson responded via text message. "Honestly it feels like you're undermining our democracy. It does." Carlson added, "I don't want to see you become a stooge of the Kremlin."

The laptop contains texts and emails revealing the extent of problems in Hunter's personal life, including fights with Hallie and within the family about his relationship with Hallie. Much of it has already provided months of tabloid fodder.

And it contains communications related to Hunter's far-flung business ventures, which may lead to more news revelations in the months ahead. One series of emails appears to show Hunter arranging a private April 2015 dinner at Cafe Milano in Georgetown with the intention of including both his father and Vadym Pozharskyi, the Burisma advisor whose email about meeting Joe was at the heart of the initial *Post* story.[811]

The British tabloid *Daily Mail* has said that it commissioned a firm founded by forensics expert Brad Maryman, a three-decade veteran of the FBI, to examine the files. The report concluded that they "appear to be authentic."[812] When asked about this, a White House spokesman referred me to a June 2021 *Washington Post* report about the dinner. The report quoted two attendees who said that Joe did drop by the dinner but that he spoke only to Alex Karloutsos, a prominent leader in the Greek Orthodox Church, while there.

John Scott-Railton, a cybersecurity expert, cautioned me that technical analysis would likely not be adequate to authoritatively verify the files. Scott-Railton is senior researcher at the Citizen Lab, a Toronto-based initiative that is a leader in tracking state-backed hacking operations. He said the fact that the files had passed through the hands of partisans, and that manipulations by highly sophisticated nation-state actors would be extremely difficult to detect, made such analyses less useful here.[813]

But other evidence points to the conclusion that the files in the cache, which I obtained from supporters of Trump, are at least largely genuine:

- A person who corresponded with Hunter in late 2018 confirmed to me the authenticity of an email in the cache. Another person who corresponded with Hunter in January 2019 confirmed the authenticity of a different email exchange with Hunter in the cache. Both of these people spoke on the condition of anonymity, citing fears of being embroiled in a global controversy.
- A third person who had independent access to Hunter's emails confirmed to me that the emails published by the *New York Post* related to Burisma and the CEFC venture matched the substance of emails Hunter had in fact received. (This person was

not in a position to compare the published emails word-for-word to the originals.)

- The National Property Board of Sweden, part of the Swedish Finance Ministry, has released correspondence between Hunter and House of Sweden employees to me and to a Swedish newspaper, *Dagens Nyheter*, under the country's freedom of information law. Emails released by the property board match emails in the cache.

- Hunter has not publicly disputed the authenticity of any of the communications from the *Post*'s stories. He told CBS News the laptop "certainly" could be his in an interview filmed several months after the election.[814]

As for the provenance of the laptop, the story of Hunter dropping it off with a legally blind repairman, who gave it to Giuliani's lawyer before it wound its way into the press just in time to shake up the final weeks of the presidential campaign, is a wild one, but it can't be ruled out.

Hunter has sought to cast doubt on Mac Isaac's story. "It could be that I was hacked. It could be that it was the—that it was Russian intelligence," he told CBS. "It could be that it was stolen from me."[815] Indeed, it is hard to believe that the son of a prominent politician would lose track of a laptop full of sensitive material just as his father is launching a presidential campaign.

It would be premature to rule out the possibility that foreign hackers were the ultimate source of these files, or that they were tampered with in some way.

But the more banal explanation—carelessness and bad luck—is consistent with Hunter's lifestyle.

He has conceded that he does not know whether or not he dropped off the laptop at Mac Isaac's shop, while saying he does not remember doing so. "I wasn't keeping tabs on possessions very well for about a four-year period of time," he has admitted.[816]

This would not even be the only laptop that was abandoned by Hunter before winding its way into the federal government's hands. In a bizarre twist, the laptop he left behind at Keith Ablow's Newburyport office had also briefly ended up in the possession of the Trump administration. In February 2020, the DEA raided Ablow's office and a nearby pharmacy,[817] sweeping up that laptop in the process. After a few weeks of haggling, the government turned the laptop back over to Hunter, because the raid was unrelated to him.[818]

Since the election, Mac Isaac has shuttered his store and left Delaware. In December, he published a video to YouTube entitled, "The Truth—It Was Him." In the video, Mac Isaac says it was in fact Hunter who dropped off the laptop. He says he initially expressed uncertainty about the identity of his customer because he was intimidated by the onslaught of reporters and mindful that his disability would sow doubt about any eyewitness identification he made.[819]

Barring more revelations, this leaves us with Mac Isaac's version of events against Hunter's vague suggestion that something else may have happened.

A month after the election, as more evidence of the criminal investigation of Hunter trickled into public view, he acknowledged it while maintaining his innocence. He hired Chris Clark, a partner at Latham & Watkins, to defend him. A few weeks later, on his first day in office, Joe appointed another Latham partner, Nicholas McQuaid, as the acting head of DOJ's criminal division. McQuaid had worked with Clark on several cases at the firm, and under federal rules, he would need an ethics waiver to participate in the case.

When contacted by the news outlet Axios, a Justice Department spokesperson declined to directly address McQuaid and the Hunter investigation, saying only, "All department employees are governed by the department's ethics rules."[820]

Before the election, Tony Bobulinski told Tucker Carlson that back in 2017, he wondered about the political complications posed by CEFC, with its apparent ties to the Chinese government. He wanted to know how the deal they were pursuing squared with Joe's potential presidential run, when his family's relationship to a Chinese oil company would likely come under intense scrutiny. He said he asked Jim Biden: "How are you guys getting away with this?" and that Jim laughed and said, "Plausible deniability."[821] Jim did not respond to a question about this alleged comment.

The phrase fits a decades-long pattern in which Joe's relatives, in mixing business and politics, have played close enough to the line to invite scrutiny and attacks, without getting caught far enough over it to derail Joe's career.

The Bidens pride themselves on integrity, and are fond of pledging "my word as a Biden" when they really mean something. Given that pattern, the public has been left to rely on Joe's word as a Biden that his relatives have not unduly influenced him.

But the evidence marshaled in the closing weeks of the campaign built on a picture in which Joe's relatives trade regularly on their connections to him, while the separation between their private dealings and his public duties is not as far and wide as he has claimed.

The influence and exploits of family perennially figure into presidential politics. They can offer a minor sideshow, in the case of someone like Jimmy Carter's colorful, wheeling-and-dealing brother, Billy. Or they can create serious issues in an administration and a campaign, as they did in Trump's case. Part of what makes the Bidens unusual is the combination of the family's centrality to Joe's political image, the scale of their involvement in his campaigns over several decades, and the sheer number of relatives whose private dealings have intersected with his role in public life.

Another opponent might have successfully painted the Bidens as symbols of a self-dealing Washington establishment. Trump and his supporters wagered the White House on this line of attack and lost.

The plot against the Bidens didn't just fail, it probably backfired. Because Trump was so untrustworthy and Giuliani so sloppy, their efforts created the impression that there was nothing to the Hunter Biden fuss beyond a smear campaign. In a media environment primed, above all else, to counter right-wing disinformation, this proved an especially egregious miscalculation. To many voters, any questions about Hunter or the family's business dealings seemed like they must be the result of some Russian plot or QAnon-style conspiracy theory. Like the false meme claiming to show a Biden ancestor who fought for the Confederacy, the distorted claims peddled by Trump's side generated reams of debunking headlines that inoculated Joe against less sensational, but still potentially damaging, truths.

In the contest of political optics, the other image of the Biden clan won out. They were a family with relatable problems that endured tragedies, hung together no matter what, and did not put on airs. Joe's longevity in Washington proved an asset. He had earned the benefit of the doubt from a large swath of voters and the media.

In November, he vanquished Trump. A half century after entering the American political arena, the Bidens had finally arrived.

Acknowledgments

This book is indebted to the hundreds of journalists whose reporting undergirds it. It leans especially heavily on decades' worth of in-depth reporting from the *News Journal*, a reminder of the value of robust local news outlets. In addition, Jules Witcover's Biden biography and Richard Ben Cramer's *What It Takes* were invaluable resources—as were the Bidens' own memoirs, Adam Entous's profile of Hunter for the *New Yorker*, and ProPublica's investigation of Jim's finances. Celia Cohen mailed me a copy of her *Only in Delaware*, an exhaustive account of the state's recent political history. Maureen Milford gave me the lay of the land in Delaware politics. Mattias Carlsson provided me with copies of emails he obtained from Sweden's government. Many others, named and unnamed, gave me information and their time to aid my reporting.

My editor at Twelve, Sean Desmond, immediately got the concept for this book. He steered it to completion with a light touch and able hands. Matt Carlini and Matt Latimer showed me why Javelin has quickly become known as the best in the business.

Lisa Rivlin provided sharp, concise legal advice. Derek Robertson provided a thorough fact-check on a tight deadline. Any errors that might remain are my own.

Tim Alberta, Dan Alexander, Garrett Graff, Joshua Green, and Patrick McGinnis shared their book-writing wisdom with me.

Blake Hounshell, who understands the value of speed, nonetheless gave me the time to pursue my initial reporting about the Bidens for *Politico* and kept it focused. Carrie Budoff Brown and Matt Kaminski encouraged me to report without fear or favor. Peter Canellos took over the task of editing me. He has watched my back and remained a constant source of encouragement and sage advice throughout.

My *Politico* reporting benefited immensely from the many skilled, dedicated colleagues who collaborated on stories and contributed multimedia elements, editing, reporting, insights, fact-checking, and more. In no particular order they include Lily Mihalik Bhandari, Erin Aulov, Katie Ellsworth, Brooke Minters, Mary Newman, Krystal Campos, Jenny Ament, Ruairí Arrieta-Kenna, Shawna Chen, Alexandra Manzano, Annie Yu, Michelle Bloom, Zack Stanton, Emily Knapp, Steve Heuser, Mike Zapler, Marc Caputo, Tara Palmeri, Natasha Korecki, and Melissa Cooke. To anyone I forgot to list here, let me know, and I'll owe you a beer when we are all back in Rosslyn.

Countless others in the world of journalism and beyond have supported me personally and as a reporter. At a time of inflamed political passions I suspect many of them would just as soon not be thanked by name in a book that deals with sensitive subjects and ongoing controversies. I will have to find another opportunity to acknowledge more of them at a later date.

The book-writing process would have been much lonelier without Lucas, Sam, Sam, Zach, Gervase, Matt, Andy, Aram, Andrew, Daniel, Daniel, Alex, Marco, and John. And of course, thank you for everything, Hazel.

Finally, Mom, Dad, Michael, Anna, and the rest of my family keep me tethered to the much more important world that exists outside of Washington, politics, and media. And Grandma, I know it ain't law school, but I hope that a book is the next best thing.

Endnotes

1. Account of gun incident drawn from Tara Palmeri and Ben Schreckinger, "Sources: Secret Service Inserted Itself into Case of Hunter Biden's Gun," *Politico*, March 25, 2021, https://www.politico.com/news/2021/03/25/sources-secret-service-in serted-itself-into-case-of-hunter-bidens-gun-477879. The two sources familiar with the involvement of Secret Service agents were a person with firsthand knowledge and a person briefed by a Secret Service agent after the fact.
2. "Fox News' Keith Ablow: Joe Biden Showed Signs of Dementia at Vice-Presidential Debate," *Huffington Post*, Oct. 15, 2012
3. Amy Miller, " 'Final Analysis' Opens This Weekend at the Ring," Fosters.com, Aug. 3, 2019, https://www.fosters.com/news/20190803/final-analysis-opens-this -weekend-at-ring
4. Jeannè McCartin, "Theater Review: 'Crippled Inside' a Developing Play with Promise," SeaCoastOnline.com, Jan. 30, 2020, https://www.seacoastonline.com /news/20200130/theater-review-crippled-inside-developing-play-with-promise
5. Stephanie Saul, "Politics, Money, Siblings: The Ties Between Joe Biden and Valerie Biden Owens," *New York Times*, Feb. 25, 2020, https://www.nytimes .com/2020/02/25/us/politics/valerie-joe-biden-sister.html
6. Kenneth P. Vogel, "Giuliani Is Drawing Attention to Hunter Biden's Work in Romania. But There's a Problem," *New York Times*, Oct. 25, 2019, https://www.ny times.com/2019/10/25/us/politics/giuliani-hunter-biden-romania.html
7. Ben Schreckinger and Darren Samuelsohn, "Giuliani Ukraine Associate Had Checkered Past Even Before Indictment," *Politico*, Oct. 17, 2019, https://www .politico.com/news/2019/10/17/lev-parnas-giuliani-ukraine-past-049677
8. Aubrey Belford and Veronika Melkozerova, "Meet the Florida Duo Helping Giuliani Investigate for Trump in Ukraine," OCCRP, July 22, 2019, https://www .occrp.org/en/investigations/meet-the-florida-duo-helping-giuliani-dig-dirt -for-trump-in-ukraine

9. Investigators' interest in potential FARA violations and Jim's activities from an interview with a person familiar with the investigation.
10. Evan Perez and Pamela Brown, "Federal Criminal Investigation into Hunter Biden Focuses on His Business Dealings in China," CNN, Dec. 10, 2020, https://www.cnn.com/2020/12/09/politics/hunter-biden-tax-investigtation/index.html
11. Interview with a person familiar with the investigation. The payments are referenced in "Hunter Biden, Burisma, and Corruption: The Impact on U.S. Government Policy and Related Concerns," U.S. Senate Committee on Finance Majority Staff Report, pp. 78–79, https://www.hsgac.senate.gov/imo/media/doc/HSGAC_Finance_Report_FINAL.pdf
12. Biden, Hunter. *Beautiful Things.* New York: Gallery Books, 2021, pp. 207–15
13. Adam Entous, "Will Hunter Biden Jeopardize His Father's Campaign?" *New Yorker*, July 1, 2019, https://www.newyorker.com/magazine/2019/07/08/will-hunter-biden-jeopardize-his-fathers-campaign
14. Author visit, Nov. 2020
15. Biden, Joe. *Promises to Keep.* New York: Random House, paperback edition, 2008, pp. 6–7
16. Richard Ben Cramer. *What It Takes.* Open Road, pp. 469–70, Kindle
17. Cramer, pp. 468–72; *Promises to Keep*, pp. 16–17
18. Interview with Russell Preno III, Oct. 2020
19. "Vice President Joe Biden Is Inducted into the Irish America Hall of Fame," acceptance speech, March 22, 2013, Irish America, YouTube, video, https://www.youtube.com/watch?v=PTM68gtBnYA
20. John M. Broder, "Father's Tough Life an Inspiration for Biden," *New York Times*, Oct. 23, 2008, https://www.nytimes.com/2008/10/24/us/politics/24biden.html
21. Timing of Val's and Jimmy's births from Jules Witcover. *Joe Biden: A Life of Trial and Redemption.* New York: William Morrow, paperback edition, 2019, pp. 7–9; Frank's birth from Ryan Parry et al. "Meet Frank Biden," *Daily Mail*, Feb. 6, 2020, https://www.dailymail.co.uk/news/article-7961825/Meet-Frank-Biden-Joes-brother-place-inner-circle-resume-raises-questions.html
22. Cramer, p. 473
23. Valerie Biden Owens interview, *Frontline*, PBS, July 21, 2010, https://www.pbs.org/wgbh/frontline/interview/valerie-biden-owens/
24. Maureen Milford, "Owens' Reach Goes Far Beyond 'Vice Sister,'" *News Journal*, Nov. 14, 2010
25. Celia Cohen. *Only in Delaware: Politics and Politicians in the First State.* Newark, DE: Grapevine Publishing, 2002, p. 203
26. Witcover, p. 15
27. Cramer, p. 475
28. Cramer, p. 543
29. Cramer, p. 475
30. Witcover, pp. 15–16

31. Witcover, p. 13
32. Biden, Jill. *Where the Light Enters.* New York: Flatiron Books, 2019, p. 64
33. Witcover, p. 17
34. Ryan D'Agostino, "Things My Father Taught Me: An Interview with Joe and Hunter Biden," *Popular Mechanics,* June 2016, https://www.popularmechanics.com/home/a20655/things-my-father-taught-me/
35. Valerie Biden Owens interview, *Frontline*
36. Author visit to Scranton, Oct. 2020
37. *Promises to Keep*, pp. 5–6
38. Author visit to Delaware, Nov. 2020
39. Cohen, p. 203
40. *Promises to Keep*, p. 103 [Biden writes he wrote the paper when he was twelve. At Cohen, 203, she writes that Joe wrote the paper in fifth grade, citing an interview with Val. It's not clear if this episode occurred at Holy Rosary or St. Helena's.]
41. Witcover, p. 21; *Promises to Keep*, pp. 21–22
42. *Promises to Keep*, pp. 9–11
43. *Promises to Keep*, p. 14
44. Daniel Golden et al., "The Benefits of Being Joe Biden's Brother," ProPublica, Feb. 14, 2020, https://www.propublica.org/article/the-profitable-business-of-being-joe-bidens-brother
45. Valerie Biden Owens interview, *Frontline*
46. Valerie Biden Owens interview, *Frontline*
47. *Promises to Keep*, p. 22
48. See, e.g., Saul, "Politics, Money, Siblings: The Ties Between Joe Biden and Valerie Biden Owens"
49. Cramer, p. 750
50. Lois Romano, "Joe Biden and the Politics of Belief," *Washington Post,* June 9, 1987, https://www.washingtonpost.com/lifestyle/2020/11/07/joe-biden-candidate-profile-1987/
51. *Promises to Keep*, pp. 27–32
52. Witcover, p. 107
53. Lisa Rab, "Mavericks Charter Schools Don't Live Up to Big Promises," *Miami New Times,* Dec. 29, 2011, https://www.miaminewtimes.com/news/mavericks-charter-schools-dont-live-up-to-big-promises-6385627
54. Newspaper clippings from the time show he attended Mount Pleasant High, then Archmere, then Wilmington Friends School
55. See, e.g., Jeff Pocaro, "Tatnall's Veale Still Specialist," *Evening Journal,* Jan. 22, 1972, p. 21
56. Chuck Durante, "Schools Get Their Kickers," *Philadelphia Inquirer,* Oct. 19, 1975, p. 10-D
57. Milford, "Owens' Reach Goes Far Beyond 'Vice Sister'"
58. That is the alternate explanation provided in Romano, "Joe Biden and the Politics of Belief"

59. *Promises to Keep*, p. 33

60. Stephanie Gibbs, "Biden's CNY Days Showed Ambition," *Syracuse Post-Standard*, June 10, 1987, p. A1

61. D'Agostino, "Things My Father Taught Me: An Interview with Joe and Hunter Biden"

62. Romano, "Joe Biden and the Politics of Belief"

63. Gibbs, "Biden's CNY Days Showed Ambition"

64. *Promises to Keep*, p. 40

65. 2309 Woods Road, Wilmington, Delaware, https://www.google.com/maps/place/2309+Woods+Rd,+Wilmington,+DE+19808/@39.7498736,-75.6399591,2986m/data=!3m1!1e3!4m5!3m4!1s0x89c6fe0fd252b0f3:0x9f13c684027ba468!8m2!3d39.7496591!4d-75.6319242

66. *Promises to Keep*, pp. 48–49

67. *Promises to Keep*, p. 42

68. Carl P. Leubsdorf, "Lifelong Ambition Led Joe Biden to Senate, White House Aspirations," *Dallas Morning News*, 1987, republished Aug. 23, 2008, https://web.archive.org/web/20080919060037/http://www.dallasnews.com/sharedcontent/dws/news/washington/cleubsdorf/stories/082308dnpolbiden87profile.4d6e19b.html

69. Witcover, p. 59

70. *Promises to Keep*, p. 54

71. James Rubin, "Rehnquist Supporter Says Biden Lived in Home with Restrictive Deed," Associated Press, Aug. 7, 1986

72. Cohen, p. 203

73. Cohen, p. 5. She cites 1998 interviews with Biden and Roth. The dog names are also mentioned in Gibbs, "Biden's CNY Days Showed Ambition."

74. Witcover, pp. 72–73

75. Al Cartwright, "She's Got to Be Best-Looking Campaign Manager," *Evening Journal*, Nov. 6, 1972, p. 3

76. See, e.g., *Promises to Keep*, pp. 59–75

77. Norm Lockman, "Biden Cut Israel Paper to Fit Support, Ex-aide Says," *Morning News*, Nov. 2, 1972, pp. 1–2

78. Norm Lockman, "Boggs vs. Biden: A Tough Tussle," *Evening Journal*, Oct. 24, 1972, pp. 27–33

79. Broder, "Father's Tough Life an Inspiration for Biden"

80. Lockman, "Boggs vs. Biden: A Tough Tussle"

81. Witcover, pp. 67–68

82. *Promises to Keep*, p. 59

83. "Elections '72: They Say That He Is Ambitious," *Time*, Nov. 6, 1972, http://content.time.com/time/subscriber/article/0,33009,942587,00.html

84. "29-Year-Old Elected to U.S. Senate," Associated Press via *Wilkes-Barre Times Leader*, Nov. 9, 1972, p. 36

85. Kitty Kelley, "Death and the All-American Boy," *Washingtonian*, June 1974, https://www.washingtonian.com/1974/06/01/joe-biden-kitty-kelley-1974-profile-death-and-the-all-american-boy/

86. *Promises to Keep*, p. 60

87. Witcover, p. 87

88. *Promises to Keep*, p. 21

89. 2014 Equine Advocates Summit video, posted April 18, 2014, 5:10, https://www.youtube.com/watch?v=Vqn9ZOzi_AQ&feature=emb_logo

90. Robert Sam Anson, "Senator Joe Biden is Back in the Race," *Esquire*, June 1982

91. Valerie Biden Owens interview, *Frontline*

92. Cramer, p. 1084

93. Interview with Tom Stiltz, Sept. 2020

94. Witcover, p. 76

95. Brian Naylor, "Biden's Road to Senate Took Tragic Turn," *All Things Considered*, NPR, Oct. 8, 2007

96. *Promises to Keep*, pp. 66–67

97. *Promises to Keep*, p. 67

98. Witcover, pp. 82–83

99. "Ted Beats Party Drum in Delaware," *Evening Journal*, Oct. 2, 1972, pp. 1–3

100. Curtis Wilkie, "Boggs Shifts Gears, Lashes Biden for Ad on Tax Stance," *Morning News*, Oct. 18, 1972

101. *Promises to Keep*, p. 72

102. Lockman, "Biden Cut Israel Paper to Fit Support, Ex-aide Says," p. 1

103. Robert Schwabach, "Biden Doesn't Really Support Israel, Ex-aide Charges," *Philadelphia Inquirer*, Nov. 5, 1972

104. Robert Hodierne, "Papers Publishing After Two-Day Halt," *Evening Journal*, Nov. 6, 1972

105. Cohen, pp. 203–4

106. Bob Frump, "Shriver Stops in New Castle, Assails Nixon," *Evening Journal*, Nov. 6, 1972, p. 3

107. Terry Zintl and Norm Lockman, "State Elects the Youngest U.S. Senator," *Evening Journal*, Nov. 8, 1972, p. 1

108. *Where the Light Enters*, p. 39

109. Interview with Bill Stevenson, Nov. 2020

110. Anson, "Senator Joe Biden Is Back in the Race"

111. Cartwright, "She's Got to Be Best-Looking Campaign Manager"

112. "Women Senators," U.S. Senate official list, https://www.senate.gov/senators/ListofWomenSenators.htm

113. "Capitol Hill First," *Sacramento Bee*, Oct. 12, 1971, p. A2

114. Cartwright, "She's Got to Be Best-Looking Campaign Manager"

115. Lockman, "Boggs vs. Biden: A Tough Tussle"

116. "Elections '72: They Say That He Is Ambitious," *Time*

117. "The Class of '69," *Life*, June 20, 1969

118. Hillary Clinton. *What Happened*. New York: Simon & Schuster, 2017, p. 198

119. Norm Lockman, "Biden Staff Joined by Veteran Senate Aide," *Morning News*, Dec. 22, 1972, p. 2

120. *Promises to Keep*, p. 79

121. Valerie Biden Owens interview, *Frontline*

122. *Promises to Keep*, p. 79

123. Valerie Biden Owens interview, *Frontline*

124. Witcover suggests the doctor was for their physical injuries; Cramer writes that it was a "shrink"

125. Bide, Joe. *Promise Me, Dad*. New York: Flatiron Books, 2017, p. 196

126. Witcover, pp. 98–99

127. *Promises to Keep*, pp. 80–82

128. See, e.g., Natalia Alamdari, "The Story Behind the Biden Family Bible," *News Journal*, Jan. 21, 2021

129. Norm Lockman, "TV Newsman Draws Second Oath from Biden," *Morning News*, Jan. 6, 1973, p. 2

130. *Promises to Keep*, p. 80

131. *Beautiful Things*, pp. 25, 56

132. Romano, "Joe Biden and the Politics of Belief"

133. Semiannual Report of the Architect of the Capitol for Jan. 1 through June 30, 1973, Government Printing Office, Aug. 27, 1973, p. 58; Semiannual Report of the Architect of the Capitol for July 1 through Dec. 31, 1973, Government Printing Office, p. 54

134. *Promises to Keep*, p. 81

135. Norm Lockman, "Out of the Woods? Don't Know, Biden Says," *News Journal*, Jan. 4, 1974

136. See "Remarks at a St. Patrick's Day Reception," U.S. Government Publishing Office, March 15, 2016, https://www.govinfo.gov/content/pkg/DCPD-2016001 52/pdf/DCPD-201600152.pdf

137. Joe Biden interview in *Irish America* magazine, 1987, republished by IrishCentral, Oct. 12, 2020, https://www.irishcentral.com/news/joe-biden-first-irish-interview -1987

138. Witcover, p. 109

139. This account of the dinner drawn from Witcover, pp. 108–9, and "Irish History, Heritage Recited at 68th Dinner," *Scrantonian*, March 18, 1973, p. 23

140. "How Joe Biden's Irish Ancestor Saved Thousands of Lives During the Famine," National University of Ireland Maynooth, undated, https://www.may noothuniversity.ie/research/spotlight-research/how-joe-bidens-irish-ancestor -saved-thousands-lives-during-famine; Niall O'Dowd, "President Joe Biden's Irish Roots—From Fleeing Famine Ireland to Winning the White House," IrishCentral, Jan. 20, 2021, https://www.irishcentral.com/news/politics/joe-biden -irish-famine-white-house

141. " 'Friendly Sons' to Hear Biden," *Scrantonian*, Feb. 18, 1973, p. 25

142. "Hotel Casey Symbolized City's Affluence, Culture," *Scranton Times-Tribune*, Nov. 8, 2009, p. D1

143. *Promises to Keep*, pp. xiv–xv

144. Author visit, Oct. 2020

145. *Promises to Keep*, p. 44

146. *Promises to Keep*, p. xxii

147. *Promises to Keep*, pp. 32–37

148. Cohen, pp. 306–7

149. *Promises to Keep*, p. 105

150. Joe Biden interview in *Irish America* magazine, 1987

151. "Remarks to the Community in Londonderry, Northern Ireland," U.S. Government Publishing Office, Nov. 30, 1995, https://www.govinfo.gov/content/pkg/PPP-1995-book2/pdf/PPP-1995-book2-doc-pg1809.pdf

152. "U.S. Senator Joseph Biden Delivers Remarks at New America Foundation," Political Transcript Wire, Sept. 6, 2005

153. *Promises to Keep*, pp. 246–7

154. Susan Rasky, "Extradition Plan with Britain," *New York Times*, Aug. 2, 1985

155. Linda Greenhouse, "Senate Panel Accepts Revised Extradition Treaty," *New York Times*, June 13, 1986

156. "Intelligencer: Biden a Cyber Target," *Irish Voice*, Jan. 21, 2003

157. *Promises to Keep*, p. 17

158. Tom Rosentiel, "Obama's Catholic Voter Problem?" Pew Research Center, April 25, 2008, https://www.pewresearch.org/2008/04/25/obamas-catholic-voter-problem/

159. See, e.g., Ed Stoddard, "Can Biden Help Obama Woo the Catholic Vote?" Reuters, Aug. 27, 2008

160. David D. Kirkpatrick, "Abortion Issue Again Dividing Catholic Votes," *New York Times*, Sept. 16, 2008, https://www.nytimes.com/2008/09/17/us/politics/17catholics.html

161. "Bishops Renew Plea to Congress and Administration to Repair Affordable Care Act," U.S. Conference of Catholic Bishops, press release, June 28, 2012, https://www.usccb.org/news/2012/bishops-renew-plea-congress-and-administration-repair-affordable-care-act

162. Jason Horowitz, "Biden, a Catholic School 'Kid,' Praises Nuns Under Fire from the Vatican," *New York Times*, Sept. 17, 2014, https://www.nytimes.com/2014/09/18/us/politics/biden-drawing-on-his-past-expresses-common-cause-with-activist-nuns.html

163. Jason Horowitz, "Joe Biden: Digging Back into His Roots to Move Obama Forward," *Washington Post*, March 15, 2012, https://www.washingtonpost.com/politics/joe-biden-digging-back-into-his-roots-to-move-obama-forward/2012/03/14/gIQARwYBDS_story.html

164. Vice President Biden's speech at Health Datapalooza, May 9, 2016, video uploaded to Vimeo by Dave deBronkart, https://vimeo.com/165932127

165. Ben Schreckinger, "Meet the O'Bamas," *Politico Magazine*, Nov. 27, 2013, https://www.politico.com/magazine/story/2013/11/letter-from-moneygall-obama-cousin-ireland-100418

166. "Vice President Joe Biden is Inducted into the Irish America Hall of Fame," acceptance speech

167. Horowitz, "Joe Biden: Digging Back into His Roots to Move Obama Forward"

168. Account of Shiner's life drawn from John G. Sharp, "The Diary of Michael Shiner Relating to the History of the Washington Navy Yard 1813–1869," produced by the Naval History and Heritage Command, introduction, 2015, https://www.history.navy.mil/research/library/online-reading-room/title-list-alphabetically/d/diary-of-michael-shiner.html

169. See, e.g., Joe Biden interview in *Irish America*, 1987; "Vice President Biden Answers Your Family History Questions," Ancestry.com, June 27, 2016, https://www.ancestry.com/corporate/blog/vice-president-biden-answers-your-family-history-questions/

170. See, e.g., David Williams, "Protesters Tore Down a George Washington Statue and Set a Fire on Its Head," CNN, June 19, 2020, https://www.cnn.com/2020/06/19/us/portland-george-washington-statue-toppled-trnd/index.html

171. Ella Lee, "Fact Check: Joe Biden's Great-Grandfather Didn't Own Slaves, Fight for Confederacy," *USA Today*, June 29, 2020, https://www.usatoday.com/story/news/factcheck/2020/06/29/fact-check-joe-bidens-great-grandfather-did-not-own-slaves/3264488001/; Tom Kertscher, "No Evidence Joe Biden's Great-Grandfather Was Confederate Soldier, Enslaved People," Politifact, June 26, 2020, https://www.politifact.com/factchecks/2020/jun/26/viral-image/no-evidence-joe-bidens-great-grandfather-was-confe/; Dan Evon, "Did Joe Biden's Great-Grandfather Own Slaves?" Snopes, June 25, 2020, https://www.snopes.com/fact-check/joe-biden-slaves-great-grandfather/

172. Dan Evon, "Did Joe Biden's Great-Great-Great Grandfather Own a Slave?" Snopes, Aug. 24, 2020, https://www.snopes.com/fact-check/joe-biden-ancestors-own-slaves/

173. Norman Lockman, "Biden Denies Report He'll Wed Reporter," *Morning News*, March 18, 1974

174. "Reporter Couple Says Vow," *Fort Worth Star-Telegram*, Nov. 30, 1974

175. Interviews with Tom Stiltz, Sept. and Nov. 2020

176. Anson, "Senator Joe Biden Is Back in the Race"

177. Romano, "Joe Biden and the Politics of Belief"

178. *Promises to Keep*, pp. 152–3

179. Kelley, "Death and the All-American Boy"

180. "Neilia Biden Had It All and Then..." *Evening Journal*, Dec. 19, 1972, p. 3

181. Tom Phillips, "Mom Goes to Washington; She's Proud of Joey's Desk," *Scrantonian Tribune*, Sept. 1, 1974, p. 14

182. Bill Stevenson. *Stone Balloon: The Early Years*. Wilmington, DE: Cedar Tree Book, 2017, p. 77, first digital edition

183. Stevenson, p. 65

184. Stevenson, p. 54

185. *Where the Light Enters*, pp. 37–42

186. "Friends Set June 14 Rites," *Morning News*, May 22, 1972, supplement p. 14

187. *Where the Light Enters*, p. 38

188. Superior Court announcements, *Morning News*, May 13, 1975, p. 38

189. *Promises to Keep*, p. 100

190. *Where the Light Enters*, p. 45

191. Harriet Alexander, "Jill Biden's First Husband Calls Joe a Hypocrite," *Daily Mail*, Sept. 21, 2020, https://www.dailymail.co.uk/news/article-8758025/I-betrayed -Bidens-Jill-Bidens-ex-husband-says-affair-Joe.html

192. Interview with Bill Stevenson in Newark, Delaware, Nov. 2020

193. Alexander, "Jill Biden's First Husband Calls Joe a Hypocrite"

194. *Where the Light Enters*, pp. 43–47; *Promises to Keep*, pp. 100–102

195. *Where the Light Enters*, p. 49

196. *Where the Light Enters*, p. 8

197. *Where the Light Enters*, p. 19

198. *Where the Light Enters*, pp. 49–51

199. *Promises to Keep*," p. 114; *Where the Light Enters*," pp. 65–66

200. Chuck Lewis, "Rugby Tourney Set at Rehoboth," *Evening Journal*, Aug. 14, 1974, p. 25

201. Interview with Bill Stevenson, Nov. 2020

202. Stevenson, p. 38; repossession notice, *Morning News*, Nov. 26, 1977, p. 27

203. D'Agostino, "Things My Father Taught Me: An Interview with Joe and Hunter Biden"

204. Stevenson, p. 70

205. Stevenson, pp. 70, 139

206. Stevenson, p. 77

207. Jim Nicholson, "Sour Notes in Disco Loan to Senator's Kin," *Philadelphia Daily News*, June 5, 1978, p. 3

208. Ralph Moyed and Joe Trento, "Probe Fixes on Investor," *Morning News*, March 5, 1978

209. Ben Schreckinger, "Biden Inc." *Politico Magazine*, Aug. 2, 2019, https://www .politico.com/magazine/story/2019/08/02/joe-biden-investigation-hunter -brother-hedge-fund-money-2020-campaign-227407

210. "Valerie Biden, John T. Owens Wed in United Nations Chapel," *Morning News*, Oct. 18, 1975, p. 12

211. Milford, "Owens' Reach Goes Far Beyond 'Vice Sister'"

212. "Biden Backs Shapp's Bid for Presidency," *Evening Journal*, July 22, 1975, p. 1

213. Witcover, p. 126

214. Schreckinger, "Biden Inc."

215. Schreckinger, "Biden Inc."

216. Repossession notice, *Morning News*

217. *Promises to Keep*, p. 115

218. Romano, "Joe Biden and the Politics of Belief"

219. *Where the Light Enters*, pp. 60–70

220. Witcover, p. 130

221. D'Agostino, "Things My Father Taught Me: An Interview with Joe and Hunter Biden"

222. Al Cartwright, "Son Told Joe to Marry Jill," *Sunday News Journal*, July 17, 1977, p. 3

223. Al Cartwright, "Delaware," *Morning News*, July 24, 1977, p. 3

224. Nicholson, "Sour Notes in Disco Loan to Senator's Kin"

225. Richard Sandza, "Small Gifts Aid Venema Fund Drive," *Morning News*, July 13, 1978, p. 9

226. Hugh Cutler, "Baxter's New Charge Claims Junket Was a Family Affair," *Morning News*, Nov. 2, 1978, p. 12

227. Richard Sandza, "For Biden, Justice Isn't Just a Word," *Evening Journal*, Oct. 10, 1980, p. A3

228. *Where the Light Enters*, p. 88

229. Celia Cohen, "I Heard You Picket Newspapers," *Delaware Grapevine*, July 13, 2005 http://www.delawaregrapevine.com/7-05sheeran.asp

230. Interview with Charles Brandt, Dec. 2020

231. See, e.g., Julie Miller, "The Irishman: The Inconvenient Truth About the Movie's Central Confession," *Vanity Fair*, Nov. 1, 2019, https://www.vanityfair.com/hollywood/2019/11/the-irishman-true-story-frank-sheeran

232. "The Publisher of *I Heard You Paint Houses* Responds to 'The Lies of the Irishman,'" *Slate*, Aug. 16, 2019, https://slate.com/culture/2019/08/the-irishman-book-publisher-reply-bill-tonelli.html

233. Charles Brandt. *I Heard You Paint Houses*. Hanover, NH: Steerforth Press, paperback edition, 2005, pp. 223–25

234. Cohen, "I Heard You Picket Newspapers"

235. "Blast Hits Newsprint Boxcar," *Morning News*, Nov. 14, 1972

236. "Sen. Joseph R. Biden Jr. Delivers Remarks from the Senate Floor," *CQ Transcriptions*, June 26, 2007

237. "Biden Got Big Boost by Labor," *Evening Journal*, March 23, 1973, p. 26

238. *Promises to Keep*, p. 70

239. Ida Crist, "Biden Wouldn't Resign Senate Post for Carter Administration Slot," Selbyville (DE) *Delmarva News*, May 6, 1976, p. 1

240. Pat Ordovensky, "Some Political Balloons Needled," *Morning News*, April 29, 1979

241. "Thornburgh to Address Pa. AFL-CIO Convention," *Philadelphia Daily News*, June 5, 1979, p. 3-B

242. "Official Named in Indictment," United Press International, Oct. 6, 1979; "Union VP to Plead in Fraud," United Press International, Feb. 18, 1981

243. Name-change notice, *Philadelphia Daily News*, Aug. 12, 1980, p. 52

244. Paul Maryniak, "Probe Nearly Cost CLI $1M Grant in '87," *Philadelphia Daily News*, Feb. 3, 1989, p. 6

245. See, e.g., *News Journal*, March 16, 1978, p. 18

246. "The Housing Recession," *Newsweek*, Sept. 21, 1981, p. 85

247. See, e.g., *Philadelphia Inquirer*, Jan. 24, 1982, p. 180, or Dec. 11, 1981, p. 66

248. "Maier Feels Mired in Sea of Disputes," *Philadelphia Daily News*, March 26, 1981, p. 10

249. Interviews with Rich Thoma

250. Kit Konolige, "Leonard: Elections Office Overused Overtime," *Philadelphia Daily News*, April 29, 1982, p. 21

251. Maryniak, "Probe Nearly Cost CLI $1M Grant in '87"

252. Kathy Sheehan and Dan Lovely, "Probes of Job-Training Agency Urged," *Philadelphia Daily News*, Feb. 1, 1989, p. 10

253. Maryniak, "Probe Nearly Cost CLI $1M Grant in '87"

254. Paul Maryniak, "Job Programs Aren't Looking Good on Paper," *Philadelphia Daily News*, April 20, 1989, p. 5

255. Advertisement, *News Journal*, Jan. 16, 1987, p. 13

256. Robert Shogan, "Presidential Klieg Lights Test Biden's Substance," *Los Angeles Times*, Feb. 8, 1987, p. 15

257. "Divided Opinion on Facing Labor Violence," United Press International, May 1, 1984

258. Jess Bravin, "Big Political Names Drop In on Union Linked with Mob," *Chicago Tribune*, June 11, 1986

259. Tom Fiedler, "Delaware's Biden Brings Passion into Politics," *Miami Herald*, Sept. 22, 1985, p. E5

260. Anson, "Senator Joe Biden is Back in the Race"

261. Valerie Biden Owens interview, *Frontline*

262. Summary of Joe's criminal justice record from Sheryl Gay Stolberg and Astead W. Herndon, "'Lock the S.O.B.s Up': Joe Biden and the Era of Mass Incarceration," *New York Times*, June 25, 2019, https://www.nytimes.com/2019/06/25/us/joe-biden-crime-laws.html

263. Rick Shaughnessy, "Speech Writer Left in Dust of Biden Collapse," *San Diego Union-Tribune*, Sept. 24, 1987

264. Maureen Dowd, "Biden Is Facing Growing Debate on His Speeches," *New York Times*, Sept. 16, 1987

265. Walter Shapiro et al. "Getting Ready for 1988," *Newsweek*, July 30, 1984

266. Robert Shogan, "Style, Substance Pose Key Test for a Biden Candidacy," May 24, 1987

267. Romano, "Joe Biden and the Politics of Belief"

268. Robert Shogan, "Character Issue Emerging As Larger Campaign Factor," *Los Angeles Times*, May 9, 1987, p. 1. See also Shogan, "Presidential Klieg Lights Test Biden's Substance."

269. Cramer, p. 557

270. Witcover, p. 169

271. Robert Wagman, "Fund-Raising Donors Revamp Politics! Just Ask Biden," Newspaper Enterprise Association via *Scranton Times-Tribune*, Aug. 9, 1987, p. B-3

272. Golden et al. "The Benefits of Being Joe Biden's Brother"

273. Maureen Dowd, "Biden's Debate Finale: An Echo from Abroad," *New York Times*, Sept. 12, 1987

274. Witcover, p. 191

275. *Promises to Keep*, p. 189

276. E. J. Dionne, "Biden Admits Errors and Criticizes Latest Report," *New York Times*, Sept. 22, 1987

277. Dowd, "Biden Is Facing Growing Debate on His Speeches"

278. *Promises to Keep*, p. 180

279. Cramer, pp. 1126–27

280. Valerie Biden Owens interview, *Frontline*

281. Jill Biden interview, *Frontline*, PBS, Aug. 5, 2020, https://www.pbs.org/wgbh/frontline/interview/jill-biden/

282. *Promises to Keep*, pp. 185–86

283. David Hench, "Biden Says He's Not Bitter, Vows, 'I'll Be Back,'" Associated Press, Sept. 25, 1987

284. Arthur Herman, "Biden Meets Kinnock," United Press International, Jan. 12, 1988

285. Mickey Kaus et al., "Biden's Belly Flop," *Newsweek*, Sept. 28, 1987

286. Laura King, "Biden Works Steadily to Win Back Political Respectability; Hart Takes Plunge," Associated Press, Sept. 25, 1987

287. Evan Osnos. *Joe Biden: The Life, the Run, and What Matters Now*. New York: Scribner, 2020, p. 46

288. *Promises to Keep*, pp. 156–58, and p. 167

289. *Promises to Keep*, p. 232

290. Susan Rasky, "Biden Return Brings Purrs to the Senate," *New York Times*, Sept. 8, 1988

291. Witcover, p. 53

292. Witcover, p. 125

293. Cramer, pp. 444–48

294. D'Agostino, "Things My Father Taught Me: An Interview with Joe and Hunter Biden"

295. See, e.g., *Promises to Keep*, p. 89

296. *Beautiful Things*, p. 48

297. Witcover, pp. 53–54

298. *Where the Light Enters*, p. 114

299. David Kamp, "Why Joe Biden Didn't Run...And Why He's Not Ruling Out 2020," *Vanity Fair*, Oct. 25, 2017, https://www.vanityfair.com/news/2017/10/why-joe -biden-didnt-run-for-president-and-why-hes-not-ruling-out-2020

300. Lucia Blackwell, "Beau Biden Funeral: How The Day Unfolded," *News Journal*, June 6, 2015, https://www.delawareonline.com/story/news/2015/06/06/beau-bid en-funeral-saturday-wilmington-delaware/28594017/

301. *Promises to Keep*, p. 24

302. *Beautiful Things*, p. 77

303. Paul Kane, "Beau Biden, Vice President's Son, Dies at 46 of Brain Cancer," *Washington Post*, May 31, 2015, https://www.washingtonpost.com/politics/2015/05 /30/e1ac5a2a-0731-11e5-a428-c984eb077d4e_story.html

304. Interview with Charles Brandt, Dec. 2021

305. *Beautiful Things*, p. 65

306. *Beautiful Things*, p. 74

307. "River of Power" anecdote from Cramer, pp. 876–78

308. Transcript of Hearing before the Committee on Commerce, Science, and Transportation; U.S. Senate; 109th Congress; June 8, 2016; https://www.govinfo.gov /content/pkg/CHRG-109shrg65181/html/CHRG-109shrg65181.htm; *Beautiful Things*, p. 76

309. *Beautiful Things*, p. 94

310. *Beautiful Things*, pp. 142–43

311. "Biden's Son to Wed," *News Journal*, May 29, 1993, p. E4; Entous, "Will Hunter Biden Jeopardize His Father's Campaign?"

312. Described in a series of tweets by Naomi Biden, Twitter, Sept. 23, 2020, e.g., https://twitter.com/naomibiden/status/1308824006481584128

313. Sheryl Gay Stolberg and Carl Hulse, "Joe Biden Expresses Regret to Anita Hill, but She Says 'I'm Sorry' Is Not Enough," *New York Times*, April 25, 2019, https:// www.nytimes.com/2019/04/25/us/politics/joe-biden-anita-hill.html

314. Michael Kranish and Matt Viser, "After the Anita Hill Hearings in 1991, Joe Biden Began a Long Quest to Redeem Himself with Women," *Washington Post*, Aug. 2, 2020, https://www.washingtonpost.com/politics/after-the-anita-hill-hearings-in -1991-joe-biden-began-a-long-quest-to-redeem-himself-with-women/2020/07 /31/ee939b8a-9576-11ea-82b4-c8db161ff6e5_story.html

315. S.1043—Police Officers' Bill of Rights Act of 1991; 102nd Congress (1991–1992), https://www.congress.gov/bill/102nd-congress/senate-bill/1043

316. Summary of Joe's criminal justice record from Stolberg and Herndon, " 'Lock the S.O.B.s Up': Joe Biden and the Era of Mass Incarceration"

317. Franklin Foer, "Paul Manafort, American Hustler," *Atlantic*, March 2018, https:// www.theatlantic.com/magazine/archive/2018/03/paul-manafort-american -hustler/550925/

318. See, e.g., Robert Kaiser, "Citizen K Street: Conclusion," *Washington Post*, April 2007, https://web.archive.org/web/20080828172846/http://blog.washingtonpost

.com/citizen-k-street/chapters/conclusion/; Lee Drutman, "How Corporate Lobbyists Conquered American Democracy," *Atlantic*, April 20, 2015, https://www.theatlantic.com/business/archive/2015/04/how-corporate-lobbyists-conquered-american-democracy/390822/

319. Ben Schreckinger, "Lobbyist Bought Tropical Land from Biden's Brother," *Politico*, Jan. 28, 2020, https://www.politico.com/news/2020/01/28/james-biden-lobbyist-virgin-islands-099318

320. Barack Obama, "Remarks by the President in Eulogy in Honor of Beau Biden," June 6, 2015, https://obamawhitehouse.archives.gov/the-press-office/2015/06/06/remarks-president-eulogy-honor-beau-biden

321. Lacrisha Butler, "Did Biden Name Help Young Lawyer's Prospects?" *News Journal*, June 17, 1996, p. A1

322. Evan Osnos, "Will Joe Biden's History Lift Him Up or Weigh Him Down?" *New Yorker*, April 26, 2019, https://www.newyorker.com/news/daily-comment/will-joe-bidens-history-lift-him-up-or-weigh-him-down

323. Sara Biden deposition, *Caroline Biden v. David A. Staffenberg, M.D. et al.*; 0805311/2015; Supreme Court of the State of New York; County of New York; Oct. 18, 2018

324. Engagement announcements, Owensboro (KY) *Messenger-Inquirer*, July 30, 1995, p. 7F

325. Wedding announcements, Owensboro (KY) *Messenger-Inquirer*, Sept. 17, 1995, p. 9F

326. Golden et al., "The Benefits of Being Joe Biden's Brother"

327. Delaware Department of State; Division of Corporations; The Lion Hall Group L.L.C.

328. Debra Cassens Weiss, "Who Are the World's Richest Practicing Lawyers? Some on the List Went to Prison," *ABA Journal*, June 30, 2016, https://www.abajournal.com/news/article/who_are_the_worlds_richest_practicing_lawyers_some_on_the_list_went_to_pris

329. Schreckinger, "Biden Inc."

330. *Promises to Keep*, p. 290

331. Cris Barrish, "Analysis: Biden's Wealth in His House," *News Journal*, Sept. 6, 2008, p. A1

332. Lowell Bergman and Patrick McGeehan, "Expired: How a Credit King Was Cut Off," *New York Times*, March 7, 2004, https://www.nytimes.com/2004/03/07/business/expired-credit-king-was-cut-off-founder-mbna-meets-anxious-board-loses.html

333. Margaret Aitken interview, *Frontline*, PBS, July 21, 2020, https://www.pbs.org/wgbh/frontline/interview/margaret-aitken/

334. Milford, "Owens' Reach Goes Far Beyond 'Vice Sister'"

335. Valerie Biden Owens, LinkedIn profile, https://www.linkedin.com/in/valerie-biden-owens-20a80512/

336. Naomi Biden, Twitter, Sept. 23, 2020, https://twitter.com/naomibiden/status /1308824006481584128

337. *Beautiful Things*, p. 84

338. Nancy Kessler, "Biden's Son, a Lawyer, to Join MBNA," *News Journal*, Nov. 11, 1996, p. A1

339. Interview with a former Biden aide, 2020

340. Theodoric Meyer, "Inside Biden and Warren's Yearslong Feud," *Politico Magazine*, March 12, 2019, https://www.politico.com/magazine/story/2019/03/12 /biden-vs-warren-2020-democratic-primaries-bankruptcy-bill-225728

341. Christopher Drew and Mike McIntire, "Obama Aides Defend Bank's Pay to Biden Son," *New York Times*, Aug. 24, 2008, https://www.nytimes.com/2008/08/25 /us/politics/25biden.html; Bergman and McGeehan, "Expired: How a Credit King Was Cut Off"

342. Weddings, *Morning News*, Oct. 13, 1985, p. G8

343. Butler, "Did Biden Name Help Young Lawyer's Prospects?"

344. Mike Clary, "Officials Seek Source of Powder Sent to Biden's Brother," *South Florida Sun Sentinel*, Oct. 2, 2011, https://www.sun-sentinel.com/news/fl-xpm -2011-10-02-fl-biden-ocean-ridge-powder-20111002-story.html

345. Account of fatal car accident and its aftermath drawn mainly from filings in *Albano et al. v. Turton et al.*, GIN-007199, Superior Court of California, for the County of San Diego, North County Branch, filed Aug. 14, 2000; see the original complaint, the register of actions, and Plaintiffs' Motion to Default Defendant Francis W. Biden, filed July 9, 2002. See also Onell Soto, "Man Pleads Guilty in '99 Felony Hit-Run That Killed Pedestrian," *San Diego Union-Tribune*, July 15, 2000, and Onell Soto, "Hit-Run Driver Who Killed Man Gets 180 Days," *San Diego Union-Tribune*, Sept. 30, 2000.

346. Rab, "Mavericks Charter Schools Don't Live Up to Big Promises"

347. Joseph Flannery, "Preno's Legacy Passes to Smith's," *Scranton Times-Tribune*, Nov. 18, 1999, p. 10

348. Interview with Russell Preno III, Oct. 2020

349. Carl Weiser, "Delaware Delegation Is Back on Hill," *News Journal*, Sept. 13, 2001, p. 7A

350. Margaret Aitken interview, *Frontline*

351. Joseph Robinette Biden Sr. Obituary, *News Journal*, Sept. 5, 2002, p. 20, https:// www.newspapers.com/clip/54947966/obituary-for-joseph-robinette-biden/

352. "Senator's Daughter Arrested in Chicago," *Chicago Tribune*, Aug. 4, 2002, https:// www.chicagotribune.com/news/ct-xpm-2002-08-04-0208040276-story.html

353. "Biden Daughter's Charges Dropped," Associated Press, Oct. 29, 2002, https:// apnews.com/article/c9380e65cba3dc869c024db9a546984e

354. Entous, "Will Hunter Biden Jeopardize His Father's Campaign?"

355. New Castle County property records for 1002 Overbrook Road in Westover Hills

356. Interview with Charles Brandt, 2020

357. Membership disclosed in transcript of Hearing before the Committee on Commerce, Science, and Transportation, U.S. Senate, 109th Congress

358. Cris Barrish and Merritt Wallick, "Freebery, the Clubhouse, the Heiress and $2.7 Million," *News Journal*, June 27, 2004

359. *Beautiful Things*, p. 86

360. *Promise Me, Dad*, p. 21

361. *Beautiful Things*, pp. 86–88

362. Michael Kranish, "Joe Biden Let Police Groups Write His Crime Bill. Now, His Agenda Has Changed," *Washington Post*, June 8, 2020, https://www.washington post.com/politics/joe-biden-let-police-groups-write-his-crime-bill-now-his-agenda-has-changed/2020/06/08/82ab969e-a434-11ea-8681-7d471bf20207_story.html

363. "Police Union Head Named in Conspiracy Case," *New York Times*, March 27, 2001

364. "Feds Nab 120 for Fraud" CNN Money, June 14, 2000, https://money.cnn.com/2000/06/14/companies/fraud/

365. Schreckinger, "Biden Inc."

366. Golden et al., "The Benefits of Being Joe Biden's Brother"

367. Interview conducted in 2020

368. Golden et al., "The Benefits of Being Joe Biden's Brother"

369. Senate financial disclosures (no headline in original), Associated Press, June 14, 1995

370. Schreckinger, "Lobbyist Bought Tropical Land from Biden's Brother"

371. See, e.g., Thomas J. Scharf. *History of Delaware, 1609–1888*, vol. 1. Philadelphia: L. J. Richards & Co., 1888, pp. 68–81, https://babel.hathitrust.org/cgi/pt?id=coo.31924095608091&view=1up&seq=103

372. Richard Conniff, "Go Ahead, Kiss Your Cousin" in *Discover* magazine, Aug. 1, 2003, https://www.discovermagazine.com/health/go-ahead-kiss-your-cousin#.UuiJgWQo46g

373. Barbara Klaw, Review of *Blood Relations: The Rise and Fall of the duPonts of Delaware*, *American Heritage* 31:4, June–July 1980, https://www.americanheritage.com/blood-relations-rise-and-fall-du-ponts-delaware#1

374. Ruthe Stein, "3 Hours of Makeup Later, Steve Carell Becomes John du Pont for 'Foxcatcher,'" *San Francisco Chronicle* via *Seattle Times*, Nov. 18,2014, https://www.seattletimes.com/entertainment/movies/3-hours-of-makeup-later-steve-carell-becomes-john-du-pont-for-lsquofoxcatcherrsquo/

375. *Promises to Keep*, p. 4

376. Niall O'Dowd, "News Biden's Irish Roots," IrishCentral, March 13, 2009, https://www.irishcentral.com/news/news-biden-s-irish-roots-788-237601931

377. Michael Fleming, "The Irish, Du Pont and a Church by the Banks," Town Square Delaware, May 11, 2016; Joe Biden interview in *Irish America* magazine, 1987

378. See, e.g., "Joe Biden Starts Election Day with Visit to Son's Grave," WABC-TV, Nov. 3, 2020, https://abc7ny.com/joe-biden-beau-grave-visits-beaus/7611401/

379. *Promises to Keep*, p. 10
380. See, e.g., TyLisa C. Johnson, "Etched in Memory: The National Guard Occupied Wilmington for Nine Months in 1968. The City Was Never the Same," *Philadelphia Inquirer*, Dec. 7, 2018, https://www.inquirer.com/news/a/wilmington-del-riots-occupation-martin-luther-king-jr-national-guard-20181207.html
381. See, e.g., *Evening Journal*, Nov. 30, 1971
382. See, e.g., "About the News Journal Media Group," Delaware Online, https://static.delawareonline.com/aboutus/
383. Kelly, "Death and the All-American Boy"
384. Anecdote related in *Promises to Keep*, pp. 72–73
385. Witcover, p. 89. He cites the anecdote to an interview with Valerie Biden.
386. See, e.g., "History of Hotel du Pont," Historic Hotels of America, National Trust for Historic Preservation, https://www.historichotels.org/us/hotels-resorts/hotel-du-pont/history.php
387. Phillips, "Mom Goes to Washington; She's Proud of Joey's Desk"
388. Jack Nolan, "Biden Vows He Won't Be a Fence-Sitter," *Morning News*, March 27, 1972, p. 13
389. See, e.g., Norm Lockman, "Biden, at 30, Hits Ultimate Goal," *Morning News*, Nov. 9, 1972, p. 1
390. "Busing Clash Wins Biden Few Friends," *Morning News*, July 10, 1974, p. 14
391. Larry Nagengast, "Judges Order State to Submit 2 School Desegregation Plans," *Morning News*, July 13, 1974, p. 1
392. Pat Ordovensky, "Biden, Roth, Evans Visiting Carter to Plug Antibusing Bill," *Evening Journal*, June 14, 1977, p. 4
393. "Busing of Schoolchildren," Hearings Before the Committee on the Judiciary, U.S. Senate, 95th Congress 1st session, s1651, July 22, 1977, U.S. Government Printing Office, p. 251, https://babel.hathitrust.org/cgi/pt?id=uiug.30112104078842&view=1up&seq=3&q1=jungle
394. Astead W. Herndon and Sheryl Gay Stolberg, "How Joe Biden Became the Democrats' Anti-Busing Crusader," *New York Times*, July 15, 2019. See also Stuart Emmrich, "Meet the Joe Biden Whisperer, His Sister Valerie Owens," *Vogue*, Nov. 11, 2020; Kristen Heffner, "Advocating for Justice and Equality: An Interview with Ashley Biden," *New Visions for Public Affairs* 6, May 2014; Maureen Milford and Jonathan Starkey, "Remembering Beau Biden: 'An Outstanding Man,'" *New Journal*, May 31, 2015.
395. See Leslie Wayne, "How Delaware Thrives as a Corporate Tax Haven," *New York Times*, June 30, 2012, https://www.nytimes.com/2012/07/01/business/how-delaware-thrives-as-a-corporate-tax-haven.html; Alana Semuels, "Loose Tax Laws Aren't Delaware's Fault," *Atlantic*, Oct. 5, 2016, https://www.theatlantic.com/business/archive/2016/10/dont-blame-delaware/502904/
396. See, e.g., Joseph Newman, "Delaware State of the Out-of-Staters," *American Banker*, March 4, 1983

397. See, e.g., Jeff Gerth, "New York Banks Urged Delaware to Lure Bankers," *New York Times*, March 17, 1981

398. Cohen, p. 302

399. Cohen, pp. 330–31

400. "Stories About Pell's Missing Car Become Complicated," NBC 10 Providence, March 11, 2014, https://turnto10.com/archive/stories-about-pells-missing-car -become-complicated

401. Cohen, p. 337

402. "'We Owe You So Much,' Kosovo to Tell Biden as Street Named After Late Son," Reuters, Aug. 15, 2016, https://www.reuters.com/article/us-kosovo-biden-street -idUSKCN10Q17X

403. "Another Biden to Take on the Brady Bunch?" *News Journal*, Aug. 7, 2001

404. Chuck Neubauer and Tom Hamburger, "Biden Family Ties Pose Questions," *Los Angeles Times*, Aug. 28, 2008, https://www.latimes.com/archives/la-xpm-2008 -aug-28-na-biden28-story.html

405. "Brady's in Hot Seat Right Next to Schaeffer," *News Journal*, July 6, 2005

406. Cris Barrish, "The Biden Machine," *News Journal*, Nov. 30, 2009

407. Biden for Attorney General, 2006 year-end campaign finance report, filed with the office of the Delaware state election commissioner

408. "Even Republicans Question State GOP's Use of Attack Ads," *News Journal*, June 10, 2006

409. Interview with Matt Frendewey, Sept. 2020

410. *Promise Me, Dad*, p. 226

411. Cris Barrish, "Rival Says Beau Goes Where He Shouldn't," *News Journal*, Sept. 29, 2006

412. Interview with Rhett Ruggerio, Sept. 2020

413. *News Journal*, Oct. 22, 2006, p. 1B; interview with Frendewey

414. Cris Barrish, "Voters Choose Biden's 'Community' Approach," *News Journal*, Nov. 8, 2006

415. Interview with Charlie Copeland, Sept. 2020

416. See, e.g., Alamdari, "The Story Behind the Biden Family Bible"

417. Ben Schreckinger, "Delaware Beer Distributor: I Wore a Wire to Probe Biden's Fundraising," *Politico Magazine*, July 21, 2020, https://www.politico.com/news /magazine/2020/07/21/christopher-tigani-joe-biden-fundraising-373724

418. David Catanese, "Biden Exit Has Dems Bracing in Del.," *Politico*, Jan. 26, 2010, https://www.politico.com/story/2010/01/biden-exit-has-dems-bracing-in -del-031992

419. Larry Nagengast, "The Past, Present and Future of DuPont," *Delaware Today*, March 16, 2014, https://delawaretoday.com/life-style/the-past-present-and-fu ture-of-dupont/

420. Jacob M. Schlesinger, "DuPont's Up-and-Down History Shaped Biden's Views on Business," *Wall Street Journal*, Nov. 23, 2020, https://www.wsj.com/articles /duponts-up-and-down-history-shaped-bidens-views-on-business-11606157282

421. Cris Barrish, "Beau Biden Defends Handling of du Pont Heir Sex Case," *News Journal*, April 3, 2014, https://www.delawareonline.com/story/news/crime/2014/04/03/beau-biden-defends-handling-du-pont-heir-sex-case/7255629/

422. Terry Conway, "A New Vibe," *Hunt Magazine*, https://thehuntmagazine.com/feature/a-new-vibe/

423. Account of Tigani saga drawn primarily from Schreckinger, "Delaware Beer Distributor: I Wore a Wire to Probe Biden's Fundraising"

424. Joel Friedlander, "Is Delaware's 'Other Major Political Party' Really Entitled to Half of Delaware's Judiciary?" *Arizona Law Review* 58, 1140–68

425. See, e.g., Glenn Rolfe, "Burying of the Hatchet: Return Day's Post-Election Traditions Unique to Sussex County," *Delaware State News*, Nov. 7, 2016

426. See, e.g., *Wilmington Daily Commercial*, Nov. 12, 1872, p. 4

427. Ralph Moyed, column, *News Journal*, May 15, 1981, p. A14

428. Eric Ruth, "Emissions Panel Draws Challenges," *News Journal*, Dec. 18, 1991, p. B5

429. Arlette Saenz, "Biden Almost Announces He's Running for President in Delaware Speech," CNN, March 16, 2019, https://www.cnn.com/2019/03/16/politics/biden-delaware-speech/index.html

430. Melanie Mason, "Joe Biden Personifies 'the Delaware Way.' In Wilmington, That Clubby Style of Politics Is Being Questioned," *Los Angeles Times*, Feb. 23, 2020, https://www.latimes.com/politics/story/2020-02-23/presidential-candidate-joe-biden-wilmington-delaware-hometown

431. Cohen, pp. 2–3

432. Jeff Montgomery, "Appeal to Justice Paid Off for Developer," *News Journal*, July 17, 1992, p. 1

433. "Justice Indicted," *News Journal*, July 16, 1992, p. 10

434. Cohen, pp. 350–59

435. Cohen, p. 363

436. Cohen, p. 409

437. Barrish and Wallick, "Freebery, the Clubhouse, the Heiress and $2.7 Million"

438. "Delaware Man Arrested in Murder-for-Hire Killing," Associated Press, Sept. 17, 1988

439. Douglas Hanks, "Du Pont Heir's Stake in Golf Club at Issue," *News Journal*, Sept. 10, 1999

440. Barrish and Wallick, "Freebery, the Clubhouse, the Heiress and $2.7 Million"

441. "Delaware Man Arrested in Murder-for-Hire Killing"

442. Mary Allen, "Indicted," *News Journal*, May 27, 2004

443. Maureen Milford and Jeff Montgomery, "Paying to Play," *News Journal*, July 31, 2011, p. A1

444. Maureen Milford and Cori Anne Natoli, "Prominent Property for Sale in Three Parts," *News Journal*, April 8, 2012, p. A1

445. Bob Yearick, "The Trials of Chris Tigani," *Delaware Today*, Dec. 7, 2010, https://delawaretoday.com/life-style/the-trials-of-chris-tigani/

446. Maureen Milford "Friendly Deal for Mansion, Jet Turns Messy," *News Journal,* April 19, 2008, p. A2

447. Ginger Gibson and Maureen Milford, "Minner '07 Flight Paid For by Liquor Distributor," *News Journal,* April 30, 2010

448. *Where the Light Enters,* pp. 149–50

449. *Promises to Keep,* pp. 355-59

450. *Where the Light Enters,* p. 151

451. Golden et al., "The Benefits of Being Joe Biden's Brother"

452. Interview with a former Biden aide, summer 2020

453. Xuan Thai and Ted Barrett, "Biden's Description of Obama Draws Scrutiny," CNN, Feb. 9, 2007, https://www.cnn.com/2007/POLITICS/01/31/biden.obama/

454. Golden et al., "The Benefits of Being Joe Biden's Brother"

455. Witcover, pp. 376–77

456. Schreckinger, "Delaware Beer Distributor: I Wore a Wire to Probe Biden's Fundraising"

457. Joseph Toner obituary, *News Journal,* April 9, 2006, https://www.legacy.com/obituaries/delawareonline/obituary.aspx?n=joseph-toner&pid=145753118; see also newspaper coverage of the council from 1971

458. Nov. 2007 Biden campaign emails provided by Tigani

459. "Biden's Campaign Manager Talks Strategy," *All Things Considered,* NPR, Oct. 22, 2007, https://www.npr.org/templates/story/story.php?storyId=15528730

460. Patt Johnson, "Bistro Montage Helped Expand Des Moines' Palate," *Des Moines Register,* Dec. 12, 2016, https://www.desmoinesregister.com/story/money/business/2016/12/12/bistro-montage-closing-enosh-kelley/95330320/

461. Witcover, p. 390

462. *Where the Light Enters,* p. 61

463. *Where the Light Enters,* pp. 154–56

464. Glenn Thrush, "Obama and Biden's Relationship Looks Rosy. It Wasn't Always That Simple," *New York Times,* Aug. 16, 2019, https://www.nytimes.com/2019/08/16/us/politics/biden-obama-history.html

465. "Family Affair—Senate," report, Citizens for Responsibility and Ethics in Washington, 2008, https://s3.amazonaws.com/storage.citizensforethics.org/wp-content/uploads/2016/07/20021533/Family%20Affair%20-%20Full%20Report.pdf

466. *Where the Light Enters,* pp. 156–57

467. *Promise Me, Dad,* p. 63

468. Thrush, "Obama and Biden's Relationship Looks Rosy"

469. "Sen. Biden's Delaying Tactics Shortchange Court Without a Judge," *News Journal,* July 24, 2008

470. Ron Williams, "What Really Sunk Connolly's District Court Nomination," *News Journal,* June 6, 2010

471. *Where the Light Enters,* pp. 158–61

472. Petrusia Sawchak, "Philadelphia Center Recognizes Philanthropist John Hynansky," *Ukrainian Weekly*, March 25, 2001, p. 8, https://www.scribd.com/fullscreen/12842854?access_key=key-2iab08r8h2r2n3ul1wt

473. Ben Schreckinger, "Donor with Deep Ukraine Ties Lent $500,000 to Biden's Brother," *Politico*, Aug. 15, 2019, https://www.politico.com/story/2019/08/15/james-biden-bungalow-ukraine-donor-1463645

474. See, e.g., Maureen Milford, "Battle over $5 Million Chateau Country Estate Ends for Tigani," *News Journal*, April 10, 2015, https://www.delawareonline.com/story/news/local/2015/04/10/battle-million-chateau-country-estate-ends-tigani/25601795/

475. Maureen Milford and Jeff Montgomery, "Veasey's Ties Stir Up More Debate," *News Journal*, July 31, 2011

476. Maureen Milford, "Tigani Avoids Added Jail Time," *News Journal*, May 8, 2013

477. Norman Veasey, "Report of Independent Counsel on Investigation of Violations of Delaware Campaign Finance and Related State Laws," Dec. 28, 2013

478. Joseph Distefano, "Del. Plan for Market in Stocks Falls Short," *Philadelphia Inquirer*, Nov. 5, 2018

479. Xerxes Wilson and Margie Fishman, "Attorney: Stock Exchange Loan Is Unlawful," *News Journal*, April 1, 2016

480. Randall Chase, "Judge Tosses Defamation Suit Filed by Former Biden Aide," Associated Press, Oct. 2, 2020

481. "Improve On-Premise Security," *Bar Business Magazine*, Oct. 15, 2009, https://www.barbizmag.com/news/improve-on-premise-security/

482. Schreckinger, "Biden Inc."; interviews with the chief compliance officer, summer 2019 and Nov. 2020

483. Valerie Biden Owens interview, *Frontline*

484. *Promises to Keep*, pp. 85, 129

485. *Promises to Keep*, pp. 83–84

486. *Promises to Keep*, p. 81

487. Norm Lockman, "Biden Aims High in New Committee Scramble," *Morning News*, Jan. 6, 1975, p. 2

488. Martha Angle, "A Back-Row Senator Is Heard on the Hill," originally published in the *Washington Star*, reprinted in the *Chicago Tribune*, Oct. 19, 1975

489. *Promises to Keep*, pp. 143–45

490. Mariah Blake, "The Fall of the House of Moon," *New Republic*, Nov. 12, 2013, https://newrepublic.com/article/115512/unification-church-profile-fall-house-moon

491. Schreckinger, "Biden Inc."

492. Entous, "Will Hunter Biden Jeopardize His Father's Campaign?"

493. Blake, "The Fall of the House of Moon"

494. Provini began the job in January 2007, per the complaint in *Provini v. Paradigm Global Advisors*, filed in United States District Court, District of New Jersey, June 12, 2008

495. Interview with Chuck Provini, July 2020

496. Stipulation of dismissal with prejudice in *Provini v. Paradigm Global Advisors,* United States District Court, District of New Jersey, Dec. 12, 2008

497. See, e.g., Foer, "Paul Manafort, American Hustler," *Atlantic,* March 2018

498. "Biden's Career Provides Grist for McCain's Mill," Associated Press via NBC News, Aug. 24, 2008, https://www.nbcnews.com/id/wbna26367811#.XRpG94hKg2x

499. Entous, "Will Hunter Biden Jeopardize His Father's Campaign?"; property records pulled from Nexis; a Redfin listing for the house, https://www.redfin .com/DC/Washington/4829-Loughboro-Rd-NW-20016/home/9946830

500. *Beautiful Things,* pp. 84–85

501. *Beautiful Things,* p. 201

502. Sen. Joseph Biden interview, *Squawk Box,* CNBC, Sept. 16, 2008, via Federal News Service

503. Matthew Barakat, " 'Cowboy' Mentality Must Go, Biden Says of Financial Crisis," Associated Press, Sept. 20, 2008

504. John Nichols, "Inaugural Matters: Baldwin's Co-chair Gig Is a (Sort of) Antidote to Rick Warren," Madison.com, Jan. 19, 2009, https://madison.com/news/inau gural-matters-baldwin-s-co-chair-gig-is-a-sort/article_8d074534-474e-5de8 -873c-e0ba5b2a371e.html

505. Esteban Parra, "Beau Biden Back from Iraq for Swearing-In," *News Journal,* Jan. 16, 2009

506. "Biden Worships at Church JFK Attended," Associated Press via NBC News, Jan. 18, 2009, https://www.nbcnews.com/id/wbna28721302

507. Morgan Winsor, "2009 vs. 2017: Comparing Trump's and Obama's Inauguration Crowds," ABC News, Jan. 25, 2017, https://abcnews.go.com/Politics/2009 -2017-comparing-trumps-obamas-inauguration-crowds/story?id=44927217

508. See, e.g., Jill Serjeant, "Michelle Obama Picks Yellow for Inauguration Dress," Reuters, Jan. 20, 2009, https://www.reuters.com/article/us-obama-fashion/mich elle-obama-picks-yellow-for-inauguration-dress-idUSTRE50J7ZA20090120

509. Tracey Lomrantz Lester, "Guess What Jill Biden and Miley Cyrus Have in Common?" *Glamour,* Jan. 21, 2009, https://www.glamour.com/story/who-wore-it -better-jill-biden

510. Schreckinger "Biden Inc."

511. Susan Schmidt et al., "Stanford Had Links to a Fund Run by Bidens," *Wall Street Journal,* Feb. 24, 2009, https://www.wsj.com/articles/SB123543815326954907

512. Schreckinger, "Biden, Inc."

513. See, e.g., "Sen. Biden Files Financial Disclosure Forms," Associated Press, June 11, 1999

514. Kenneth P. Vogel, "Biden Carries Big Debt," *Politico,* May 15, 2009, https://www .politico.com/story/2009/05/biden-carries-big-debt-022580

515. Walter Roche, "Vice President Biden Able to Collect $180,000 in Pension Benefits," *Pittsburgh Tribune-Review,* April 23, 2009, https://archive.triblive.com /news/vice-president-biden-able-to-collect-180000-in-pension-benefits/

516. For descriptions of the Naval Observatory, see, e.g., Derrick Bryson Taylor, "Do You Know Where the Vice President Lives?" *New York Times*, Jan. 22, 2021, https://www.nytimes.com/2021/01/20/us/politics/naval-observatory-vice-president.html; and Jura Koncius, "As the Bidens Pack Up, a Look at Their Mark on the Vice President's Residence," *Washington Post*, Jan. 11, 2017, https://www.washingtonpost.com/lifestyle/as-the-bidens-pack-up-a-look-at-their-mark-on-the-vice-presidents-residence/2017/01/11/7ec556c8-d37c-11e6-945a-76f69a399dd5_story.html

517. See *Where the Light Enters*, p. 146

518. Rachel Kipp, "A New Life, But She's Still Jill," *News Journal*, May 3, 2009

519. See, e.g., Matthew Stabley, "Biden May Need New Bunker," NBC 4 Washington, May 18, 2009, https://www.nbcwashington.com/news/local/biden-may-need-new-bunker/1875436/; and Mark Silva, "VP Bunker Exposed—Sort Of," *Chicago Tribune*, May 19, 2009, https://www.chicagotribune.com/news/ct-xpm-2009-05-19-0905180391-story.html

520. Katie Glueck and Steve Eder, "Why Jill Biden Is Taking Time Off to Help Her Husband Get a Job," *New York Times*, Feb. 1, 2020, updated Jan. 20, 2021, https://www.nytimes.com/2020/02/01/us/politics/joe-jill-biden-2020.html

521. *Where the Light Enters*, pp. 112–13

522. Kipp, "A New Life, But She's Still Jill"

523. Ronald Kessler. *The First Family Detail*. Crown Forum, 2014, pp. 6–13, Kindle

524. *Where the Light Enters*, p. 56

525. Andrew Malcolm, "Joe Biden Update: He's Now Charging the Secret Service Rent for a Cottage to Protect Him," *Los Angeles Times*, Aug. 2, 2011, https://latimesblogs.latimes.com/washington/2011/08/joe-biden-update-hes-charging-secret-service-rent-for-cottage-to-protect-him.html

526. Jodi Kantor. *The Obamas*. New York: Back Bay Books, updated paperback edition, Jan. 2017, p. 48

527. Executive branch personnel Public Financial Disclosure Reports for Vice President Joseph Biden—see 2011 disclosure: https://obamawhitehouse.archives.gov/sites/default/files/biden_278_cy_2011_final_-_scanned_pdf_oge_certified.pdf; and 2014 disclosure: https://obamawhitehouse.archives.gov/sites/default/files/docs/oge_278_cy_2014_biden.pdf

528. *Promise Me, Dad*, pp. 57–59

529. "Obama's Prime-Time Press Briefing," transcript via Federal News Service, *New York Times*, Feb. 9, 2009, https://www.nytimes.com/2009/02/09/us/politics/09text-obama.html; "2/9/09: Presidential Press Conference," YouTube, video, around 43:00, https://www.youtube.com/watch?v=XuqK_-nKccM

530. Entous, "Will Hunter Biden Jeopardize His Father's Campaign?"

531. Stephanie Toone, "President Biden Alludes to Not Being Invited to White House 'Residence' as Vice President," *Atlanta Journal-Constitution*, Feb. 24, 2021, https://www.ajc.com/news/president-biden-alludes-to-not-being-invited-to-white-house-residence-as-vice-president/RM3ARK7WEFD3ZPUYE3AFBXYD3Q/

532. Amie Parnes, "The Bidens' 'Regular' Lives," *Politico*, June 28, 2011, https://www
    .politico.com/story/2011/06/the-bidens-regular-lives-057887

533. Philip Bump, "Robert Gates Thinks Joe Biden Hasn't Stopped Being Wrong for
    40 Years," *Atlantic*, Jan. 7, 2014, https://www.theatlantic.com/politics/archive
    /2014/01/robert-gates-thinks-joe-biden-hasnt-stopped-being-wrong-40
    -years/356785/

534. *Promise Me, Dad*, pp. 91–92

535. *Promise Me, Dad*, p. 108

536. *Where the Light Enters*, pp. 164–65

537. *Where the Light Enters*, pp. 136–37

538. District of Columbia corporate registration, Aug. 12, 2008

539. See lobbying disclosures for Hunter Biden and Eric Schwerin in the database
    maintained at https://lda.senate.gov/system/public/. Clients include Regis Uni-
    versity and Achaogen.

540. Aime Williams et al., "Hunter Biden's Web of Interests," *Financial Times*, Oct. 9, 2019

541. Interview with a person familiar with the encounter, 2021

542. Interview with a person familiar with the arrangement, 2021

543. Delaware corporate registration database, registered May 28, 2013

544. Interview with the Navy officer, 2020

545. Colleen McCain Nelson and Julian E. Barnes, "Biden's Son Hunter Discharged
    from Navy Reserve after Failing Cocaine Test," *Wall Street Journal*, Oct. 16, 2014,
    https://www.wsj.com/articles/bidens-son-hunter-discharged-from-navy-reserve
    -after-failing-cocaine-test-1413499657; Entous, "Will Hunter Biden Jeopardize
    His Father's Campaign?"

546. *Beautiful Things*, p. 156

547. Chao Deng, "Bohai, Harvest and U.S. Investment Firms Expand Target for Out-
    bound Fund," *Wall Street Journal*, July 10, 2014, https://www.wsj.com/articles
    /bohai-harvest-and-u-s-investment-firms-expand-target-for-outbound-fund
    -1404956572

548. Entous, "Will Hunter Biden Jeopardize His Father's Campaign?"

549. "Explainer: Trump's Claims and Hunter Biden's Dealings in China," Reuters,
    Oct. 3, 2019, https://www.reuters.com/article/us-usa-trump-whistleblower-hun
    terbiden-c/explainer-trumps-claims-and-hunter-bidens-dealings-in-china-id
    USKBN1WI2HK

550. "BHR and AVIC Auto Acquire Henniges Automotive," BHR, press release,
    Sept. 15, 2015, https://www.prnewswire.com/news-releases/bhr-and-avic-auto
    -acquire-henniges-automotive-300143072.html

551. "CFIUS Scorecard: US-China Transactions, Jan 2014–September 2018," report
    by Pillsbury Winthrop Shaw Pittman LLP, https://www.pillsburylaw.com
    /images/content/1/1/119897.pdf

552. "Ashley Biden Ties the Knot in Vera Wang," *Washingtonian Magazine*, June 4, 2012,
    https://www.washingtonian.com/2012/06/04/ashley-biden-ties-the-knot-in
    -vera-wang/; *Beautiful Things*, p. 40

553. See, e.g., "Philadelphia Browlift Surgeon Dr. Howard Krein Discusses Browlift Facial Rejuvenation in New Video," SB Wire, press release, July 1, 2013, http://www.sbwire.com/press-releases/philadelphia-browlift-surgeon-dr-howard-krein-discusses-browlift-facial-rejuvenation-in-new-video-275170.htm; and Krein's directory listing at Thomas Jefferson University, https://www.jefferson.edu/university/jmc/departments/otolaryngology/faculty/krein.html

554. "Health Seekers Get Their Own Social Networking Site," OrganizedWisdom, press release, Oct. 3, 2006, https://www.globenewswire.com/news-release/2006/10/03/348976/106107/en/Health-Seekers-Get-Their-Own-Social-Networking-Site.html

555. John George, "StartUp Health: 'We Want the Best of the Best,'" *Philadelphia Business Journal*, Aug. 21, 2015, via Philadelphia Impact, https://philadelphiapact.com/startup-health-we-want-the-best-of-the-best/

556. Ben Schreckinger, "Biden's Son-in-Law Advises Campaign on Pandemic While Investing in Covid-19 Startups," *Politico*, Oct. 13, 2020, https://www.politico.com/news/2020/10/13/howard-krein-covid-startups-biden-429123

557. "Ashley Biden and Howard Krein," wedding announcement, *New York Times*, June 3, 2012, https://www.nytimes.com/2012/06/03/fashion/weddings/ashley-biden-howard-krein-wedding.html

558. Jim Biden deposition, *Biden v. Staffenberg*

559. Kevin O'Connor alumnus profile, New York Institute of Technology, https://www.nyit.edu/box/profiles/kevin_oconnor

560. Sara Biden deposition, *Biden v. Staffenberg*

561. Caroline Biden deposition, *Biden v. Staffenberg*

562. Shayna Jacobs, "Former Vice President Joe Biden's Niece Evades Jail After Pleading Guilty in $110G Credit Card Scam," New York *Daily News*, June 9, 2017, https://www.nydailynews.com/new-york/manhattan/joe-biden-niece-pleads-guilty-110g-credit-card-scam-article-1.3235665

563. Listing accessed on Realtor.com, address withheld

564. See Ulster County, New York, property records

565. Alyson Krueger, "Jamie Biden: A D.J. Related to a V.P.," *New York Times*, July 16, 2014, https://www.nytimes.com/2014/07/17/fashion/jamie-biden-a-dj-related-to-vp-Joseph-R-Biden-Jr.html

566. Beatrice Thomas, "US Construction Firm Admits Mistake over Iraq Investment," *Arabian Business*, Feb. 24, 2014, https://www.arabianbusiness.com/us-construction-firm-admits-mistake-over-iraq-investment-540113.html

567. "Hill International Names Four Executives to Lead New Subsidiary HillStone International," CNN Money, Sept. 24, 2010, https://money.cnn.com/news/newsfeeds/articles/globenewswire/202295.htm

568. See, e.g., "Patrick-Justice," wedding announcement, *News Journal*, July 21, 1991, p. G4

569. White House visitors log records Justice and Prolow visiting on Nov. 4, 2010. Hill announced Jim's role in a press release on Nov. 23, 2010. See "James B.

Biden Joins Hill International Subsidiary as Executive Vice President," Globe-Newswire, Nov. 23, 2010, https://www.globenewswire.com/news-release/2010 /11/23/434923/207583/en/James-B-Biden-Joins-Hill-International-Subsidiary -as-Executive-Vice-President.html.

570. Joseph DiStefano, "NJ Firm up 55% on Iraq Contract to House 1 Million+," *Philly Deals* (blog), *Philadelphia Inquirer*, June 2, 2011; "Libya Plans Network of 25 Universities," MEED, https://www.meed.com/libya-plans-network-of-25-univer sities/#:~:text=The%20US'%20Hill%20International%20was,such%20project %20in%20the%20world

571. "Hill International Recoups $10mn of Libyan Debt," *Construction Week*, March 12, 2014, https://www.constructionweekonline.com/article-27057-hill-international -recoups-10mn-of-libyan-debt

572. "Stately Fashion: Outfits from the State Dinner," CBS News, Oct. 14, 2011, https:// www.cbsnews.com/pictures/stately-fashion-outfits-from-the-state-dinner/21/

573. "Hill Wins Two Saudi Contracts," *Building*, March 9, 2012, https://www.build ing.co.uk/news/hill-wins-two-saudi-contracts/5033343.article

574. "Hill International Wins Jeddah Airport PM Contract," *Construction Week*, July 22, 2012, https://www.constructionweekonline.com/article-17752-hill-inter national-wins-jeddah-airport-pm-contract

575. "Hill to Manage Construction of Saudi Medical Cities," *Trade Arabia*, Oct. 10, 2012 http://www.tradearabia.com/news/CONS_223555.html

576. Charlie Gasparino, "The Ties That Biden," Fox Business, Oct. 22, 2012, https:// www.foxbusiness.com/politics/the-ties-that-biden

577. Gasparino, "The Ties That Biden"

578. Jennifer Beeson, "Biden Family's Keewaydin Vacation Home Sold for $1.35 Million to Local Architects," *Naples Daily News*, June 27, 2018, https://www .naplesnews.com/story/money/real-estate/2018/06/27/biden-familys-keeway din-vacation-home-sells-1-35-m-architecture-firm-naples-buyer-florida /698194002/

579. Entous, "Will Hunter Biden Jeopardize His Father's Campaign?"

580. Max Seddon, "Biden's Son, Polish Ex-president Quietly Sign On to Ukrainian Gas Company," *BuzzFeed*, May 13, 2014, https://www.buzzfeednews.com/article /maxseddon/bidens-son-polish-ex-president-quietly-sign-on-to-ukrainian

581. *Beautiful Things*, p. 138

582. "Hunter Biden, Burisma, and Corruption: The Impact on U.S. Government Pol-icy and Related Concerns," p. 24

583. Adam Taylor, "Hunter Biden's New Job at a Ukrainian Gas Company Is a Problem for U.S. Soft Power," *Washington Post*, May 14, 2014, https://www.washington post.com/news/worldviews/wp/2014/05/14/hunter-bidens-new-job-at-a-ukrai nian-gas-company-is-a-problem-for-u-s-soft-power/

584. Entous, "Will Hunter Biden Jeopardize His Father's Campaign?"

585. *Beautiful Things*, p. 131

586. Paul Sonne et al., "The Gas Tycoon and the Vice President's Son: The Story of Hunter Biden's Foray into Ukraine," *Washington Post*, Sept. 28, 2019, https://www.washingtonpost.com/world/national-security/the-gas-tycoon-and-the-vice-presidents-son-the-story-of-hunter-bidens-foray-in-ukraine/2019/09/28/1aadff70-dfd9-11e9-8fd3-d943b4ed57e0_story.html

587. Registration for 1018 PL LLC filed with Delaware Division of Corporations, accessed at https://icis.corp.delaware.gov/ecorp/entitysearch/namesearch.aspx; primary residence mortgage filed with Montgomery County, Penn., recorder of deeds

588. Ben Schreckinger, "Donor with Ukraine Ties Helped Biden's Brother with Florida Vacation Home," *Politico*, Aug. 15, 2019, https://www.politico.com/states/florida/story/2019/08/15/donor-with-ukraine-ties-helped-bidens-brother-with-florida-vacation-home-1144215

589. Joseph N. DiStefano, "Joe Biden's Friends and Backers Come Out on Top—At the Expense of the Middle Class," *Nation*, Nov. 7, 2019, https://www.thenation.com/article/archive/biden-delaware-way-graft/

590. Overview of loan published by U.S. International Finance Corporation (OPIC's successor organization), "Public Summary—LLC Winner Imports Ukraine, Ltd," https://www.dfc.gov/sites/default/files/2019-08/072612-llcwinterimports.pdf

591. Schreckinger, "Donor with Ukraine Ties Helped Biden's Brother with Florida Vacation Home"

592. "Remarks by Vice President Joe Biden to the Ukrainian Rada," as published by the White House, Dec. 9, 2015, https://obamawhitehouse.archives.gov/the-press-office/2015/12/09/remarks-vice-president-joe-biden-ukrainian-rada

593. Email cited in "Hunter Biden, Burisma, and Corruption: The Impact on U.S. Government Policy and Related Concerns," p. 23

594. Jessica Donati, "Firm Hired by Ukraine's Burisma Tried to Use Hunter Biden as Leverage, Documents Show," *Wall Street Journal*, Nov. 5, 2019, https://www.wsj.com/articles/firm-hired-by-ukraines-burisma-tried-to-use-hunter-biden-as-leverage-documents-show-11573009615

595. Search of the FARA database; Karen Tramontano interview with Homeland Security and Finance committees; Aug. 28, 2020, pp. 133–34, https://www.hsgac.senate.gov/imo/media/doc/2020-08-28-Tramontano%20Interview%20with%20Exhibits.pdf

596. Ashley Parker, "Biden Relies on His Closest Adviser, His Sister," *New York Times*, Oct. 1, 2008, https://www.nytimes.com/2008/10/02/us/politics/02valerie.html

597. Jeanne Marie Laskas, "Have You Heard the One About President Joe Biden?" *GQ*, July 18, 2003, https://www.gq.com/story/joe-biden-presidential-campaign-2016-2013

598. Byron Tau and Tarini Parti, "Gibbs, Messina, Plouffe's Energy Trip," *Politico*, May 30, 2013, https://www.politico.com/story/2013/05/robert-gibbs-jim-messina-david-plouffe-azerbaijan-trip-092054

599. Scott Higham et al., "10 Members of Congress Took Trip Secretly Funded by Foreign Government," *Washington Post*, May 13, 2015, https://www.washingtonpost.com/investigations/10-members-of-congress-took-trip-secretly-funded-by-foreign-government/2015/05/13/76b55332-f720-11e4-9030-b4732caefe81_story.html

600. "President Obama Announces More Key Administration Posts," White House, press release, Sept. 13, 2016, https://obamawhitehouse.archives.gov/the-press-office/2016/09/13/president-obama-announces-more-key-administration-posts

601. Casey (Owens) Castello, LinkedIn profile, https://www.linkedin.com/in/casey-owens-castello-90540b1/

602. See, e.g., Ryanne Persinger, "Blacks and Sugar-Sweetened Drinks," *Philadelphia Tribune*, March 26, 2016, https://www.phillytrib.com/news/blacks-and-sugar-sweetened-drinks/article_38c4b875-9277-5176-bad1-d5dc63d27500.html

603. See, e.g., "Remarks by First Lady Michelle Obama at the Let's Move Launch," Federal News Service, Feb. 9, 2010

604. Mark Bittman, "Soda: A Sin We Sip Instead of Smoke?" *New York Times*, Feb. 13, 2010, https://www.nytimes.com/2010/02/14/weekinreview/14bittman.html

605. Nancy Benac, "First Lady Applauds NYC Plan to Ban Sugary Drinks," Associated Press via Yahoo! News, June 5, 2012, https://news.yahoo.com/first-lady-applauds-nyc-plan-ban-sugary-drinks-185334720.html

606. White House visitor logs show Missy entered the White House around 9 a.m. and left around 11:30 a.m.

607. Email exchange with Harley Feldbaum, June 2021

608. Dr. Jill Biden, "Promoting Empowerment and Education in the Americas," White House blog, June 5, 2013, https://obamawhitehouse.archives.gov/blog/2013/06/05/promoting-empowerment-and-education-americas

609. See, e.g., "Soda Industry Spent $67 Million Opposing State, City Soda Taxes and Warning Labels, Total Big Soda Federal Lobbying at About $14 Million a Year," State News Service, Sept. 21, 2016

610. Josh Gerstein, "Experts: W.H. H2O Evidence Murky," *Politico*, Sept. 12, 2013, https://www.politico.com/story/2013/09/michelle-obama-water-initiative-096703

611. Rene Lynch, "Michelle Obama Urges Americans to Drink More Water; Cue the Critics," *Los Angeles Times*, Sept. 13, 2013, https://www.latimes.com/food/dailydish/la-dd-michelle-obama-water-20130912-story.html

612. "Donald R. Keough, James B. Williams to Retire from the Coca-Cola Company Board of Directors," Coca-Cola Company, press release, Feb. 21, 2013, https://www.coca-colacompany.com/press-releases/donald-r-keough-james-b-williams-to-retire-from-board-of-directors

613. "Vice President Joe Biden Is Inducted into the Irish America Hall of Fame," acceptance speech

614. "World Cup Trophy Unveiled by Joe Biden and John Kerry During Pre-tournament World Tour—Video," Reuters via *Guardian*, April 15, 2014, https://www.theguardian.com/football/video/2014/apr/15/world-cup-trophy-joe-biden-john-kerry-video

615. Susan Jones, "Biden: Taking Grandkids on Trips 'One of the Great Advantages of Being Vice President,'" CNS News, April 15, 2014, https://www.cnsnews.com/news/article/susan-jones/biden-taking-grandkids-trips-one-great-advantages-being-vice-president

616. Carol E. Lee, "Biden Plies a Mixed Agenda in Davos," *Wall Street Journal*, Jan. 21, 2016, https://www.wsj.com/articles/biden-plies-a-mixed-agenda-in-davos-1453408972

617. Eliza Collins, "Canadian Stars Dot the State Dinner Guest List," *Politico*, March 10, 2016, https://www.politico.com/story/2016/03/canadian-state-dinner-guest-list-220593

618. "Coca-Cola Starts Local Production in Myanmar," Coca-Cola Company, press release, June 4, 2013, https://www.coca-colacompany.com/press-releases/coca-cola-starts-local-production-in-myanmar

619. Belén Marty, "Coca-Cola Ready to 'Open Happiness' in Cuba," *PanAm Post*, March 2, 2015, https://web.archive.org/web/20150316113200/http://panampost.com/belen-marty/2015/03/02/coca-cola-ready-to-open-happiness-in-cuba/

620. Marc Frank, "Jill Biden, Wife of U.S. Vice President, Arrives in Cuba," Reuters, Oct. 6, 2016

621. "Vice President Joe Biden During a Naturalization Ceremony in Al Faw Palace on Camp Victory, Iraq," White House photo, https://obamawhitehouse.archives.gov/photos-and-video/photos/vice-president-joe-biden-during-a-naturalization-ceremony-al-faw-palace-camp

622. Kim Gamel, "Biden Spends July 4 with Son, Other Troops in Iraq," Associated Press via *San Diego Union-Tribune*, July 4, 2009, https://www.sandiegouniontribune.com/sdut-ml-iraq-070409-2009jul04-story.html

623. *Promise Me, Dad*, pp 117–18

624. *Promise Me, Dad*, pp. 24–25

625. Samuel P. Jacobs, "Biden's 'U.S. President' Gaffe Points to 2016 Ambitions," Reuters, Jan. 20, 2013, https://www.reuters.com/article/uk-usa-inauguration-iowa/bidens-u-s-president-gaffe-points-to-2016-ambitions-idUKBRE90J03X20130120

626. Peter Nicholas, "Biden Flashes Signs of a 2016 Run," *Wall Street Journal*, Jan. 20, 2013, https://www.wsj.com/articles/SB10001424127887323485704578254211027776062

627. Mike Allen et al., "Biden 'Intoxicated' by 2016 Run," *Politico*, Jan. 23, 2013, https://www.politico.com/story/2013/01/no-joke-joe-biden-makes-2016-moves-086600

628. Lucien Bruggeman, "How Frank Biden Leveraged His Famous Name for Business Gain," ABC News, Jan. 17, 2020, https://abcnews.go.com/Politics/frank-biden-leveraged-famous-business-gain/story?id=68202529

629. Rab, "Mavericks Charter Schools Don't Live Up to Big Promises"

630. Valerie Strauss, "Brother of VP Biden Promotes Charters, Invoking Family Name," *Washington Post*, Dec. 10, 2011, https://www.washingtonpost.com/blogs /answer-sheet/post/brother-of-vp-biden-promotes-charters-invoking-family -name/2011/11/22/gIQAnhLFfO_blog.html

631. Interview with a person involved with Mavericks, 2021

632. Karen Yi and Amy Shipley, "Mavericks in Education: Failing to Make the Grade," *South Florida Sun Sentinel*, Oct. 10, 2014, https://www.sun-sentinel.com/news /education/fl-mavericks-charter-investigation-20141010-story.html

633. Thomas Sutterfield profile, https://ballotpedia.org/Thomas_Sutterfield

634. Ben Schreckinger, "The Strange Tale of Biden's Bid to Ban Horse Meat," *Politico*, Nov. 6, 2019, https://www.politico.com/news/2019/11/06/joe-biden-frank -biden-horse-meat-ban-066394

635. See Pinellas County Schools, Regular School Board Meeting minutes, March, 24, 2009, http://pinellasschool.iqm2.com/Citizens/FileOpen.aspx?Type=1&ID=10 43&Inline=True pp 360

636. Alli Langley, "Mavericks in Education, Two of Its Pinellas Charters, Find Themselves at Odds over Proposed Curriculum Changes," *Tampa Bay Times*, July 31, 2012, https://www.tampabay.com/news/education/k12/mavericks-in-education -two-of-its-pinellas-charters-find-themselves-at/1243452/

637. *Shane et al. v. Mavericks in Education Florida, LLC et al.*; 8:14-cv-01496-MSS -EAJ; Florida Middle District Court; June 20, 2014

638. Interview with a person with firsthand knowledge of the lawsuit and the circumstances surrounding it, 2021

639. Schreckinger, "The Strange Tale of Biden's Bid to Ban Horse Meat"

640. Andrew Conte, "Biden Name Drives Costa Rican Golf Dream," *Pittsburgh Tribune-Review*, April 26, 2014, https://archive.triblive.com/local/pittsburgh-allegheny /biden-name-drives-costa-rican-golf-dream/

641. Jaime Lopez, "Major Solar Energy Project Planned in Guanacaste," *Costa Rica Star*, Jan. 23, 2014, https://news.co.cr/major-solar-energy-project-planned-in-gua nacaste/31894/

642. "VP Biden to Colombia, Dominican Republic in June," Associated Press, May 29, 2014, https://apnews.com/article/74f3329239124293bbecb6b6aececbd7

643. "International Development and Foreign Assistance, Economic Affairs, International Environmental Protection and Peace Corps Subcommittee Hearing on 'U.S. Security Implications of International Energy and Climate Policies and Issues,'" Federal News Service, July 22, 2014

644. "OPIC Supports 20 MW J'can Solar Energy Facility," U.S. Embassy in Jamaica, press release, June 25, 2015, https://jm.usembassy.gov/opic-supports-20-mw-jcan -solar-energy-facility/

645. Sue Weakley, "The World of Victoria McCullough," *Equestrian Living*, circa 2013, https://eqliving.com/the-world-of-victoria-mccullough/

646. Lobbying Registration, AIM, https://lda.senate.gov/filings/public/filing/9478 b927-9959-453f-9101-32624c779a20/print/

647. Account of the Abruzzo-McCullough-Frank collaborations drawn primarily from Schreckinger, "The Strange Tale of Biden's Bid to Ban Horse Meat"

648. Brian Schwartz, "Biden Brother Linked to Firm Involved in Effort to Lobby Obama Administration, Congress in 2016," CNBC, Feb. 1, 2021

649. Delmarva Group LLC, Electronic Articles of Organization for Florida Limited Liability Company, filed May 29, 2015 at http://search.sunbiz.org

650. Marc Caputo and Ben Schreckinger, "Biden Pledges 'Absolute Wall' to Separate Relatives' Business Dealings," *Politico*, Aug. 28, 2019, https://www.politico.com /story/2019/08/28/biden-brother-business-2020-1476815

651. Maureen Milford and Cris Barrish, "In Times of Crisis, Bidens Rally for Beau," *News Journal*, Aug. 26, 2013

652. Entous, "Will Hunter Biden Jeopardize His Father's Campaign?"

653. Milford and Barrish, "In Times of Crisis, Bidens Rally for Beau"

654. Quinn Ostrom et al. "CBTRUS Statistical Report: Primary Brain and Other Central Nervous System Tumors Diagnosed in the United States in 2012–2016," *Neuro-Oncology* 21, Suppl. 5 (Nov. 2019): v1–v100, https://www.ncbi.nlm.nih .gov/pmc/articles/PMC6823730/

655. "Statement from the Vice President and Dr. Jill Biden," White House, Aug. 21, 2013, https://obamawhitehouse.archives.gov/the-press-office/2013/08/21/statement -vice-president-and-dr-jill-biden

656. *Promise Me, Dad*, pp. 22–32

657. Jonathan Starkey, "Beau Biden Alters Usual Political Path," *News Journal* via *USA Today*, April 20, 2014, https://www.usatoday.com/story/news/politics/2014 /04/20/beau-biden-2016-governors-race/7945615/

658. *Promise Me, Dad*, p. 76

659. *Promise Me, Dad*, p. 21

660. *Promise Me, Dad*, pp. 112–18

661. John Hudson et al., "Diplomat Tells Investigators He Raised Alarms in 2015 About Hunter Biden's Ukraine Work but Was Rebuffed," *Washington Post*, Oct. 18, 2019, https://www.washingtonpost.com/politics/diplomat-tells-investi gators-he-raised-alarms-in-2015-about-hunter-bidens-ukraine-work-but-was-re buffed/2019/10/18/81e35be9-4f5a-4048-8520-0baabb18ab63_story.html

662. Ben Schreckinger, "A Town, and Country, Mourns as Beau Biden Lies in Honor," *Politico*, June 4, 2015, https://www.politico.com/story/2015/06/beau-biden-ser vice-118646

663. Ben Schreckinger, "Thousands Pay Tribute to Beau Biden," *Politico*, June 5, 2015, https://www.politico.com/story/2015/06/beau-biden-tributes-delaware-118679

664. *Promise Me, Dad*, pp. 77–78

665. Quoted in Alex Thompson, "'The President Was Not Encouraging': What Obama Really Thought About Biden," *Politico Magazine*, Aug. 14, 2020, https://

www.politico.com/news/magazine/2020/08/14/obama-biden-relationship
-393570

666. Glenn Thrush, "Behind the Biden Hype," *Politico*, Aug. 26, 2015, https://www
.politico.com/story/2015/08/joe-beau-biden-president-hype-2016-121749

667. Don Sapatkin, "In Visit with Penn Scientists, Biden Launches Cancer 'Moonshot,'"
Philadelphia Inquirer, Jan. 15, 2016, https://www.inquirer.com/philly/health/can
cer/20160116_Biden_cancer_initiative_comes_at_opportune_time.html

668. See Krein tweet from Davos, Switzerland, Twitter, Jan. 20, 2016, https://twitter
.com/KreinMD/status/689741053897871361?s=20

669. Josh Lederman, "At the Vatican, Biden Seeks Common Cause with Pope on Cancer," Associated Press, April 29, 2016, https://apnews.com/article/0666e070cd19
4159befbdd6d173d59f2

670. See, e.g., "StartUp Health Insider," Jan. 20, 2016, https://us2.campaign-archive
.com/?id=5e96e78fd7&u=7b5e9c627761550fb3157fdb9

671. "Vice President Joe Biden's Keynote at Cleveland Clinic 2016 Medical Innovation
Summit," StartUp Health, Oct. 26, 2016, YouTube, video, https://www.youtube
.com/watch?v=nsxAgCQgM_k

672. "StartUp Health Announces 10 Health Moonshots with Global Army of Health
Transformers to Improve Health of Everyone in the World," StartUp Health,
press release, Oct. 16, 2016, https://healthtransformer.co/startup-health-announ
ces-10-health-moonshots-with-global-army-of-health-transformers-to-improve
-ed911c33d8d7

673. "Vice President Joe Biden's Irish Family History," Irish Family History Centre,
2016, https://www.irishfamilyhistorycentre.com/article/vice-president-joe-bide
ns-irish-family-history

674. This dynamic described in Thompson, " 'The President Was Not Encouraging':
What Obama Really Thought About Biden"

675. "Vice President Biden at the StartUp Health Festival," StartUp Health, press
release, Jan. 10, 2017, https://healthtransformer.co/vice-president-biden-at-the
-startup-health-festival-d11532b8f652

676. "Joe Biden's Welcome Home Rally 2017," WITN Channel 22, Jan. 25, 2017, You-
Tube, video, https://www.youtube.com/watch?v=kkOl576p5u0

677. "Biden and Amatus Team Up on Substance Abuse Treatment Plans," Amatus
Health, press release, Jan. 24, 2019, https://www.biospace.com/article/releases
/biden-and-amatus-team-up-on-substance-abuse-treatment-plans/

678. Lobbying Report, the Coca-Cola Company, Q4, 2017, https://lda.senate.gov
/filings/public/filing/43e675a0-935e-4112-a152-479e92971b85/print/

679. Lobbying Report, the Coca-Cola Company, Q4, 2019, https://lda.senate.gov
/filings/public/filing/0858dd91-1c6d-4436-b9f1-7e37cf70d433/print/

680. Mala Adiga, "In Observance of Veterans Day, Dr. Biden Honors the Military Community in Atlanta and D.C.," Biden Foundation, Medium, Nov. 15, 2017, https://
medium.com/@bidenfoundation/in-observance-of-veterans-day-dr-biden-hon
ors-the-military-community-in-atlanta-and-d-c-55796ddb3996

681. Trina Health of Booneville, Inc.; Mississippi corporate registration, accessed via OpenCorporates database, https://opencorporates.com/companies/us_ms/1079343

682. Golden et al., "The Benefits of Being Joe Biden's Brother" (Ellison declined my interview request)

683. *U.S.A. v. Gilbert et al.,* 2:18-cr-00116-MHT-WC, U.S. District Court for the Middle District of Alabama, Northern Division, Superseding Indictment, July 24, 2018

684. Mary Sell, "Micky Hammon: Release from Prison Expected Today," Florence (AL) *TimesDaily,* June 28, 2018

685. Melissa Brown, "CEO Sentenced for Conspiring to Bribe Alabama Legislator," *Montgomery Advertiser,* May 30, 2019

686. Interviews with former Americore executives conducted in 2020

687. Interviews with former Americore executives; and Ben Schreckinger, "James Biden's Health Care Ventures Face a Growing Legal Morass," *Politico,* March 9, 2020, https://www.politico.com/news/2020/03/09/james-biden-health-care-ventures -123159

688. Esteban Parra, "Former President Barack Obama Surprises Attendees at a Beau Biden Foundation Fundraiser," *News Journal,* Sept. 25, 2017, https://www.dela wareonline.com/story/news/local/2017/09/25/former-president-barack-obama -surprises-attendees-beau-biden-foundation-fundraiser/702496001/

689. Interviews with former Americore executive

690. Schreckinger, "James Biden's Health Care Ventures Face a Growing Legal Morass"

691. Interview with a person who discussed the alleged loan with Jim

692. Schreckinger, "Donor with Ukraine Ties Helped Biden's Brother with Florida Vacation Home"

693. Ben Schreckinger, "Execs Claim Biden's Brother Offered Biden's Help Promoting Business Venture," *Politico,* Aug. 26, 2019, https://www.politico.com /story/2019/08/26/joe-biden-brother-2020-1475897

694. Ben Schreckinger, "Biden's Brother Touted Biden Cancer Initiative Ties in Investment Pitch," *Politico,* Sept. 26, 2019, https://www.politico.com/news/2019/09 /26/joe-biden-brother-cancer-initiative-investment-pitch-001675

695. Schreckinger, "James Biden's Health Care Ventures Face a Growing Legal Morass"

696. "Joe Biden: I'm Proud of CNN Turk," CNN Turk, Aug. 24, 2016, https://www .cnnturk.com/turkiye/joe-biden-cnn-turk-ile-gurur-duyuyorum (translated from Turkish)

697. "Turkish Businessman Hosted Joe Biden's Brother on Vacation in Turkey," *Duvar English,* Feb. 25, 2021, https://www.duvarenglish.com/turkish-businessman-ekim -alptekin-hosted-joe-bidens-brother-on-vacation-in-turkey-news-56406

698. Ben Schreckinger, "Suit: Biden Brother Invoked Political Clout to Further Fraud Scheme," *Politico,* Aug. 8, 2019, https://www.politico.com/story/2019/08/08 /joe-biden-brother-fraud-scheme-1453527

699. Phone interview with Ellwood City mayor Anthony Court, Fall 2020

700. Patrick E. Litowitz, "Search Warrant Targets Ellwood City Medical Center," *New Castle News*, Jan. 19, 2019, https://www.ncnewsonline.com/news/local_news /search-warrant-targets-ellwood-hospital/article_3cd600ff-3842-5b28-9d24 -ecbdedc0aea1.html

701. Matt Viser and Anu Narayanswamy, "Joe Biden Earned $15.6 Million in the Two Years After Leaving the Vice Presidency," *Washington Post*, July 9, 2019, https:// www.washingtonpost.com/politics/joe-biden-earned-156-million-in-the-two -years-after-leaving-the-vice-presidency/2019/07/09/55aad492-a27e-11e9-b8c8 -75dae2607e60_story.html

702. Charlie Gasparino and Brian Schwartz, "Joe Biden's Beef with Bill Ackman Sparks Heated Exchange and Presidential Chatter," Fox Business, June 27, 2017, https:// www.foxbusiness.com/politics/joe-bidens-beef-with-bill-ackman-sparks-heated -exchange-and-presidential-chatter

703. Viser and Narayanswamy "Joe Biden Earned $15.6 Million in the Two Years After Leaving the Vice Presidency"

704. Kamp, "Why Joe Biden Didn't Run . . . and Why He's Not Ruling Out 2020"

705. Author visit, Nov. 2020

706. Something Comfortable, Facebook, July 7, 2018, https://www.facebook.com /SomethingComfortable/photos/2345720192121873

707. David Kamp, "Joe Biden on Having Few Assets, and Why He Wishes He'd Had a Republican Child," *Vanity Fair*, Nov. 8, 2017, https://www.vanityfair.com /culture/2017/11/joe-biden-book-assets

708. *Beautiful Things*, p. 45

709. *Beautiful Things*, pp. 106–7

710. *Beautiful Things*, p. 180

711. Entous, "Will Hunter Biden Jeopardize His Father's Campaign?"

712. *Beautiful Things*, pp. 118–19

713. *Beautiful Things*, pp. 115–17

714. *Beautiful Things*, pp. 144–47

715. See, e.g., Hugh Dunkerley cross-examination, *U.S. v. Galanis et al.*, 1:16-cr-00371- RA, Southern District of New York, trial transcript for June 5, 2018

716. *U.S. v. Galanis*, document 402-17, filed April 11, 2018

717. Hugh Dunkerley cross-examination, *U.S. v. Galanis*, June 5, 2018

718. Dave Michaels and Theo Francis, "Hunter Biden's Name Was Used as Selling Point in Fraudulent Bond Scheme," *Wall Street Journal*, Oct. 24, 2019, https:// www.wsj.com/articles/hunter-bidens-name-was-used-as-selling-point-in-fraudu lent-bond-scheme-11571863676

719. Email cited in *U.S. v. Galanis*, Devon Archer's Memorandum in Support of His Motion In Limine, filed April 11, 2018

720. Michaels and Francis, "Hunter Biden's Name Was Used as Selling Point in Fraud- ulent Bond Scheme"

721. "Seven Defendants Charged in Manhattan Federal Court with Defrauding a Native American Tribe and Investors of over $60 Million," U.S. Department of Justice, press release, May 11, 2016, https://www.justice.gov/usao-sdny/pr /seven-defendants-charged-manhattan-federal-court-defrauding-native-ameri can-tribe-and

722. *Beautiful Things*, pp. 155–75

723. Entous, "Will Hunter Biden Jeopardize His Father's Campaign?"; attorney general's badge detail from Matthew Boyle, "Exclusive—2016 Arizona Police Report: Cocaine Pipe Found in Car Rented by Joe Biden's Son Hunter Biden, Authorities Declined to Prosecute," *Breitbart News*, May 17, 2019, https://www.breitbart .com/politics/2019/05/17/exclusive-2016-arizona-police-report-cocaine-pipe -found-in-car-rented-by-joe-bidens-son-hunter-biden-authorities-declined-to -prosecute/

724. *Beautiful Things*, pp. 177–83

725. Margie Fishman, "Divorce Filing Details Split of Kathleen, Hunter Biden," *News Journal*, March 2, 2017, https://www.delawareonline.com/story/news/2017/03 /02/kathleen-biden-files-divorce-hunter/98638454/

726. Entous, "Will Hunter Biden Jeopardize His Father's Campaign?"

727. Scott Cendrowski, "The Unusual Journey of China's Newest Oil Baron," *Fortune*, Sept. 28, 2016, https://fortune.com/2016/09/28/cefc-ye-jianming-40-under-40/

728. Alexandra Stevenson et al., "A Chinese Tycoon Sought Power and Influence. Washington Responded," *New York Times*, Dec. 12, 2018

729. Jim's involvement with Hunter's Chinese contacts attested to by a person familiar with the FBI investigation of Hunter as well as a former Americore executive, in addition to Bobulinski's public statements

730. Andrew Duehren and James T. Areddy, "Hunter Biden's Ex–Business Partner Alleges Father Knew About Venture," *Wall Street Journal*, Oct. 23, 2020, https:// www.wsj.com/articles/hunter-bidens-ex-business-partner-alleges-father-knew -about-venture-11603421247

731. Stevenson et al., "A Chinese Tycoon Sought Power and Influence. Washington Responded"

732. Email first reported by Emma-Jo Morris and Gabrielle Fonrouge, "Emails Reveal How Hunter Biden Tried to Cash In Big on Behalf of Family with Chinese Firm," *New York Post*, Oct. 15, 2020, https://nypost.com/2020/10/15/emails -reveal-how-hunter-biden-tried-to-cash-in-big-with-chinese-firm/

733. Duehren and Areddy, "Hunter Biden's Ex–Business Partner Alleges Father Knew About Venture"

734. Delaware corporate registration database, registered May 15, 2017

735. Delaware corporate registration database, registered May 22, 2017; interviews with people familiar with the CEFC venture

736. "Hunter Biden, Burisma, and Corruption: The Impact on U.S. Government Policy and Related Concerns," pp. 78–79

Endnotes

737. Henry Foy and Neil Hume, "CEFC China Energy Buys $9bn Stake in Rosneft," *Financial Times*, Sept. 8, 2017, https://www.ft.com/content/25b18d2e-94a4-11e7 -a9e6-11d2f0ebb7f0

738. Lucy Hornby and Don Weinland, "Opaque Chinese Oil Group Makes Clear Gains in Former Soviet Bloc," *Financial Times*, Sept. 13, 2017, https://www.ft .com/content/e3f8cbd2-983f-11e7-a652-cde3f882dd7b

739. Copies of these emails were initially provided to me by Mattias Carlsson, reporter for the Swedish newspaper *Dagens Nyheter*. I later obtained copies of the emails directly from the National Property Board of Sweden, which released them under Sweden's freedom of information law.

740. *Beautiful Things*, p. 231

741. Interview with a person with firsthand knowledge of those conversations, 2020

742. Stephenson et al., "A Chinese Tycoon Sought Power and Influence. Washington Responded"

743. "Hunter Biden, Burisma, and Corruption: The Impact on U.S. Government Policy and Related Concerns," p. 79

744. "Patrick Ho, Former Head of Organization Backed by Chinese Energy Conglomerate, Sentenced to 3 Years in Prison for International Bribery and Money Laundering Offenses," U.S. Department of Justice, press release, March 25, 2019

745. Lucy Hornby and Archie Zhang, "CEFC Chairman Ye Jianming Said to Be Detained," *Financial Times*, Feb. 28, 2018, https://www.ft.com/content/9c6caaba -1cf9-11e8-aaca-4574d7dabfb6

746. *Beautiful Things*, pp. 187–94

747. See, e.g., Dalton's 2017 Form 990, https://990s.foundationcenter.org/990_pdf _archive/132/132751872/132751872_201806_990.pdf

748. Timothy Anderson cross-examination, *U.S. v. Galanis*, trial transcript for May 29, 2018

749. "What Is a Suspicious Activity Report?" Thomson Reuters, undated, https://legal .thomsonreuters.com/en/insights/articles/what-is-a-suspicious-activity-report

750. Hallie Biden, "Opinion: Delaware Takes Beau Biden's Quest to Protect Children Nationwide," *News Journal*, Jan. 8, 2019, https://www.delawareonline.com /story/opinion/contributors/2019/01/08/opinion-delaware-takes-beau-bidens -quest-protect-children-nationwide/2501955002/

751. Palmeri and Schreckinger, "Sources: Secret Service Inserted Itself into Case of Hunter Biden's Gun"

752. *Beautiful Things*, p. 207

753. Jonathan Martin et al., "Biden Faced His Biggest Challenge, and Struggled to Form a Response," *New York Times*, Oct. 5, 2019, https://www.nytimes.com /2019/10/05/us/politics/biden-trump-ukraine.html

754. *Beautiful Things*, pp. 219–30

755. *Beautiful Things*, pp. 215–43

756. Kenneth P. Vogel and David Stern, "Ukrainian Efforts to Sabotage Trump

288

Backfire," *Politico*, Jan. 11, 2017, https://www.politico.com/story/2017/01/ukraine-sabotage-trump-backfire-233446

757. Andrew Kramer et al., "Secret Ledger in Ukraine Lists Cash for Donald Trump's Campaign Chief," *New York Times*, Aug. 14, 2016, https://www.nytimes.com/2016/08/15/us/politics/what-is-the-black-ledger.html

758. Darren Samuelsohn and Ben Schreckinger, " 'It's Extremely Insulting': Giuliani Fires Back at Allegations of Erratic Behavior," *Politico*, May 8, 2018, https://www.politico.com/story/2018/05/08/giuliani-trump-lawyer-insulting-576749

759. For more on the role of Soros in central and eastern Europe, which is often exaggerated by his antagonists, see Emily Tamkin, "Who's Afraid of George Soros?" *Foreign Policy*, Oct. 10, 2017, https://foreignpolicy.com/2017/10/10/whos-afraid-of-george-soros/

760. *Promise Me, Dad*, pp. 92–95

761. See, e.g., David L. Stern, "Trump Called This Ex–Ukrainian Prosecutor 'Very Good.' But He Resigned in Disgrace," *Washington Post*, Sept. 25, 2019, https://www.washingtonpost.com/world/europe/trump-called-this-ex-ukrainian-prosecutor-very-good-but-he-resigned-in-disgrace/2019/09/25/d1410aa2-dfb1-11e9-be7f-4cc85017c36f_story.html

762. "Court Seizes Property of Ex-minister Zlochevsky in Ukraine," Interfax-Ukraine, Feb. 4, 2016, https://web.archive.org/web/20160206023204/https://en.interfax.com.ua/news/general/322395.html

763. See, e.g., Adam Entous, "The Ukrainian Prosecutor Behind Trump's Impeachment," *New Yorker*, Dec. 16, 2019, https://www.newyorker.com/magazine/2019/12/23/the-ukrainian-prosecutor-behind-trumps-impeachment

764. Ben Schreckinger, " 'I'm the Real Whistleblower': Giuliani's Quixotic Mission to Help Trump in Ukraine," *Politico*, Sept. 27, 2019, https://www.politico.com/news/2019/09/27/giuliani-trump-ukraine-005098

765. Rebecca Davis O'Brien and Christopher M. Matthews, "Ukraine Energy Official Says Giuliani Associates Tried to Recruit Him," *Wall Street Journal*, Nov. 24, 2019, https://www.wsj.com/articles/ukraine-energy-official-says-giuliani-associates-tried-to-recruit-him-11574652499

766. See, e.g., Ben Protess et al., "Giuliani Pursued Business in Ukraine While Pushing for Inquiries for Trump," *New York Times*, Nov. 27, 2019, https://www.nytimes.com/2019/11/27/nyregion/giuliani-ukraine-business-trump.html

767. "The *Hill*'s Review of John Solomon's Columns on Ukraine," *Hill*, Feb. 19, 2020, https://thehill.com/homenews/news/483600-the-hills-review-of-john-solomons-columns-on-ukraine

768. Donati, "Firm Hired by Ukraine's Burisma Tried to Use Hunter Biden as Leverage, Documents Show"

769. Salvador Rizzo, "Fact-Checking President Trump's Wild Jabs at Joe Biden," *Washington Post*, May 23, 2019, https://www.washingtonpost.com/politics/2019/05/23/fact-checking-president-trumps-wild-jabs-joe-biden/

770. Martin et al., "Biden Faced His Biggest Challenge, and Struggled to Form a Response"

771. Caputo and Schreckinger, "Biden Pledges 'Absolute Wall' to Separate Relatives' Business Dealings"

772. Caitlin Emma and Connor O'Brien, "Trump Holds Up Ukraine Military Aid Meant to Confront Russia," *Politico*, Aug. 28, 2019, https://www.politico.com/story/2019/08/28/trump-ukraine-military-aid-russia-1689531

773. Interview with Rudy Giuliani, Sept. 2019

774. "Hunter Biden, Burisma, and Corruption: The Impact on U.S. Government Policy and Related Concerns," pp. 67–68

775. Interviews with people familiar with the investigative efforts

776. Adam Goldman et al., "Material from Giuliani Spurred a Separate Justice Dept. Pursuit of Hunter Biden," *New York Times*, Dec. 11, 2020, https://www.nytimes.com/2020/12/11/us/politics/hunter-biden-justice-department-pittsburgh.html

777. Michael S. Schmidt et al., "Giuliani Is Said to Be Under Investigation for Ukraine Work," *New York Times*, Oct. 11, 2019, https://www.nytimes.com/2019/10/11/us/politics/rudy-giuliani-investigation.html

778. See, e.g., Ellen Nakashima et al., "FBI Was Aware Prominent Americans, Including Giuliani, Were Targeted by Russian Influence Operation," *Washington Post*, May 1, 2021, https://www.washingtonpost.com/national-security/rudy-giuliani-fbi-warning-russia/2021/04/29/5db90f96-a84e-11eb-bca5-048b2759a489_story.html

779. "Foreign Threats to the 2020 US Federal Elections," National Intelligence Council, Intelligence Community Assessment, March 10, 2021, p. i, https://www.dni.gov/files/ODNI/documents/assessments/ICA-declass-16MAR21.pdf

780. Interviews with people familiar; Goldman et al., "Material from Giuliani Spurred a Separate Justice Dept. Pursuit of Hunter Biden"

781. Natasha Korecki et al., " 'For Christ's Sake, Watch Yourself': Biden Warns Family over Business Dealings," *Politico*, Jan. 28, 2021, https://www.politico.com/news/2021/01/28/frank-biden-business-dealings-463662

782. Ryan Grim, "New Evidence Supporting Credibility of Tara Reade's Allegation Against Joe Biden Emerges," *Intercept*, April 24, 2020, https://theintercept.com/2020/04/24/new-evidence-tara-reade-joe-biden/

783. Amber Phillips and Matt Viser, "Former Neighbor of Biden Accuser Confirms She Was Told of an Incident in the 1990s," *Washington Post*, April 29, 2020, https://www.washingtonpost.com/politics/former-neighbor-of-biden-accuser-confirms-she-was-told-of-an-incident-in-the-1990s/2020/04/29/9bac8864-8a81-11ea-8ac1-bfb250876b7a_story.html

784. For a summary see Amber Phillips, "New Reporting Puts Focus on Tara Reade's Inconsistencies," *Washington Post*, May 23, 2020, https://www.washingtonpost.com/politics/2020/05/23/reporting-tara-reade-credibility/

785. Meghan Keneally, "List of Trump's Accusers and Their Allegations of Sexual Misconduct," ABC News, Sept. 18, 2020, https://abcnews.go.com/Politics/list-trumps-accusers-allegations-sexual-misconduct/story?id=51956410

786. Author visit

787. Dustin Volz, "Commentator Who Amplified Macron Hacks Given White House Press Access," Reuters, May 10, 2017, https://www.reuters.com/article/us-usa -france-cyber-activist/commentator-who-amplified-macron-hacks-given-white -house-press-access-idUSKBN187008

788. John Whitesides, "Trump's Handling of Coronavirus Pandemic Hits Record Low Approval: Reuters/Ipsos Poll," Reuters, Oct. 8 2020, https://www.reuters.com /article/us-usa-election-trump-coronavirus/trumps-handling-of-coronavirus -pandemic-hits-record-low-approval-reuters-ipsos-poll-idUSKBN26T3OF

789. Frank Bajak, "Russians Hacked Company Key to Ukraine Scandal: Researchers," Associated Press, Jan. 14, 2020, https://apnews.com/article/9a4a6d6f21b48375b 762b88587c45411

790. Garrett Graff, "The Right Way to Cover Hacks and Leaks Before the Election," *Wired*, Oct. 7, 2020

791. See, e.g., Bo Erickson and Stefan Becket, "What We Know—and Don't Know— About Hunter Biden's Alleged Laptop," CBS News, Oct. 16, 2020, https://www .cbsnews.com/news/hunter-biden-laptop-new-york-post-story/

792. Karl Baker, "Meet the Computer Repairman at the Center of *New York Post*'s Hunter Biden Laptop Story," *News Journal*, Oct. 14, 2020, https://www.delaware online.com/story/news/2020/10/14/meet-wilmington-repairman-who-report edly-gave-biden-laptop-giuliani-associate/3655753001/

793. See, e.g., Katie Glueck et al., "Allegation on Biden Prompts Pushback from Social Media Companies," *New York Times*, Oct. 14 2020, https://www.nytimes .com/2020/10/14/us/politics/hunter-biden-ukraine-facebook-twitter.html

794. "Twitter: Censoring *NY Post*'s Hunter Biden Story a 'Mistake,'" Sen. John Cornyn, press release, Nov. 17, 2020, https://www.cornyn.senate.gov/content/news/twitter -censoring-ny-post%E2%80%99s-hunter-biden-story-%E2%80%98mistake%E2 %80%99

795. Interview with a person familiar with the situation

796. "FBI Probing If Russia Involved in Hunter Biden Email Story," Associated Press via Delaware Online, Oct. 16, 2020, https://www.delawareonline.com /story/news/politics/2020/10/16/fbi-investigating-hunter-biden-emails-russia -disinformation/3683566001/

797. Katie Robertson, "*New York Post* Published Hunter Biden Report Amid News-room Doubts," *New York Times*, Oct. 18, 2020, https://www.nytimes.com/2020 /10/18/business/media/new-york-post-hunter-biden.html

798. Peter Schweizer and Seamus Bruner, "Exclusive—'This Is China, Inc.': Emails Reveal Hunter Biden's Associates Helped Communist-Aligned Chinese Elites Secure White House Meetings," Breitbart News, Oct. 16, 2020, https://www .breitbart.com/politics/2020/10/16/exclusive-this-is-china-inc-emails-reveal -hunter-bidens-associates-helped-communist-aligned-chinese-elites-secure -white-house-meetings/

799. "Full Statement from Tony Bobulinski to the *New York Post*," Scribd, Oct. 21, 2020, https://www.scribd.com/document/481146289/Full-Statement-From-Tony -Bobulinski-to-the-New-York-Post

800. Bobulinski donor records from OpenSecrets.org, https://www.opensecrets.org /donor-lookup/results?name=+Bobulinski

801. Ben Smith, "Trump Had One Last Story to Sell. The *Wall Street Journal* Wouldn't Buy It," *New York Times*, Oct. 25, 2020, https://www.nytimes.com/2020/10/25 /business/media/hunter-biden-wall-street-journal-trump.html

802. Duehren and Areddy, "Hunter Biden's Ex–Business Partner Alleges Father Knew About Venture"

803. "Tony Bobulinski Statement on Hunter Biden," CSPAN, Oct. 22, 2020, https:// www.c-span.org/video/?477307-1/tony-bobulinski-statement-hunter-biden

804. See, e.g., Kerry Breen, "'A Powerful Message': Debate Watchers React to Joe Biden's Response about Son's Drug Use," Today.com, Sept. 30, 2020, https:// www.today.com/health/joe-biden-speaking-son-hunter-s-drug-problem-garners -praise-t192883

805. Michael Goodwin, "'Look Out for My Family'—Hunter's Biz Partner Tells All on Meetings with Joe Biden: Goodwin," *New York Post*, Oct. 27, 2020, https://nypost.com/2020/10/27/hunters-biz-partner-tells-all-on-meeting -with-joe-biden-goodwin/

806. Video included in tweet by Sinclair reporter James Rosen, Twitter, Oct. 29, 2020, https://twitter.com/JamesRosenTV/status/1321932396091068417?s=20

807. Alex Pappas and Marisa Schultz, "Jim Biden Refuses to Answer Questions About Family's Business Dealings," Fox News, Oct. 28, 2020, https://www.foxnews .com/politics/jim-biden-refuses-to-answer-questions-family-business-dealings

808. My initial requests for the files, for example, were rebuffed. See also Ken Dilanian and Tom Winter, "Here's What Happened When NBC News Tried to Report on the Alleged Hunter Biden Emails," NBC News, Oct. 30, 2020, https://www .nbcnews.com/politics/2020-election/here-s-what-happened-when-nbc-news -tried-report-alleged-n1245533.

809. This has been reported in Emma-Jo Morris and Gabrielle Fonrouge, "Text Messages Show Raw and Intimate Exchange Between Joe and Hunter Biden," *New York Post*, Oct. 16, 2020, https://nypost.com/2020/10/16/texts-show-raw-intimate -exchange-between-joe-and-hunter-biden/.

810. "Tucker Carlson Speaks on Relationship with Hunter Biden, Corruption on Capitol Hill," Fox News, Jan. 26, 2020, video, around 1:10, https://video.foxnews .com/v/6126574453001#sp=show-clips

811. These emails were first reported in Miranda Devine, "Hunter Biden Brought VP Joe to Dinner with Shady Business Partners," *New York Post*, May 26, 2021, https:// nypost.com/2021/05/26/hunter-biden-arranged-secret-dinner-with-busi ness-partners-and-vp-joe/.

812. Josh Boswell, "EXCLUSIVE: What WASN'T in Hunter Biden's Book: How He Got Unauthorized Secret Service Protection, Begged Joe to Run for WH to Salvage

His Own Reputation and Made Porn Films with Prostitutes. Forensic Experts Prove Laptop IS President's Son's," *Daily Mail*, April 8, 2021, https://www .dailymail.co.uk/news/article-9445105/What-Hunter-Biden-left-tell-memoir -revealed.html

813. WhatsApp exchange with the author, Nov. 2020

814. Marshall Cohen and Evan Perez, "Hunter Biden Dodges Questions on Laptop Seized by FBI," CNN, April 2, 2021, https://www.cnn.com/2021/04/02/poli tics/hunter-biden-laptop/index.html

815. "Hunter Biden Opens Up About Family Intervention and Addresses Laptop Reports," CBS News, April 3, 2021, https://www.cbsnews.com/news/hunter-biden -laptop-reports-intervention-memoir/

816. "Hunter Biden Defends His Position on Burisma Board, Says Trump Used It in 'Illegitimate Way' During 2020 Election," CBS News, April 5, 2021, https:// www.cbsnews.com/news/hunter-biden-burisma-board-2020-election-trump/

817. See, e.g., Dave Rogers, "DEA Agents Raid Office of Port Psychiatrist," *Daily News of Newburyport*, Feb. 14, 2020, https://www.newburyportnews.com/news /local_news/dea-agents-raid-office-of-port-psychiatrist/article_93e249d5-036d -55d7-8dd5-b01a9140aa2f.html

818. Interview with a person familiar with the situation. See also Dilanian and Winter, "Here's What Happened When NBC News Tried to Report on the Alleged Hunter Biden Emails."

819. John Paul Mac Isaac, "The Truth—It Was Him," Dec. 11, 2020, YouTube, video, https://www.youtube.com/watch?v=THYjft9aH88

820. Lachlan Markay, "Ex-colleague of Hunter Biden's Lawyer Gets Top DOJ Post," Axios, Feb. 2, 2021, https://www.axios.com/hunter-biden-ex-colleague-doj-job -be5c0c8e-c65d-4ce0-a2f9-761a118e7b08.html

821. Bobulinski interview on *Tucker Carlson Tonight*, Fox News, Oct. 27, 2020, Facebook, video, https://www.facebook.com/watch/?v=359475435162576

Index

Index

About the Author

Ben Schreckinger is a national political correspondent at *Politico*. Before that he served as *GQ* magazine's Washington correspondent, and as a campaign reporter for *Politico* he covered the rise of Donald Trump. He has been a regular guest on radio and television, including NPR, CNN, and MSNBC. He is also the cowinner of a 2021 National Headliner Award for best magazine column. Ben hails from New England and lives in Washington, DC.